The Skills of Primary School Management

Les Bell and Chris Rhodes

ROUTLEDGE

London and New York

First published 1996
by Routledge
11 New Fetter Lane, London EC4P 4EE

Simultaneously published in the USA and Canada
by Routledge
29 West 35th Street, New York, NY 10001

Typeset in Garamond by Florencetype Ltd, Stoodleigh, Tiverton, Devon.

Printed and bound in Great Britain by
Mackays of Chatham PLC, Chatham, Kent.

British Library Cataloguing in Publication Data
A catalogue record for this book is available from the British Library

Library of Congress Cataloguing in Publication Data
A catalogue record for this book has been requested

ISBN 0–415–09757–6

The Skills of Primary School Management

This book is for all teachers who have curriculum and management responsibilities or who aspire to those positions. Taking into account the many radical changes which have influenced the management of primary schools since 1988, it describes the responsibilities facing teachers. It also offers practical guidelines on how to form effective management strategies, whilst recognising that good management is not an end in itself. The focus throughout the book is on how to achieve quality in schools through good management, so that children are offered the best education possible. Topics covered include:

- inspections
- the school development plan
- curriculum management
- professional development
- teacher appraisal
- appointing staff
- managing the budget

Les Bell is Professor of Educational Management and Director of the School of Education and Community Studies at Liverpool John Moores University. He is the author of many books on education management. **Chris Rhodes** is the Director of Educational Services in Warwickshire and a registered OFSTED inspector. He has seventeen years' experience as a primary school teacher.

Educational management series
Series editor: Cyril Poster

To Gill, Sue, Georgina, Katherine and Susan

Contents

Figures

Acknowledgements

Chris Rhodes and I are grateful to our many friends and colleagues, too numerous to mention by name, among primary school teachers and head-teachers in Birmingham, Coventry, Solihull and Warwickshire, who read the various versions of the manuscript and made extremely constructive comments. They continually reminded us of the realities of primary school management. We are especially grateful to Cynthia Beckett for her advice on aspects of governors' responsiblities; Angela Bird for her contribution to our thinking about school development and curriculum management; Stella Blackmore and Chris Rayers for their advice about quality and school inspections; and Patricia McMillan for her help in producing the final manuscript. We have also welcomed the editorial advice of Cyril Poster, to whom we are grateful for his tolerance and attention to detail when we failed to reach his high standards. We have also appreciated the support of Helen Fairlie, Samantha Larkham and the staff at Routledge.

I would also like to pay tribute to my friend and colleague Barry Troyna. I have long benefited from his contribution to research and scholarship. He has now set us all an outstanding example of personal integrity and courage in the face of extreme adversity.

Les Bell
Liverpool, May 1995

Chapter 1

Managing primary schools in a new era

This book is for the majority of primary school teachers who have curriculum and management responsibilities and for those who aspire to senior management positions. It will provide an analysis of those responsibilities and of how they may best be exercised in the changing climate within which all of us involved in primary education now work. It will take account of the many radical policy changes that have influenced the management of primary schools since 1988. Above all it will offer practical guidelines on which effective strategies for managing primary schools may be based while recognising that good management is not an end in itself. The main purpose of schools is to contribute to the education of children. The processes of teaching and learning are central to this. The purpose of school management must be to promote and facilitate these processes.

All staff in primary schools, including caretakers and secretaries, have a direct and important part to play in the management of the schools in which they work. Teachers have a particular and direct contribution to make. This might be made through work in year or subject teams or as part of a senior management team. It might be made as part of the collegial decision-making or through the acceptance of specific management responsibility for some aspect of the school's work.

Most teachers in all primary schools are likely to have such responsibilities. The Department for Further Education's *School Teachers' Pay and Conditions of Employment Document* (DFE 1994a) places significant emphasis on the management role of all teachers. Their duties now include:

- advising and cooperating with the headteacher and other teachers . . . on the preparation and development of courses of study, teaching materials, teaching programmes, methods of teaching and assessment and pastoral arrangements;
- participating in meetings which relate to the curriculum for the school or the administration or organisation of the school;
- contributing to the selection for appointment and professional development of other teachers;

- coordinating or managing the work of other teachers;
- taking such part as may be required in the review, development and management of activities relating to the curriculum, organisation and pastoral functions of the school.
- participating in administrative and organisational tasks . . . including the management and supervision of persons providing support for the teachers . . . and the ordering and allocation of equipment and materials.

(adapted from DFE 1994a: paras 37.6–37.12)

This same document, for the first time, defines the management role of the deputy headteacher who shall:

Play a major role under the overall direction of the headteacher in:

1 formulating the aims and objectives of the school;
2 establishing the policies through which they shall be achieved;
3 managing staff and resources to that end; and;
4 monitoring progress towards their achievement.

(adapted from DFE 1994a: para. 34.1)

This is a significant departure for deputy headteachers whose role, hitherto, tended to be determined almost entirely by the headteacher. It gives a clear management focus to the position of deputy. The circular which accompanies this document states that a clear distinction needs to be established between the job of deputy and that of other senior staff. This distinction rests on deputy headteachers having permanently delegated responsibilities which are both school-wide and of considerable weight (DFE 1994b).

Nevertheless, the responsibility for the overall management and administration of the school rests with the headteacher working through and with the governing body. As local education authorities (LEAs) come to terms with their changing roles and their reduced capability to control and organise their schools, more power and responsibility is vested in the staff of individual schools, especially the headteacher who is responsible for the internal organisation and management of the school and whose duties include:

- formulating the overall aims of the school;
- participating in the selection and appointment of staff;
- deploying and managing all teaching and non-teaching staff and allocating duties to them;
- determining, organising and implementing an appropriate curriculum;
- reviewing the work and the organisation of the school;
- evaluating standards of teaching and learning;
- supervising and participating in arrangements for the appraisal of teachers;
- ensuring that all staff have access to advice and training appropriate to their needs;
- ensuring that newly-qualified teachers and those returning to teaching have access to adequate support;

- allocating, controlling and accounting for those financial and material resources of the school which are under the control of the headteacher.

(adapted from DFE 1994a: paras 32.1–32.18)

Many of the newly delegated powers, however, are vested in the school's governing body rather than the headteacher. It is not our intention in this book to examine in detail the developing role of governing bodies (see Beckett *et al.*, 1991 for this). Nevertheless, the partnership between governors and primary school staff forms part of the context within which primary schools are managed and will, therefore, be discussed at various points throughout this book. For the moment it must be recognised that the delegation of powers to governors can cause confusion over who does what. Any such difficulty is best resolved at school-level, based on an understanding that governors must seek to govern, that is to establish broad policy and to monitor its implementation. Headteachers working with their staff must manage the implementation of policy, including the detail of organising, assessing, reviewing, appraising and resourcing such activities. If this division of responsibility is to be successful each party must understand the role of the other and be willing to collaborate and cooperate. For this to happen, schools must establish a sound management framework.

THE FRAMEWORK FOR SCHOOL MANAGEMENT

A management framework is:

> a defined set of relationships and responsibilities within an organisation. It establishes accountability and provides clarity for individuals within the organisation by answering the basic questions of 'Who does what?' and 'Who is responsible for what?'.

(DFE 1993: 7)

Although each school should establish a management framework to reflect its own needs and circumstances, there are a number of broad areas that might be common to all frameworks. These include:

- a timetable and procedures for planning the school's annual budget, for reviewing the development plan and ensuring that it is consistent with the budget;
- an outline of the respective roles of the headteacher and governing body in setting and approving the annual budget;
- a statement on the frequency and level of detail at which the governing body wishes to receive reports from the headteacher about the general performance of the school and about budget expenditure;
- the terms of reference and delegated powers of any committees of the governing body;

- the delegated authority of the headteacher including the ability to commit expenditure;
- arrangements for authorising payments and monitoring financial expenditure;
- agreed procedures for filling staff vacancies, including governors' involvement in the process;
- the management arrangements to be made in the event of the absence of the headteacher, chair of governors or other key individuals.

(adapted from DFE 1993: 8–9)

As might be expected from a document written by accountants and management consultants, this framework says nothing about the main concern of the school, the progress of pupils' learning. A management framework for primary schools must include an explicit statement about the duties and responsibilities of all staff in regard to the management of pupils' learning and the curriculum. The management of the curriculum involves all members of the school community working together as a team. Teamwork is essential within the governing body, between the governing body and the staff of the school, within the staff of the school and between staff and parents.

Schools are no longer made up of large numbers of autonomous individuals acting independently of each other. Children are organised into classes, sets, teams and in many other ways. They are treated as groups and expected to act, in some ways, as groups. In a similar way teachers have collective as well as individual professional responsibilities and must exercise those collectively through their curriculum, year and management groups. Equally teachers are held accountable to colleagues, parents, governors and other parties with a legitimate interest for what is done in schools. Thus the exercise of responsibility, whether individually or as part of a group, takes place within a collective framework. This will be derived from the overall aims of the school and the development plan based on those aims. It is almost self-evident, therefore, that effective primary school management be based largely on teamwork within the schools.

Such teamwork must be based on a clear sense of purpose and a set of agreements about where the school is going and how it will get there. This sense of purpose will find expression through the school's development plan which involves the recognition that the main function of all primary schools is to foster learning and to provide an education which is appropriate for its children. Children, therefore, are at the centre of all the activities of all primary schools and it is for the benefit of children that all schools must be managed. Styan (1989) has argued that effective management has a vital part to play in enabling teachers to meet the needs of their children: 'Teachers have the right to expect well managed schools which provide the conditions for good teaching and learning. Headteachers and senior staff have the major responsibility for creating these conditions' (Styan 1989: 1).

At the same time teachers generally have a similar responsibility for making children the main focus of what they do:

> teachers need to work together collectively to produce an atmosphere in the school which encourages children to respond in a positive and responsible fashion. . . . The value of clear objectives for each lesson and the need for children to understand these objectives are often demonstrated. . . . The members of staff (should) work as a team so that they can offer leadership and guidance in areas of the curriculum that might present difficulties to individual teachers. In this way weaknesses and omissions are assessed and, as far as possible, remedied.
>
> (DES 1985: paras 13–30)

Thus the management of any primary school involves the whole staff of that school to a significant degree. This responsibility has to be exercised, however, within the framework created by legislation on the curriculum, assessment and the management of schools and the teachers within those schools.

THE CONTEXT OF SCHOOL MANAGEMENT

In the period from 1944 to the late 1980s schools worked within the context of a partnership between the Department of Education and Science (DES), now the Department for Education (DFE), the LEAs and the schools themselves. Each partner could offer advice to the others but tended to operate only through influence. For example, the governing body of a school could not impose its views on the content of the curriculum or on how it might best be taught. The same was also true of the DES and LEAs. Advice could be given and certain courses of action such as giving greater emphasis to reading within the primary school curriculum could be encouraged and supported by additional resources and in-service courses. Changes, however, might only take place through agreement. Consensus was the overriding principle (Blanchard *et al.* 1989).

After the 1986 Education Act no. 2 the situation became very different. This Act increased parental and community representation on governing bodies, gave governors power to modify an LEA's curriculum policy to suit the needs of individual schools, and enabled them to exercise some limited control of the school's budget. The same act gave, for the first time, a clear indication that governors were accountable to parents for their stewardship of the school. This accountability was to be rendered through an annual report from the governors to parents. This report had to describe the work of the governing body during the year and had to be presented and discussed at an annual parents' meeting.

The 1988 Education Reform Act (ERA) gave governing bodies even greater responsibilities. Schools were to assume responsibility for their own finances. The task of ensuring that the budget is effectively managed rests with the governing body. Governors can also decide staffing levels and make recommendations about appointments and dismissals. They may also seek to take their schools out of LEA control by applying for grant-maintained status. At the same time the governing body of each school has to satisfy itself that the school is meeting the requirements of the National Curriculum.

The National Curriculum poses particular difficulties for most primary schools. Its structure is extremely complex and this alone is creating significant management problems for primary schools. Each subject is divided into four key stages which are deemed appropriate for pupils of specified age ranges. For each subject and for each key stage, programmes of study set out what pupils should be taught and attainment targets set out the expected standards of pupil performance. At the end of Key Stages 1, 2 and 3, for all subjects except art, music and physical education, standards of pupil performance are set out in eight levels of increasing difficulty. The attainment targets are to be achieved by teaching programmes of study which are the matters, skills and processes which are required to be taught to pupils of different abilities and maturities during each key stage. The extent to which children attain these targets and thus achieve specific levels is assessed at each key stage by formal and external Standard Assessment Tests and by teacher assessment.

This type of structure marks a radical change in the approach to the curriculum for many primary schools. To begin with it is based on subjects rather than themes or projects. Not all teaching in primary schools was, prior to the National Curriculum, based on projects or entirely devoid of subject content. The requirement to structure much teaching on a subject basis and to cover a wide variety of subject content, is placing a considerable strain on the management skills and resources of many schools. David Pascal, Chair of the National Curriculum Council, recognised this when he stated that:

> I was concerned by the long hours dedicated primary teachers were working and their feeling that the curriculum might well be overloaded. ... We intend to address teachers' immediate needs for guidance, initial teacher training and the wider question of complexity and overload. ... We also wish to move away from the sterile debate about topics versus subjects.
>
> (*Guardian*, 6 October 1992: 22–3)

Others have also expressed concern about the likely effect of the National Curriculum over a longer period of time on primary schools. Nias *et al.* (1989) point out that the whole school approach which is now required to plan and implement the National Curriculum is alien to the deeply rooted traditions of individualism, self-reliance and curricular autonomy that are found in most primary schools. Nias does, however, remind us that an ability to engage wholeheartedly in the formation of whole school policies may be a hallmark of professional maturity. It is possible that teaching styles and methods are likely to become more traditional in the face of the curriculum and assessment demands currently being made on primary school teachers. This in turn may hasten the decline of vertical grouping and mixed age and ability classes.

There is no doubt that the National Curriculum is helping to determine the nature of management tasks that face all teachers in primary schools. It is intended to encourage all schools to change. The National Curriculum Council's *Information Pack Number 1* states that the National Curriculum will:

- give a clear incentive for the weaker schools to catch up with the best and the best will be challenged to do even better;
- provide teachers with detailed and precise objectives;
- provide parents with clear and accurate information;
- ensure continuity and progression from one year to another, from one school to another;
- help teachers to concentrate on the task of getting the best possible results from each individual child.

(adapted from NCC 1989: overhead transparency (OHT) 1)

These things will not just happen. They need to be managed at a variety of different organisational levels within the school. They have clear implications for the planning and implementation of processes of teaching and learning related to both content and method within classes, year groups and schools. There are also wider implications concerning provision for pupils with special educational needs, equal opportunities, the form and nature of information collected and transmitted about pupils and their performance and the provision of guidance and counselling for pupils. There is little doubt, however, that the National Curriculum has emphasised the importance of sound curriculum management for all staff, and especially senior managers, in primary schools. The curriculum, its content and the processes for delivering that content, is now the central focus of management activity in these schools. This also includes the monitoring, reviewing and evaluating of those processes in the light of pupil performance. The reinstating of the curriculum to the centre of management activity in the primary school means that much more detailed consideration is now being given to the management of teaching and learning.

There have been, however, considerable difficulties associated with this transformation. The National Curriculum has proved to be a set of rapidly changing guidelines rather than a fixed framework within which all work can be planned. It is still too detailed and is difficult to encompass within the confines of the time available for teaching in primary schools. It also assumes that all primary schools have the specialist expertise available to cover the whole curriculum. This is unlikely to be the case in many schools. The demands of assessment, its recording and reporting have also placed great strain on teachers, especially as this work had to be done while coping with classes of up to 35 pupils. Little wonder that one study has shown that: 'The pressure that teachers were under within the school day was creating a sense of working hard but achieving little ... they simply did not have time in the school day to do all the things which had to be done' (Campbell *et al.* 1993: 16).

These issues have been addressed by Sir Ron Dearing in his review of the National Curriculum. His report, based on the assumption that teachers broadly support the ten-subject National Curriculum and regard it as an entitlement for all pupils (Dearing 1993), makes a number of recommendations which are intended to reduce teacher work load and create opportunities for teachers to use time more flexibly. The recommendations include:

- the slimming down of Key Stages 1, 2 and 3 so that the equivalent of one day a week of teaching time is freed for schools to use at their discretion;
- the revision of all curriculum orders at the same time;
- no further changes to be made for five years;
- the retention of the 10-level scale and its improvement by reducing the number of statements of attainments and attainment targets;
- the restriction of national testing to core subjects and the simplification of tests and the reduction of the time needed to administer them;
- giving assessment of pupils by teachers equal weight to test results in reports to parents.

(adapted from Dearing 1994)

It remains to be seen how effective these reforms are. It has been argued that Dearing has failed to address the main issue, that of the disparity of staffing between primary and secondary schools when the level of educational demands are broadly similar. In spite of attempts to slim down the National Curriculum the statutory curriculum remains undeliverable for most primary schools because the detail which remains specified within the National Curriculum and the number of statements of attainment is too great (Campbell 1994). Teachers are still left trying to get a quart into a pint pot. The effect of this, and of the continued emphasis on the assessment of the core subjects, is that any time that becomes free for flexible use by teachers will, almost inevitably, be devoted to the core subjects rather than be used to broaden curriculum provision. Dearing's attempt to address the question of curriculum balance entirely in terms of the time allocated to different subjects seems to be both superficial and misplaced.

Whatever the outcome of the Dearing Report, a number of key questions will still need to be addressed by primary school teachers about the management of the curriculum. These include:

- How can we ensure that all the pupils in our school study the core and foundation subjects for a reasonable period of time?
- How will the curriculum need to change and develop as we become familiar with the demands of the National Curriculum?
- What are the staffing implications of those changes in terms of recruitment and professional development?
- What are the funding and resource management implications of these changes for both primary and secondary schools?
- How do we ensure that all staff feel involved in and confident about the planning and implementation of the National Curriculum?

(adapted from NCC 1989: OHT 21)

These questions draw attention to the importance of curriculum management as well as to the detail of resource and staff management. They also highlight the need to consult staff and involve them in the decision-making about the planning and implementation of the school's teaching and assessment of the National Curriculum. Primary schools must, therefore, have a management structure that will enable all staff to play an active part in the continued management of the curriculum.

Primary school teachers with a curriculum responsibility are required to carry out certain tasks in order to implement and monitor the effectiveness of work in their particular subject area. These tasks include:

- extracting relevant information from reports of the working groups and NCC advice to the Secretary of State;
- studying the statutory orders and non-statutory guidance for the relevant subject;
- comparing the programmes of study in the statutory orders with existing teaching schemes and other material in the school;
- drawing up a plan of action to ensure that all prescribed progammes of study are taught;
- preparing and adapting resource material;
- providing support and guidance for colleagues;
- planning for the continuous assessment and the recording of pupils' progress;
- monitoring the implementation of the plans for teaching and assessing work in the subject area;
- monitoring, reporting to colleagues and acting upon any changes that may be made to the statutory orders.

(developed from NCC 1989: OHT 22)

Any teacher will recognise just how time-consuming these processes can be. Coping with them requires much more than a simple adaptation of existing teaching programmes and a modification of existing resources. Nevertheless primary schools are now required to deploy the resources at their disposal in order to provide pupils with that to which they are now entitled. This is a broad and balanced curriculum which will promote spiritual, moral, cultural, mental and physical development and which will provide a preparation for the opportunities, responsibilities and experiences of adult life. The management of the curriculum, and especially planning for continuity and progression has become central to the management of primary schools.

This is highlighted in the white paper, *Choice and Diversity: A New Framework for Schools* (DFE 1992). Here the curriculum is subsumed under the heading *Quality*, one of the 'five great themes for education' which are intended to inform the legislative programme for education throughout the 1990s. It is argued that:

> the National Curriculum . . . has now guaranteed to all pupils the same grounding in essential subjects. The National Curriculum provides clear objectives and a basic framework of standards for what pupils should know, do and understand. . . . Debate is no longer about the principle of a national curriculum. It is about how subjects should be developed within the National Curriculum and about the crucial testing arrangements associated with them.
>
> (DFE 1992: paras 1.11–1.12)

This, it is suggested, is the first stage in achieving quality which, in this white paper, appears to be defined entirely in terms of outcomes rather than processes or content. This issue of quality will be considered in Chapter 2 when the arrangements for school inspection will be examined.

The remaining four 'great themes' all relate to ways of ensuring that quality is maintained by holding schools to account for what they are doing and depriving them of resources if they fail to perform well. Thus *diversity* will ensure that schools are providing a form of education that is linked to local circumstances and individual needs and that alternative forms of schooling based on grant maintained schools and city technology colleges are made available. The basic principle that 'parents know best' (DFE 1992: para. 1.17) is enshrined in much of the legislation on education that was enacted during the 1980s. Here, *parental choice* emerges as a theme which will continue to be pursued by increasing parental influence over the work of schools. Schools will, it is argued, be better able to respond to the wishes of parents and others if they are free from unnecessary LEA control and are able to make decisions on the basis of locally identified need. The white paper argues that, in order to do this, schools need *greater autonomy*.

This will be achieved through delegating resource management to schools and by allowing schools to develop their own strengths and specialisations within the framework of the National Curriculum. With autonomy comes *accountability* which will be ensured by intense, interested and increasingly informed scrutiny of schools by parents, employers and the local community and will focus upon the ways that schools seek to respond to:

- the clear targets of the National Curriculum, which give schools and parents alike benchmarks against which to judge the progress of pupils, both individually and collectively;
- assessment arrangements and public examinations which measure pupils' progress in relation to those targets at regular intervals;
- the publication of the results of the National Curriculum tests and public examinations, backed by regular independent inspections, which will enable parents to hold schools to account for their performance and give them assurance about standards of teaching;
- the broadening of choice of schools which will enable parents to act on information about schools' relative performance and to choose schools which are right for their children.

(adapted from DFE 1992: para. 2.8)

These five themes have implications for the management of primary schools beyond those of how to manage a national curriculum. For example it is now necessary to establish what is meant by quality and to identify criteria by which the outcomes of children's learning can be matched with those notions of quality. Teachers in primary schools have to decide how to respond to an increased diversity by ensuring that what is offered in schools meets local circumstances and individual needs. It is far from clear how such needs will be articulated nor can the assumption be made that clearly articulated local needs will be either coherent or consistent. It is quite possible that schools may be asked to respond to needs that are, at best, rapidly changing or, at worst, mutually exclusive. Nevertheless teachers do have to come to terms with greater parental choice and the operation of market forces. This might lead to decisions being taken about specialisation, although most primary schools may find that resources are stretched to their limits if they are to implement the National Curriculum and that scope for specialisation is very limited. All primary schools will be required, however, to cope with the demands of increased levels of accountability and new forms of school inspection. How schools might respond to these demands will be dealt with in subsequent chapters of this book. What these demands mean at the very least, however, is that staff in primary schools must understand what they are trying to achieve and be able to communicate this in a clear, meaningful way to parents and others in their local community. In short we have to be clear what is meant by an effective school.

EFFECTIVE SCHOOLS AND SCHOOL EFFECTIVENESS

The Audit Commission (1991), in its report on management within primary schools stated that:

There is no accepted definition of effectiveness and there is little systematic evidence of the relationship between management action and effectiveness. But there is evidence that education quality is more likely to be high if the necessary organisational pre-conditions are in place – competent leadership, trained staff, sound buildings and adequate teaching materials.

(Audit Commission 1991: 7)

The report does not examine the implied difference between education quality and school effectiveness or show how quality is achieved by the four pre-conditions. The link between quality and effectiveness is far less problematic in *Choice and Diversity* (DFE 1992) where an effective school is defined as one that meets locally identified needs from its existing resources and ensures that its pupils attend regularly and perform well in public tests and examinations, a view focusing on quality in terms of outcomes rather than processes. This is somewhat different from the definition that might be derived from an analysis of the National Curriculum which might lead us to assume that an effective school is one which maximises pupil achievement, cares for the development of the whole individual and prepares pupils for adult life. Little wonder then, that:

It is sometimes hard to pin down what exactly makes people point at a place and say 'that's a good school'. It is not always characterised by spending more money on having smaller class sizes, larger libraries, better buildings, new facilities, or the things that many people seek in wanting to improve our schools.

(DFE 1992: para. 1.33)

In other words in order to become an effective school it is not necessary to increase the levels of resources. This is a very comforting message for those who wish schools to manage within tight resource constraints. Nevertheless some guidance is given as to what is required to achieve such effectiveness: 'Central to a good school is strong leadership ... parental involvement in its life and processes ... freedom from excessive external control and regulation ... and ... teachers of high quality' (DFE 1992: para. 1.33).

Strong leadership, it is argued, usually means articulating a clear academic mission for the school, setting standards and creating a recognisable ethos, but these are not ends in themselves.

To some extent this echoes the view expressed in *Ten Good Schools* (DES 1977) that:

The schools see themselves as places designated for learning; they take trouble to make their philosophies explicit for themselves and to explain them to parents and pupils. ... Emphasis is laid on consultation, teamwork and participation but, without exception, the most important single factor in the success of these schools is the qualities of leadership of the headteacher.

(DES 1977: section 8)

Similar criteria have been identified by others. For example Mortimore *et al.* (1988) suggest that good primary schools are characterised by:

- purposeful leadership of the staff by the headteacher;
- involvement of the deputy headteacher;
- involvement of the staff in planning;
- consistency, continuity and progression in teaching;
- structured approaches to learning;
- intellectually challenging teaching;
- a work centred environment and a positive climate;
- clearly defined tasks;
- good communication between teachers and pupils;
- written records;
- parental and community involvement;
- well displayed and valued work.

(adapted from Mortimore 1988)

These criteria are almost entirely concerned with processes and focus mainly on the staff team and whole school organisational levels. In contrast to this Her Majesty's Inspectors (HMI) point out that to be effective primary schools must provide learning and teaching of high quality. This is most likely to be achieved where teachers:

- establish and maintain a good classroom ethos in which pupils are motivated to learn;
- plan, prepare and organise lessons well and ensure that pupils are clear about what they have to learn;
- recognise the need for good classroom organisation including the organisation of resources;
- set a good example, and foster good relationships with pupils;
- have high, but attainable, expectations of pupils in respect both of academic performance and good behaviour;
- provide tasks which are well matched to the needs, aptitudes and prior knowledge of individual pupils;
- understand the role of language in learning;
- ensure that pupils acquire knowledge, understanding and skills, are encouraged to become independent, resourceful and responsible, and are able to work purposefully on their own and with others;
- check that learning has taken place by ensuring that assessment is an integral part of classroom;
- work to provide diagnostic information on pupil progress and information which can be used to evaluate their teaching and inform parents;
- support classroom learning with work done at home where this is appropriate and in accordance with school policy.

(DES 1989: adapted from para. 1.3)

It can be seen, then, that in the work of Mortimore *et al.* (1988) and in that adopted by HMI certain common factors are valued. There is an emphasis on the improvement of both teaching and learning and on the continued development of the school as a learning institution. There is an emphasis on collaboration and an awareness of the benefits of both process and outcome rather than a concern with one at the expense of the other. There is a recognition that all staff in the school have a role to play in the management of the institution.

There is, however, a distinction to be made between a good school and an effective one.

> It could be argued that effective schools develop effectively . . . by examining both the normative and procedural dimensions. This leads to the drawing of vital distinction between a 'good' and 'effective' school. The latter develops successfully in any direction; the former develops successfully according to an agreed agenda.
>
> (Reid *et al.* 1987:12)

It is difficult to know just how valid this distinction is at a time when much of the educational agenda is determined externally for most schools. What is clear, however, is that effectiveness is concerned with achieving appropriate and agreed objectives whether these are determined internally or externally. If government policy provides no coherent plan for the future of education (NAHT 1992), and the definition of a good school emphasises outcome at the expense of process, then those in schools whose responsibility it is to provide professional leadership must respond to this situation. Such a response might involve exploring with relevant constituent groups such as parents, governors, staff and even members of the wider community exactly what set of objectives might be used against which to test the effectiveness of a particular school. At the same time some of the difficulties that are encountered when seeking to establish how well a school has performed might also be examined to demonstrate how complex a task it is to compare performance within and between schools in advance of any inspection reports or the publication of league tables. A new form of educational leadership that extends beyond the immediate confines of the school is now required. Much of the responsibility for this will fall on the headteacher whose role in the primary school has changed rapidly in the last few years and will continue so to do.

THE ROLE OF THE HEADTEACHER

However difficult it is to arrive at a definition of a good school or to list those factors which contribute to school effectiveness, it is quite clear that sound classroom organisation, good teaching and leadership from staff with curriculum and whole school responsibilities are vital but the role of the headteacher is of paramount importance: 'The leadership qualities of headteachers and the manner in which they fulfill their management responsibilities are key factors in determining the effectiveness of their schools' (DES 1989: 16). This says little about what headteachers actually do or about what they should do. There is a growing body of evidence which suggests that headteachers are regularly involved in fragmented, reactive, short-term and even trivial tasks which have little or nothing to do with the overall management of the school or its curriculum (Torrington and Weightman 1989; Laws and Dennison 1991).

Nevertheless, it is possible to identify a range of tasks of a somewhat different nature that commonly face headteachers and other staff with management responsibility in schools (Morgan *et al.* 1983). These might be subsumed under four headings:

- **Technical** Those tasks which are specific to the main purpose of the school, that is the education of its pupils. These will be concerned with teaching and learning.
- **Conceptual** Those tasks related to the control and administration of the school such as the appointment and deployment of staff, establishing appropriate contractual relationships with providers of services, financial management and the management of resources.
- **Human Relations** Those tasks that involve decision-making, policy-making and staff development.
- **External Relations** Those tasks which enable managers to control the flow of information into and out of the school, to manage the legitimate interventions in the work of the school from parents, governors and others within the community, and to represent the school on external planning and development bodies.

The technical tasks have always been a significant feature of the work of primary school staff but they are now made more complex by the role that governors have in the management of the curriculum under the terms of the 1988 Education Reform Act. At the same time carrying out the conceptual tasks in primary schools has also become more demanding. With the introduction of local management of schools (LMS) through delegated budgets, the appointment, deployment and dismissal of staff have been devolved to schools in their entirety. Again governors now have a central role to play in these matters. Furthermore all staff are now subject to appraisal on a two-yearly cycle. This can provide benefits for both individual teachers and the school as a whole, but it is a time-consuming and demanding process. Closely related to the conceptual tasks are those concerned with human relations. Policy-making and the involvement of staff in decision-making is crucial but complex, while maximising the professional development opportunities that are available is an essential part of the process of enabling the school to meet the needs of its pupils. External relations have, until recently, been regarded as the province of the headteacher. While the headteacher still remains the focal point of much of this activity, many other staff are now increasingly involved through their roles as teacher governors, curriculum and year leaders and members of LEA-wide planning groups.

It has been argued that it is extremely difficult to differentiate the technical or professional from the administrative or executive aspects of these tasks (Field 1985). Hughes (1985) has drawn attention to the importance of making this distinction for understanding the role of headteachers. He argues that all headteachers carry out professional leadership and executive functions.

Professional development functions include:

- providing professional guidance to staff;
- counselling pupils, parents and others;
- teaching and curriculum development;
- acting as spokesperson for the school on relevant educational matters;
- involvement in external professional activities.

Executive functions include:

- allocating resources and monitoring their use;
- coordinating functions within the school;
- monitoring and reviewing performance;
- appraising staff;
- establishing and maintaining external relationships with members of the governing body, parents and other constituent groups.

Hughes argues that educational expertise enables the headteacher to operate both as chief executive and leading professional:

> the professional-as-administrator does not act in some matters as a leading professional and in others as a chief executive. Professional knowledge, skills and attitudes are likely to have a profound effect on the whole range of tasks undertaken by the headteacher of a professional organisation.
>
> (Hughes 1985: 279)

It has been suggested (Bell 1986) that, although they had to carry out basic administration prior to the 1988 Education Reform Act, primary head-teachers were mainly concerned with the education and welfare of children through:

- teaching and providing professional leadership;
- managing colleagues and helping to develop their expertise;
- setting educational priorities for their schools;
- building good working relationships inside their school and with colleagues in other schools.

After the Act it was anticipated that this emphasis on professional leadership would give way to a concern for system maintenance based on:

- testing and assessing the work of children and colleagues;
- directing and controlling the professional activities of teachers;
- managing resources on the basis of priorities identified by others;
- public relations and pupil recruitment;
- basic administration including financial management.

While the role of the primary school headteacher has always had these two basic dimensions, the professional or educational and the executive or managerial, the traditional view of the headteacher tended to emphasis the former, while recent developments are placing more emphasis on the latter. As Maclure has argued:

> The headteacher has always had a powerful management role. . . . The new dispensation ushered in by the Education Reform Act puts this on a new basis. . . . The element of financial delegation ensures that this change will be real. . . . The headteacher's enhanced management role cannot but change relationships within the profession as a whole.
>
> (Maclure 1989: 11–12)

Others, however, in warning against a similar change in emphasis, attribute it not to financial delegation but to the changes in the relationships between headteachers and governing bodies. A contradiction is identified between the need for a strong professional role for headteachers and the constraints placed upon them in carrying out this role by recent legislation:

> The White Paper emphasises the importance of strong leadership from . . . the headteacher. Yet it fails to follow through its thinking to a logical conclusion, i.e. that the headteacher should be the chief executive responsible to the governing body for the executive management of the school. The government has always equated the relationship of the headteacher to the governing body with that of the Chief Executive to a Board of Directors. Responsibility without power blurs the line of account-ability . . . and is a recipe for confusion, poor management practice and difficult relationships.
>
> (NAHT 1992: para. 11.1)

The discussion paper *Curriculum Organisation and Classroom Practice in Primary Schools* (Alexander *et al.* 1992) also warns of the danger of allowing the role of primary headteacher to become an administrative rather than an educational one:

> There is a view at present in England that . . . the primary headteacher must become an administrator or chief executive. We reject this view absolutely. The task of implementing the National Curriculum and its assessment arrangements requires headteachers, more than ever, to retain and develop the role of educational leader.
>
> (Alexander *et al.* 1992: 46)

The report goes on to argue that headteachers are uniquely placed to monitor and review the whole school for purposes of judging its strengths and weaknesses, identifying potential problems and drawing attention to work of distinction. It points out that primary headteachers will increasingly be responsible for quality assessment and assurance within their schools. Here, although the authors do not acknowledge it, they are placing emphasis on the chief executive rather than on the professional leadership role, since they are choosing to highlight the evaluative functions. They do note, however, that effective primary headteachers need to have a vision of what their schools should become and must seek to establish this vision through the development of shared educational beliefs which underpin evaluative judgements, school policies and decision-making. This vision will be articulated through school development planning, which will be discussed in Chapter 3. At the heart of this plan will be a clearly articulated view of what constitutes the school curriculum and how this can be translated into pupil learning. This is the essence of curriculum management and will be explored in Chapter 4.

There is no doubt that whatever developments occur in the role of primary headteachers they must retain general oversight of the curriculum and take a lead in decision-making on curriculum matters. Headteachers, however, cannot be expected to possess the subject knowledge needed to teach every aspect of the National Curriculum, nor be expected to be familiar with the detail of all relevant developments. Except in the very smallest schools, headteachers should delegate responsibility for subject, cross-curricular and age-phase matters to other members of staff while retaining for themselves the responsibility of coordinating a range of activities and the deployment and overall development of staff.

MANAGEMENT IN PRIMARY SCHOOLS

Such an approach to primary headship means that responsibility for managing the school is shared between the members of staff and that everyone involved must acquire and refine a set of appropriate management skills. Each member of the staff team has a body of professional knowledge and expertise that can and should be deployed for the benefit of the children in the school and which can be used to support the work of colleagues. Each individual member of staff can benefit from the expertise of the others. Such a collaborative framework is necessary if primary schools are to meet the challenges presented by the National Curriculum, the Parents Charter, and the five great themes. It they are to be successful then the work of the members of the primary school staff team has to be coordinated through the setting of clear objectives, decisions taken and implemented, tasks delegated, and effectiveness monitored and evaluated. All staff have a part to play in this and it is possible to identify a set of management skills which each member of staff will need to deploy. These are:

Planning   This is the identification of a course of action in order to achieve desired results. The results will be expressed in terms of objectives and will be derived from the priorities identified in the school development plan.

Decision-making   In essence, decision-making means choosing from at least two possible courses of action. It is one of the central skills of management since most of us spend most of our time making such choices. Within the context of primary schools particular care has to be taken to involve colleagues in this process.

Problem-solving   Often confused with decision-making but is distinctly different. It requires teachers to recognise when something is not working properly, or as effectively as should be the case, and individually or collectively to seek to establish the cause of this deviation from the normal situation. Once the causes of a problem are identified then decisions can be taken about how best to deal with the situation.

Organising   This means ensuring that all members of staff are working together cooperatively and that all the necessary functions and tasks are being carried out.

Coordinating   Duties have to be defined and responsibilities have to be allocated fairly. At the same time duplication of effort has to be avoided.

Commanding   This often has an unfortunate authoritarian tone which is not acceptable among a group of professional colleagues. In the context of primary school management, however, commanding is the ability to give clear instructions and information where this is appropriate.

Controlling   Again, the notion of control runs counter to the ethos of professional autonomy. It is clear, however, that control is necessary to ensure that the National Curriculum is provided, that resources are managed effectively and that the schools are able to be accountable to the various stakeholders. Controlling is the monitoring of performance to achieve objectives and tasks completed.

Delegating   When work is divided up between groups of colleagues delegation may be taking place. It requires that the tasks to be delegated are clearly identified and the person to whom the task is delegated is adequately prepared and supported.

Motivating   This can be defined as the process of encouraging colleagues to work more enthusiastically. It involves making behavioural choices, decisions about objectives and assumptions about rewards.

Developing staff   Staff development is now an integral part of school development and a responsibility of all managers in primary schools who have to ensure that colleagues within their teams are given the maximum opportunity to benefit from individual professional development.

Communicating   Decisions can only be made, plans implemented, activities coordinated and controlled, tasks delegated, staff motivated and developed, through an effective system of communication. This might be done in writing but is mainly face-to-face and is normally intended to encourage colleagues to take appropriate actions or acquire relevant information.

Influencing   This is an important sub-skill of communicating. It is achieved by knowing what is to be achieved, listening, questioning and reaching agreements.

Monitoring   The process of ensuring that appropriate actions are being taken at the right time, checking that control and coordination are working effectively.

Evaluating   The process of examining performance outcomes against previously identified and agreed criteria to ensure that those criteria are being met.

Some of these skills, such as communicating, influencing and problem-solving, may be required equally by all members of the school staff. Others, such as motivating, delegating and developing staff, are thought to be more relevant for senior managers. All of these skills, however, are interdependent. Planning requires evaluation and monitoring, while organising requires delegation and motivating is necessary to get most things done. In primary schools, management can be understood as the application of a set of skills in order to establish a professional collaboration between colleagues to achieve common objectives. With the introduction of school development plans, these objectives and the tasks to be completed in order to achieve them will be written down, known and understood by the staff of the school and its wider constituency.

It has been argued that groups of professionals do not need to be managed because they are self-directed. This position is based on the view that either all decisions are group decisions or, alternatively, any decision taken by a professional will be very much like that taken by another because it is based on the interests of the client (Rust 1985). This is an extremely simplistic view of professions and professionals. Few schools, if any, even those staffed by the most highly committed and sophisticated professional teachers, are likely to exhibit such unity and accord on all matters. Furthermore, teachers are often struggling to cope with competing pedagogic and wider professional demands in a rapidly changing context within which they may not always be fully informed and over which they may not have full control. Managing the professional development of teachers is an essential part of providing the necessary support to enable them to cope with the demands which they now face. This will be considered in Chapters 5 and 6. Appointing the most appropriate staff is a further essential element in primary school management and will be the subject of Chapter 7.

Management of professional groups within organisations such as primary schools is vitally necessary. It tends to mediate between the needs and expectations of teachers, pupils, parents and other constituents of the school. It is one function of those with management responsibility in the school to break down the physical and social separation which results from the way in which much of a teacher's day is structured. A well-managed school is one in which professional colleagues share the responsibilities associated with the work of the school. Different individuals take the lead in different areas depending on their expertise. Such an approach to management can go a long way towards minimising the professional isolation that some teachers experience. The management of the school's human resources will, therefore, be examined in Chapter 8.

Professional autonomy is not readily compatible with collegiality and collaboration which require a commitment to sharing expertise and to influencing and being influenced by the work of colleagues. Primary school teachers who work in situations where colleagues share expertise within the framework of a well-structured school organisation are more likely to be professionally interdependent than independent. This means that their freedom to act as they wish within their classrooms is, to some extent, constrained by the expectations of colleagues. Such constraints may also be derived from the National Curriculum and other legislation. These are harder to avoid and will be easier to face if approached in a collaborative way. This requires that all staff are treated as professionals by headteachers and colleagues with management responsibility throughout the school. It also requires that all staff act on the basis of a professional concern for the whole school rather than merely for their own classroom.

Teachers in primary schools have to be managed in such a way as to recognise their professional status while fostering the development of whole-school policies, the foundation of which must be professional interdependence. This requires a knowledge of those specific skills which form the broad basis of management. It also demands the ability to apply those skills at all levels of the school in order to achieve the aims and objectives and to carry out the tasks that the school has set itself. This can best be done if managers in primary schools create a stable environment within which such work can take place. Teachers cannot, therefore, be left to operate in isolation or in ignorance of how the school plans to meet the demands that face it. The school development plan, carefully formulated on the basis of wide consultation and discussion, provides the framework for meeting those demands. It is also an essential part of the process of managing material and physical resources effectively. This will be considered in Chapter 9.

A major concern for all those who have an interest in primary schools is, and will continue to be, the need to ensure that schools provide high quality education for their pupils. The concept of quality in education is extremely elusive in spite of the apparent certainties that have been expressed about it (DFE 1992). Identifying when it is present and monitoring the progress of schools towards providing it is a complex process. For the time being, at least, the task of doing this rests with the Office for Standards in Education (OFSTED). Its main vehicle for carrying out this duty is the inspection process and it is to this that we now turn.

Chapter 2

Quality and the inspection of primary schools

In the first chapter it was argued that delivering quality in education is now a major concern for teachers. Quality will be achieved through diversity and choice within a framework of school autonomy that has clearly defined processes to ensure that schools are held to account for what they do and for what their pupils achieve. This is intended to lead to increased competition between schools for pupils. The publication of examination results is intended to enable parents to make more informed choices about the selection of suitable schools for their children. In turn it is anticipated that schools will pay more attention to processes of teaching and learning and focus on the requirements of customers of the education service.

WHAT IS QUALITY?

Quality, in this context, has two distinct strands. The first relates to a national set of educational standards within the framework of the National Curriculum. These will be monitored by tests at the key stages of a child's education. Quality here is conceptualised in terms of specific and absolute outcomes and the efficient use of resources rather than of processes or relative achievements. The quality of teaching is the other strand. Quality, therefore, is to be identified by assessing the work of pupils, appraising teachers, and informing parents about the school's performance. It is now Government policy to pursue both aspects of quality through OFSTED which will ensure that schools are subjected to regular and rigorous inspections.

The purpose of inspection is: 'to identify strengths and weaknesses in schools so that they may improve the quality of education offered and raise the standards achieved by their pupils' (OFSTED 1993: 4). In some ways, the new inspection process is similar to that previously carried out by HMI. It involves a group of officials spending a short but intensive period examining the work of the school. In other ways, however, it is different. The criteria for inspection, the details of the process and the structure of the report are now published and available for staff in schools to use for themselves. The agenda for the inspection is now a public rather than a private one. Perhaps as a result of this, however, the link between inspection and follow-up advice and support no longer exists. LEA advisors are no longer able to provide this service if they have been directly involved in the inspection. The school must produce its own action plan based on the recommendation of the OFSTED inspectors.

It is doubtful, however, if quality can be guaranteed in schools by externally conducted inspections, even if these are carried out on a regular and frequent basis. At best such inspections can produce only a snapshot of the quality of education being provided, of the educational standards being achieved, of the extent to which resources are being managed efficiently and of the spiritual, moral, social and cultural development of pupils in the school. To be effective, inspection and monitoring need to be an integral part of the management of the school and its continuous process of improvement. Inspection, however, is only one element in the total process for assuring that pupils receive an education of good quality. School development planning, teacher appraisal, recording and reporting of pupil performance and other internal quality assurance measures, which will be considered in later chapters, also play an important part in quality assurance in all primary schools.

THE CONCEPT OF QUALITY

The concept of quality as applied to primary schools is both new and, to a large extent, confusing. A distinction needs to be made, therefore, between different approaches to quality.

Quality control involves checking, monitoring and inspecting by external agencies. It looks only at what the school is now achieving and measures that against specific criteria. It takes no account of how much the school has achieved or what it plans to do in future. It is neither formative nor developmental and it tends to lead to externally imposed quality control through school-based reactions to periodic inspection. Quality control leads to the rejection of what is poor and its replacement by something new, rather than to organic change and development. In schools where quality is seen in this way, much time will be spent preparing for, and responding to, external inspections. If quality is achieved, this will be because the school is merely responding to the threats of external inspection.

Quality assurance, on the other hand, recognises that external inspection is but one of a number of mechanisms for continually monitoring and improving the quality of education provided by the school for its pupils. In such schools the main concerns about inspection will not be how to prepare for it and how to react to it. They will be how to incorporate it into the existing procedures for assuring quality in the school and how to benefit from it in such a way that the school can continue to change, develop and improve. This requires that everyone in the school takes the responsibility for achieving quality through the consistent meeting of pre-determined specifications or criteria by following clearly defined processes. There is likely to be a strong emphasis on teamwork based on a clear aim, specific objectives, effective delegation and good communication. Quality is achieved through the continual improvement of provision based on an understanding that the purpose of inspection is to evaluate, not to commend or prescribe. Schools have autonomy over how they manage their responses to inspection and, therefore, are able to use the process to support their planned processes of development.

TOTAL QUALITY MANAGEMENT

When the quality assurance approach to managing schools is applied to all areas of the work of schools it is sometimes called total quality management (TQM). It is not really helpful to add yet another educational acronym to the already extensive list but the underlying principles of TQM are useful for understanding how to establish sound quality assurance in primary schools. These include the recognition that:

- quality depends on a commitment to a shared vision for the school;
- quality is defined by the receivers of education rather than by the providers;
- quality is based on 'fitness for purpose', on the idea that education does what it sets out to do;
- quality consists of meeting clearly stated standards;
- quality is achieved by ensuring that these standards are met rather than by the detection of failure;
- quality is everyone's responsibility within the school;
- staff development is fundamental to achieving quality;
- to achieve quality the school must define its own priorities in the light of the needs of its pupils and their parents. These priorities find expression in the school development plan and should be driven by the needs of the pupils and, therefore, linked closely to the curriculum;
- quality can only be achieved through continuous improvement.

(after West-Burnham 1992)

In primary schools, therefore, TQM shifts the focus away from teacher-determined programmes, processes and outcomes towards a partnership between the staff of the school and its customers, who are both the parents and the pupils. It also demands that schools cease to ask if they have succeeded and begin to ask how they can become more capable of continuing to succeed. Inspections, therefore, must be treated as formative rather than summative. The emphasis should be on taking action for further development. Such actions should not be developed independently of one another, nor should they be the result of small groups producing individual action plans for development. Rather, actions to bring about continuous improvement must be part of the strategic planning of the school. For this to happen the school's procedures have to be analysed against clearly identified measures and standards. These measures and standards help to define the principal attributes of quality. They are arrived at by conducting a quality review through:

- discovering what is being done;
- documenting what is intended;
- analysing procedures to ensure that they achieve what is intended;
- doing what is intended;
- providing evidence that the school is doing what it claims it is doing;
- sharing information within the school identifying areas for planned improvement.

It can be seen, therefore, that underpinning TQM is a process of stating what is to be done, how it will be achieved and solving problems as and when necessary. Sallis (1993) argues that every school seeking to develop quality assurance through TQM should focus its quality review on a number of aspects of its work which include:

- The school development plan which provides the long-term vision for the school, establishes its strategic plan, gives a context within which all of its other provisions and policies operate and from which its objectives are derived and expresses those objectives in priority order within the constraints of the locally managed budget.
- A defined set of management responsibilities which set out the role of the governing body, the senior management team and middle managers in the school.
- An equal opportunities policy for staff and pupils which gives details of the content of the policy and of the methods and procedures to be used to achieve its aims.
- A policy for marketing and publicity which enables the school to provide its prospective customers with clear, up-to-date and accurate information about what it offers.
- A process for dealing with enquiries and admissions that enables the correct advice to be given to those making enquiries and includes a well-documented procedure for admitting pupils and facilitating transfer from one school to another.
- A pupil induction programme which introduces children and their parents to the school, its ethos and styles and methods of teaching, learning and assessment.
- Reporting on and guiding pupil progress which follows from induction and should be a regular feature of school life for all teachers, pupils and parents. It can be based on personal development profiles, reports and records of assessment. It must be fully understood by staff and by parents and take into account the need to respond to situations in which pupils appear to be under-performing.

- The management of learning which has to ensure that progression, continuity and differentiation are all achieved and that the standard of pupil achievement and the quality of their learning is fundamental to the decisions taken.
- The management of the curriculum which has to be linked to the National Curriculum programmes of study and attainment targets and must include Curriculum policies which identify the aims, objectives and resources for each Curriculum area, schemes of work, records of work, assessment records and action plans for future development.
- Administrative arrangements for dealing with the financial and organisational aspects of the work of the school.
- Staff development policy which should include induction for new staff and appraisal, and which is linked to the school development plan and shows how needs are identified, how priorities are established, how staff development contributes to achieving the school's current objectives and the extent to which the programme is cost effective. All staff should establish and keep a professional development record or portfolio.
- Monitoring and evaluation of all aspects of the work of the school in order to establish that resources are being used efficiently and value for money is being achieved. This should be based on regular audits and reviews and on monitoring and evaluation. Staff appraisal will also be a part of this process, which then needs to feed back into the school's strategic planning.

Although this seems a detailed and possibly bureaucratic approach to primary school management, it does incorporate all the main areas of the work of the school. If a school is involved in many of the aspects of this quality review then it will be well placed to deliver a high quality education to its pupils. It will also be well prepared to meet the demands of a full inspection and to gain maximum benefit from it. This is especially true since in this quality review, as in the approach adopted by OFSTED, it is the school development plan which is central to the school's management process. It also reflects the documentary information required for an OFSTED inspection which includes the school's aims and objectives, its development plan, curriculum policy statements, school prospectus, timetable, curriculum and assessment programmes, agendas and minutes of meetings (see OFSTED 1994a: Part 2). All of these documents are a normal product of the work of a well-organised primary school where quality assurance and continuous improvement are fundamental to its management.

THE INSPECTION OF SCHOOLS

The inspection of schools as conducted by the OFSTED inspectorate provides a freeze frame view of the school based on a specific and public set of criteria.

It is a snapshot of what the school is doing at the time of inspection. It is not developmental nor formative. It does not take direct account of what the school has already achieved but may be informed by data relating to relevant special circumstances. It is essentially evaluative and judgemental but not punitive except to the extent that it can identify a school as failing. The definition of a failing school and the procedures to be followed if a school is so designated can be found in Technical Paper 13 (OFSTED 1994a: 93–102). The inspectorate do not make judgements about individuals but set out to compare the performance of each school against a standard set of criteria. They concentrate on collecting evidence about how well the school is currently performing based on documentary and observational evidence supplemented by discussions with pupils, parents, staff and governors. OFSTED is particularly concerned with the standards of pupil learning, the quality of teaching and the management of and support provided for learning and teaching. Underpinning all this is an emphasis on the implementation of whole-school policy in the classroom and the effective and efficient deployment of resources in order to achieve the priorities identified by the school development plan and to obtain value for money.

> Inspectors can estimate value for money by relating the overall judgments of quality, standards, efficiency and the development of pupils to the unit costs of the school. . . . Thus if a school achieves high standards, makes good quality educational provision, is efficiently managed, and achieves satisfactory spiritual, moral, social and cultural development of pupils, for average unit cost, it provides good value for money.
>
> (OFSTED 1994a: Part 4: 83)

How are such judgements made? The detailed programme for an inspection is set out in OFSTED (1993) and modified in OFSTED (1994a). The document, like the inspection process, is complex. It can be summarised in two parts. The first relates to the process of inspection itself. The second concerns the content or focus of the inspection, the aspects of the school's work to be inspected, the criteria used for making judgements and the collection of evidence.

THE PROCESS OF INSPECTION

It is intended that schools will be inspected regularly as part of a four-yearly cycle. There are already some doubts, however, about whether the people and resources can be found to inspect primary schools so frequently. Whatever the frequency of inspection, the process is likely to have twelve stages. These are:

1 The school is informed that invitations have been issued for appropriately qualified and trained groups to tender for its inspection. OFSTED

considers bids and awards the tender. Once the school is notified that it is to be inspected the governors have a legal responsibility to inform parents, the LEA (or Secretary of State in the case of a grant maintained school), those who appoint any foundation governors, and local business organisations.

2 The inspection team will consist of a registered inspector (RI) who leads the team, team members who are trained inspectors with educational backgrounds and who, collectively, should be competent to inspect the range of National Curriculum subjects and features of the whole school organisation such as management, special educational needs and assessment. There will also be at least one lay inspector who is trained but who will not have an educational background. This inspector will look particularly at the financial and business aspects of the school but otherwise the role is similar to that of the other team members. The whole team writes the final inspection report. Once the team is identified the RI will contact the headteacher to arrange an early visit to talk about the documentary evidence necessary for the inspection and to outline the process to the headteacher and chair of governors. At this meeting the headteacher should ask for information about the balance of the inspecting team. Headteachers and governors can request information about each member of the inspection team but the RI may decide whether or not to comply with this request. Headteachers should, at the earliest opportunity, raise any concerns there may be about the background of any member of the inspecting team. At this first meeting the headteacher should also ensure that the RI is aware of any significant aspects of the school's circumstances that may influence its work and the performance of the staff and pupils. The headteacher has the opportunity to record this in writing in section A, part 10 of the headteacher's forms (OFSTED 1993: Part 8).

3 The RI will call a meeting of parents to collect views on the school about matters including pupils' standards of work, information provided to parents, homework and behaviour (see OFSTED 1993: 51). No members of staff are allowed to attend this meeting unless they are also parents of pupils at the school.

4 After the meeting with parents, the RI will make the headteacher aware of the issues that arose from the meeting and will give the headteacher an opportunity to comment.

5 The dates and times for the inspection are agreed with the appropriate authority by the RI. The length of the inspection is determined by the size of the school (see OFSTED 1993: 9). The total duration is unlikely to exceed two weeks.

6 The inspection team will receive documentary evidence from the school. This will be a pre-inspection context and a school indicator report, together with other documentation including the headteacher's form and record of evidence.

7 The team will arrive to conduct the inspection. Its exact size and composition depends on the size and nature of the school. Detailed guidance
on the code of conduct to be adopted by the inspectors while conducting
the inspection can be found on pages 24 to 29 in OFSTED (1994). All
staff of a school being inspected should be familiar with these guidelines.
At least 60 per cent of the inspection time will consist of observing
teachers and pupils in classrooms. This will involve observing teaching,
looking at the earlier and current work of pupils and talking to them.
Part of the school's preparation for inspection should include becoming
familiar with the lesson observation proforma that the inspectors will
use (see OFSTED 1994: Part 3: 15, 20, 61). During the inspection the
school staff should take the lead in ensuring that inspectors and teachers
meet informally before the lesson observation takes place. Inspectors
are encouraged to give feedback to teachers as soon as possible after the
lesson, but they are not required to do so. In giving such feedback
the inspector should explain to the teacher the grading and the criteria
used for classroom observation. The grading has been changed for the
1994–95 and subsequent round of inspections (see OFSTED 1994, Part
3: 16). The use of the 'Sound' grading is quite normal and a perfectly
acceptable level of performance. All gradings must be based on evidence.

8 It is recommended (OFSTED 1993) that the RI talks daily to the headteacher about the progress of the inspection. The headteacher should
be available so that this can happen. The RI will determine the nature
of the conversation and its level of confidentiality and should not be
asked to make premature judgements about all or part of the work of
the school. It is legitimate, however, for headteachers to challenge any
statements with which they disagree if, in their view, they are based on
false information. Although headteachers should keep their diaries as clear
as possible during an inspection and be available for external meetings
and appointments with the RI, the normal teaching timetable should
not be abandoned for either the headteacher or the deputy. Where
headteachers have a full-time or substantial teaching commitment, they
should discuss with the RI how time can be made available for these
meetings.

9 The RI is required, within two weeks of the completion of the inspection,
to offer to discuss the main findings of the inspection with the headteacher of the school and any members of staff invited by the headteacher.
In small schools the whole staff may be invited if the headteacher so
chooses. This meeting provides an opportunity to check the accuracy of
factual information. It cannot be used to modify the judgements of the
inspection team unless these are based on factual inaccuracies. It is likely
that detailed comments on the delivery of the curriculum, subject by
subject, will be given at this meeting which is an opportunity for groups
of professionals to look at the curriculum. This may well be in more

depth than appears in the final report or than is appropriate for the meeting with governors. It will be a long meeting, up to three hours. Careful notes should be taken.

10 The RI is also required to offer a similar but separate opportunity to the governing body after the meeting with the headteacher. This meeting should summarise, in an unambiguous way, the main findings of the inspection team. These must be clearly presented so that governors can identify the features of the school which should be addressed when preparing the action plan. The report must be factually supportable. Once again, factual errors but not judgements may be challenged. Nothing at the meeting with the governors should come as a surprise to the headteacher.

11 The RI must then prepare a written report within five weeks of the end of the inspection. This should contain nothing that has not been discussed with the governing body. The structure of the report is set out in OFSTED (1994: Part 2, section 2). The central purpose of the report is to identify the strengths and weaknesses of the school. It will include basic information on the school intake, area served and the evidence used. It will comment on the standards achieved, behaviour, discipline and attendance and make observations on the quality of teaching, assessment, record keeping and reporting, range and content of the curriculum, equality of opportunity and provision of special educational needs. It will also report on the efficiency and effectiveness of management and administration, including resource management. Judgements will be made about the overall quality of education provided, the standards pupils are achieving, and what should be done if improvements are needed. In producing the report, inspectors must demonstrate that their judgements are supported by evidence and are based on first-hand observation of pupils and teachers. These judgements must be the collective view of the whole inspection team and be consistent with OFSTED criteria, cover all the aspects laid down by OFSTED and be a valid reflection of the standards normally achieved in the school. The report will be sent to OFSTED and to the governors of the school. A summary is also provided. This must be sent to all parents by the governors. It is becoming common practice for schools to draft their own press releases once the report has been received.

12 Within 40 days of receiving the report the governing body must produce an action plan to address the relevant areas identified in the Key Issues for Action section of the report. This will be used as part of the documentary evidence for subsequent inspections. Copies of this plan must be distributed to parents and staff, to the LEA, OFSTED and to anyone who may ask for it. A statement about progress on the plan must be included in each subsequent annual report to parents.

THE FOCUS OF THE INSPECTION

Each inspection will cover the same areas for every school, taking into account circumstances such as special units or the school's involvement in initial teacher education partnership arrangements. The best way to understand what an inspection will involve and to prepare for it is to become familiar with the *Handbook for the Inspection of Schools* (OFSTED 1993 and 1994a). This gives all the details of the content and processes related to inspections, including copies of all the forms to be used. Fundamental to all this information is The Inspection Schedule (OFSTED 1994a: section 2) which lists the four focal areas on which inspection will concentrate. This has several sub-sections and provides a detailed picture of what inspectors will look at, together the criteria used to make judgements and the evidence on which these judgements will be based. The focal areas are:

- **Standards and quality** Defined in terms of pupil achievement and the quality of learning. This will be judged by evaluating what pupils know, understand and can do in all relevant curriculum subjects and by examining their competence in key skills in relation to their capabilities and to National Curriculum norms. Two different types of judgement will be made here. One is about the delivery of the National Curriculum. The other is about the standards being achieved by the children. These are not the same thing and the judgements made may be different. For example, the lessons observed and the delivery of the curriculum may be sound. The standards being achieved might be excellent given the capabilities of the children, many of whom might be working at a higher level than could reasonably be expected when social and other circumstances are taken into account. Evidence for this will include National Curriculum assessments, a comparison of pupil abilities on intake with assessment scores, lesson observations, pupils' work and discussion with pupils, teachers' records and the views of parents.
- **The efficiency of the school** This will be judged by the quality of financial management and decision-making, the efficiency and effectiveness with which resources are deployed to meet the school's aims and objectives, the efficiency of financial control and the steps taken by schools to evaluate their cost-effectiveness. Evidence will include the school development plan, the school's budget and recent out-turns of expenditure, minutes of relevant meetings including governors' meetings, information about the school budget management policies and arrangements, information about the deployment of resources including staff and time throughout the school and information about the evaluation of quality and standards in the school.
- **Pupils' personal development and behaviour** Evidence will be collected in three main sub-sections. The first is the spiritual, moral, social and cultural development of pupils. Criteria for spiritual development will

include the extent to which pupils display a system of personal beliefs, an ability to communicate these beliefs and a willingness to reflect on experience and give meaning to it. Moral development will be judged by the extent to which pupils understand the difference between right and wrong, respect people, property and truth and show a concern for how their actions may affect others. The quality of relationships in school, the ability of pupils to exercise responsibility, take initiative and work in groups and the extent to which pupils understand the structures and processes of society will be used to evaluate social development. Cultural development will be assessed by examining how far pupils widen their knowledge, understanding, interests and experience through the curriculum and by participation in cultural activities. Evidence will include the extent to which the school's policies influence pupil development, the attitudes and behaviour displayed by pupils and the role models provided by staff. Discussions with parents and pupils will take place to discuss the extent of opportunities for pupils to contribute to the life of the school.

The second sub-section is pupil behaviour and discipline. Criteria here will include the extent to which pupil attitudes and actions contribute to or restrict effective learning in classrooms, the quality of life in the school, the functioning of the school as an orderly community and the development of self-discipline. Evidence will include the observation of standards of behaviour throughout the school, pupils' records, data on exclusions, views of pupils, parents and teachers on bullying and the school policy on behaviour and discipline.

The third sub-section is attendance. This will be judged by the levels of pupils' actual attendance, records of attendance and how far these comply with the requirements of DES Circular 11/91, and punctuality. Evidence will include school registers and attendance statistics for the whole school, year groups and classes, data on authorised and unauthorised absence, school policy on attendance, discussions with pupils, parents and staff.

- **Subjects of the curriculum and other curricular provision** This area has eight sub-sections, some of which are divided still further. Taken together with the inspection of standards of achievement and quality of learning, these form a detailed analysis of the work that is being done by the school, the extent to which pupils are achieving appropriate standards in all aspects of their work, and the contributions being made by the staff of the school. The first sub-section is quality of teaching. High quality teaching is based on teachers having objectives for their lessons and pupils being aware of those objectives; teachers having a command of their subject and lessons having a suitable content, activities being well chosen to promote learning and presented in ways that will engage and motivate children. Evidence will include teachers' planning of work, observation of lessons, samples of pupils' work and the ways in which it has been marked and followed up, teachers' records, input from specialist teachers and individual plans for statemented pupils.

Assessment, recording and reporting is the second sub-section. Criteria here include the extent to which the school keeps accurate and comprehensive records of the achievement of individual pupils in relation to the National Curriculum attainment targets and other objectives, how far the outcomes are constructive and helpful to pupils, teachers and parents and the extent to which outcomes inform subsequent work. Evidence will include the school's policy and guidelines in this area, arrangements for National Curriculum assessment, procedures for monitoring and reviewing the progress of individual children, the record of pupils' achievements and the arrangements for reporting to parents. Samples of pupils work will be examined and discussions held with pupils and those who write and use the reports.

The sub-section on the curriculum includes the quality and range of the curriculum and equal opportunities. The criteria for quality and range include the extent to which the school's curriculum complies with statutory requirements, contributes to the achievement of high standards, reflects the aims of the school, is broad and balanced, is organised effectively and is enhanced by extra-curricular activities. Evidence for this will come from the school's statement of aims and objectives, curriculum plans, schemes of work and timetables, the organisation and composition of teaching groups, planning for the National Curriculum and other subjects, classroom inspections and observations of work, discussions with pupils, staff, parents and governors. The equal opportunity aspect of the curriculum will be evaluated by how far all pupils, irrespective of gender, ability, ethnicity and social circumstances have access to the curriculum. Evidence will include school policies and their implementation, standards of achievement of individuals and groups of pupils, curriculum content and the organisation of teaching and learning.

The provision for pupils with special educational needs must be designed to ensure that all pupils make the greatest possible progress and gain access to a broad and balanced curriculum which includes the subjects of the National Curriculum. Evidence will include: the school's policy on special needs; the standards of achievement of individual pupils; arrangements for monitoring funding for pupils with special needs; teaching and arrangements for staffing provision, including the provision made for statemented children where money has been delegated from the LEA for this purpose; the use of external agencies for these pupils, the extent of integration within the school and screening and assessment information and procedures.

- **Management and administration**   These will be judged by the extent to which: there is an ethos in the school that promotes the quality of learning; leadership by the governors, headteacher and other staff promotes high standards; planning is carried out effectively and appropriate priorities and targets are set; plans are implemented effectively; the school is well administered and organised; good working relations exist, communication is effective; and the school uses evaluation of its performance to achieve its aims. Evidence will include a wide range of documents such as the prospectus, policies on all relevant areas, the school development plan, minutes of meetings including governors meetings, the latest budget turn out statement and monthly profile, staff job descriptions, roles and plans for professional development, policies for allocating resources.

The resources and their management sub-section is divided into three areas. The first is teaching and non-teaching staff. Evaluation here will consider availability and sufficiency of staff with suitable qualifications, and recruitment, retention, deployment and development of staff. Evidence will include staffing policy and the use made of financial incentives, the existing staffing structure and the rationale for its future development, an analysis of staff deployment, in-service training records and job descriptions and the level of non-teaching staff. Resources for learning will be evaluated by their effect on the quality of learning and the standards achieved in respect of their availability, accessibility, quality and efficient use. Evidence here will include an analysis of the relationships between resource provision and the school development plan, the spending on resources per pupil and on different parts of the curriculum, the use made of funds raised by sponsorship and an inspection of the learning resources available.

- **Accommodation**   This will be considered in respect of its availability and condition, efficiency of use, provision of specialist facilities, suitability for numbers and ages of pupils and accessibility. Evidence will include an analysis of room use including those rooms that are surplus to class teaching requirements, the observation of the condition and appearance of the buildings and whole school site and the use made of buildings outside normal teaching hours.
- **Pupils' welfare and guidance**   This will be judged by the effectiveness of the school's procedures in this area, the measures taken to identify and meet pupils' academic and personal needs and to provide curricular guidance, the quality of health education and the effectiveness of the implementation of the governing body's policy on sex education. Evidence here will include the school's child protection policy and procedures, procedures for dealing with illness, school visits and sporting events, the health education programme and liaison with specialist services.
- **Links with parents, agencies and other institutions**   These will be assessed according to how well informed parents are about the school and their contribution to school life, the quality of liaison arrangements with other schools and the quality of relationships with other agencies. Evidence will include school documentation for parents, external agencies and other schools, information from the pre-inspection parents' meeting, and liaison with other schools.

This summary of the Framework for Inspection part of *The Handbook for Inspection of Schools* shows that inspectors will be collecting evidence in order to make judgements about the standards that children are achieving, about the quality of learning, the quality of teaching and the work in classrooms and about the overall management and organisation of the school.

THE DOCUMENTARY EVIDENCE FOR THE INSPECTION

The documentary information that inspectors require to support their observations is extensive. As well as the forms in *The Handbook for the Inspection of Schools* (OFSTED 1993, 1994) there is a long list of school documents to which the inspecting team will require access. This is summarised in Figure 2.1.

The inspection processes focus, therefore on the extent to which the school is: planning effectively; establishing priorities, costing and resourcing them; and evaluating its own progress. This will include an examination of the accounting and budgeting procedures and a review of the outcomes of expenditure and an evaluation of the benefits. Schools might, for example, be asked to demonstrate that the resources devoted to professional development of teachers have provided value for money. All of this documentation, and the processes to which they refer, will already exist in well-managed schools.

PREPARATION FOR INSPECTION AND ASSURING QUALITY IN THE SCHOOL

The best preparation for inspection is for a school to be well managed and to have established its own procedures for monitoring and reviewing what it does. In this way quality assurance becomes an integral part of the management of the school. It is clear that it is the school's development plan and its implementation which is regarded by OFSTED as the key to sound school management. The development planning process should be central to the work of a school that is well managed. The emphasis of the inspection process is on how the school plans to maintain and improve the standards that the pupils are achieving, the quality of learning and the quality of teaching. In the fourth part of the handbook (OFSTED 1994b), the evaluation criteria are amplified. This is done by giving a prose description of what might be found in a school which meets the criteria for each section together with a description of a school where the criteria are not being met. These descriptions, in themselves, provide a valuable source of in-service training material for schools. They can be used to help schools and individual teachers to understand what will be required of them by an inspection, to explore how far the criteria are being met, and to identify what steps need to be taken in order to meet the criteria fully. Such an understanding might be reached by selecting various aspects of the school's work and, using the school's

- The school's aims and objectives and its development plan
- curriculum policies including schemes of work, planning guidelines and development plans
- curricula policies on sex education, special educational needs, equal opportunities and religious education
- staff development programme showing how needs are identified and provision made for training all staff for the last three years
- timetables for all classes and teachers
- planning documentation
- financial statements and the auditor's financial report
- headteacher's report to governors
- annual report to parents
- staff handbook
- school prospectus
- job descriptions
- school policy statements on areas such as admissions, marking and assessment, special educational needs, attendance, behaviour and discipline, pastoral care, equal opportunities, cross-curricular provision and use of time within 1,265 hours
- details of the nature of extra-curricular activities and of the pupils involved
- information about links and joint ventures with other schools and organisations
- links with other agencies
- pupils' attainment on admission to the school and National Curriculum assessment details
- relevant LEA policy statements such as the local financial management scheme.

Figure 2.1 Documentation for school inspection

established policies and statements about intended levels of pupil performance, asking staff working in groups to apply the criteria to the school and to provide an evaluation based on the evidence that inspectors will be using. This is a useful way of identifying what improvements might be necessary and the result might be a set of actions to be taken in advance of inspection to initiate those improvements. It is driven, however, by what the school already does rather than by a reaction to an external inspection. It also helps to share the load of preparation for inspection throughout the staff team. At the same time, staff become familiar with what inspectors are looking for and with the criteria and language that will be used during the inspection which, in turn, helps to build up staff confidence.

The OFSTED inspection criteria are a guide to how a school should be organised and administered. Inspections should confirm good practice through their evaluative processes and identify areas for improvement for the benefit of the children. Although schools being inspected will have to provide evidence about the extent to which they meet the specific criteria as set out in the inspection schedule, this must reflect what they already do, encourage them to establish and maintain sound management structures and to provide a high quality education for their pupils. There is no doubt, however, that preparing for inspection for many schools adds up to a formidable exercise and will require them to provide a considerable amount of information, some of which may not be available or easily accessible. In view of this, head-teachers and senior staff in all primary schools should embark upon a process of ensuring that their existing documentation and procedures, while based on the needs of the school, match the high quality identified in the OFSTED criteria. Two things must be done both in the interests of good management and as preparation for inspection.

First, steps must be taken to ensure, as far as possible, that all the policy documents and other data exist and are available. For example, are minutes of year group meetings kept? Can they be found and understood by somebody who did not attend the meeting? Is there a standard record-keeping system throughout the school for classes, groups and individual children and can evidence of this be produced? Are curriculum policy documents outmoded or up-to-date in all subject areas? Can the progression through a series of revised documents be seen? Can it be shown how these documents inform classroom practice through the work of classroom teachers and the curriculum coordinators? Can copies of communications with parents be found? It is vital to show that policy documents influence classroom practice. It is also helpful to be able to show how policy documents and plans have developed over time. There is no point, however, in inventing documents simply to help the school meet inspection criteria. They should be part of the management framework of all good schools.

Second, much of this information has to be presented to the inspection team in a particular way. A well-managed school will cope well with an inspection, but it may not always have the information required available in the appropriate form. The information about the school is presented on the headteacher's form in part 8 of *The Handbook for the Inspection of Schools* (OFSTED 1994a). It is worthwhile going through this form well in advance of any notification of inspection to ensure that it can be completed and to check that all the information within the school has been collected in such a way that it can be transposed on to the form. It is worthwhile delegating the completion of some sections of the form to other members of staff to give them an early insight into the inspection process.

The demands of OFSTED inspections and the criteria in the *Handbook* should not determine everything that happens in the school. The inspection processes and their related documentation should be seen for what they are, a valuable way of monitoring the effective management of all primary schools:

> The healthiest approach to inspection is one where school leaders inculcate in staff an expectation that they will be confidently operating at the highest level of quality assurance, rather than reacting to externally imposed quality control resulting from the inspection.
>
> (Ormston and Shaw 1993: vii)

In this way periodic inspection becomes an event which offers additional insights into the way the school is working but does not dominate its functioning. In well-managed schools where monitoring and evaluation are regular features of day-to-day activity, inspection rarely provides any surprises. Continuous improvement will take place in schools because of the professional commitment of teachers, not because schools are being inspected every four years.

Nevertheless, there are areas which will need attention in order to prepare for inspections. The importance of knowing and understanding the criteria for inspection and having relevant information available in an appropriate form have already been outlined above. Other steps can also be taken. Staff can be prepared by:

- Briefing them on the timing, purpose and process of inspection. Headteachers might prepare a briefing paper which gives some information about the inspection team. It might be agreed that the inspection team be asked to focus on a particular area of the school's work, remembering that inspection must look at the totality of school life. At the same time staff should be reminded that inspection involves everybody and its outcomes are non-negotiable unless based on false information.
- Reminding staff of the school's aims and objectives and of how these are expressed in the school's development plan.
- Reviewing with staff the key priorities of the school development plan and the contribution that each individual is making towards achieving specific targets related to those priorities. Policy documents play an important part in this process. Schools should establish a cycle of revision for these documents. No inspection team will expect to see a portfolio of policy documents that are dated immediately prior to the inspection. It is essential, however, that policies inform practice and that they are revised regularly, if not frequently, according to a clearly established programme.
- Reminding staff that inspectors can go anywhere and see anybody in the school including supply teachers, students, ancillary staff, secretaries and helpers. The inspectors' classroom observations are based on a specific form which is in *The Handbook for the Inspection* (OFSTED 1994a). Staff should become familiar with that form. Staff should also know that inspectors

ought to stay in lessons long enough to understand what is happening but need not see whole lessons. In the classroom inspectors will be looking for evidence that teaching is of high quality, that learning and progress is taking place and that achievement is of a high standard. They will make a judgement based on a five-point scale as follows:

1 Very good: many good features, some of them outstanding
2 Good: good features and no major shortcomings
3 Sound: acceptable but unremarkable
4 Unsatisfactory: some shortcomings in important areas
5 Poor: many shortcomings

All teachers need to be helped to understand the relevant criteria in order to identify exactly how such judgements will be made.

It is a good idea to invite the RI to talk to the whole staff about the inspection process at an early stage. Ormston and Shaw (1993) suggest that it is possible to identify some common causes of concern about teaching:

- aims in teaching were often not clear;
- teacher did not have or did not specify planned learning outcomes or did not consider them over the short- and medium-term;
- teachers frequently had expectations which were too low for below average ability pupils and which did not challenge the more able pupils;
- the variety of teaching techniques used was very limited;
- differentiation between pupils was not effective in lesson planning and delivery for pupils with both low and high ability levels;
- teaching concerns were often linked to lack of staff skills in some areas of the curriculum;
- assessment procedures were not always clear and often not linked to existing systems;
- teachers did not make sufficient use of assessments to inform their teaching;
- curriculum breadth and balance was also an issue, especially linked to the length of the school day.

Teachers who are aware of these weaknesses will be better prepared for inspection. Schools also need to plan to monitor the inspection process as it is carried out in the school to ensure that it meets the relevant criteria. The headteacher should be well prepared for the meeting with the reporting inspector before the written report is sent to the school. This might be done by a simple process of having all staff reporting to an individual or small team on what the inspectors have seen, said and done during the day. Deciding what is the most effective role for the deputy is also important. The headteacher will need support and so will all other members of staff. The role of the deputy can be particularly important here. At the same time, be clear about what roles curriculum coordinators might play. Good curriculum coordination is vital in ensuring that policy is translated into practice in primary schools.

Inspection, however well managed, can be stressful. This may affect some staff more than others. The headteacher and the reporting inspector must know if members of staff are experiencing stress of any kind that may influence their work. This may be one job that is delegated to the deputy. Another task may be to ensure that the administrative arrangements for the inspection are satisfactory. Inspectors should, if at all possible, be provided with a place to meet and given access to refreshments, although they are responsible for their own secretarial support. The deputy headteacher may monitor these arrangements while leaving the headteacher to deal with other issues. Many small primary schools, however, may not have space available. The staff room, library, and headteacher's room are all essential for the day-to-day running of the school and should not be given up to the inspecting team for their base. Headteachers may need to discuss this at an early stage with the RI.

Obtaining an outsider's view of the school in advance of inspection can often be helpful. Such a view may be gained by inviting a headteacher colleague whose school has recently been inspected to visit and comment on a school in the light of the OFSTED criteria. Some LEAs and other agencies offer pre-inspection visits and courses. These must be approached carefully. Only use the services of a group whose work has already proved to be satisfactory in the past. Remember, however, that this group's perspective may not be the same as that of the inspecting team. Regular internal auditing and monitoring is an integral part of good management.

GOVERNORS, PARENTS AND PUPILS

Governors have a vital role to play in inspections and should also be well prepared. Ormston and Shaw (1993) suggest that, without guidance, a typical reaction of governors might be to look in the *The Handbook for School Inspection* (OFSTED 1994) to see where specific mention is made of governors. Those that recalled that they had overall responsibility for policy might look at the thirty or so policy issues mentioned, and then panic! Governors, therefore, must be fully informed about the inspection and aware that aspects of their work will be subject to inspection in much the same way as the work of others in the school community. This is especially important for the chair of governors. Headteachers and chairs of governors must decide how they will communicate during the inspection. Will the chair of governors visit the school briefly every day at a pre-arranged time? Will they discuss the day on the telephone? However it is done, the two people with the overall responsibility for the school and its management must communicate effectively and regularly during inspections.

Governors need to be knowledgeable about their roles and responsibilities for the general oversight of the school. The best preparation for this is to be fully involved in the strategic planning of the school as a normal part of its management. Nothing can be a substitute for this. Governors must be aware of their statutory responsibilities which include ensuring that the National Curriculum is covered and assessed, that religious education and a daily act of worship is provided, that there is a complaints procedure and that the school provides the required information about all aspects of its work to parents and others. In order to do this, governors must be involved in the formulation of the school development plan and encouraged regularly to examine curriculum and other policy documents over a period of time. They must also understand how these policies are being implemented within the school and which staff have responsibility for specific aspects of policy. At the same time governors must know how the school is managed and administered, how decisions are taken in the school, understand about the quality, efficiency and effectiveness of decision-making procedures and about arrangements for managing resources and monitoring and evaluating resource use. All of this is an integral part of the school's strategic planning. An understanding of these aspects of school management is necessary if governors are to be able to respond to the inspection report, produce the required action plan and monitor its implementation.

Parents also have a contribution to make to the inspection process and should, therefore, be prepared for it. As with the governing body, the best preparation for parents is for them to have regular and frequent opportunities to be involved in the life of the school. Good documentation for parents, well organised parents' evenings and annual meetings, appropriate representation on governing bodies, an active parents' association, the regular seeking of parents' views about the school and using this information as a basis for action can all contribute to such preparation. As for the inspection itself, the meeting between the reporting inspector and the parents is an important part of the process. The headteacher and governors have no right to attend but the headteacher should ensure that it is effectively organised and that access to premises and facilities is arranged. Summaries of the report and copies of the action plan must be sent to all parents. Parents may respond to the action plan either through parent governors or at the annual meeting and subsequently since governors must report on the progress being made towards implementing the plan at those meetings.

Pupils should also be told about the inspection. Inspectors will visit their classrooms and will talk to them. In schools which frequently have visitors, this may be accepted as a normal part of the school day by most children. In other schools, however, this will not be the case. Pupils should be prepared for this. Pupils play an important part in receiving visitors in many schools. This might be encouraged during the inspection. They may also be asked about current or earlier work. They need to have access to it. Above all, if pupils know what is happening and why, they are less likely to be concerned and are more likely to be able to cope with the disruption that inspection inevitably causes.

It can be seen, therefore, that, as with the internal management of the school, the demands of the inspection process in respect of governors, parents and pupils serve to highlight what might normally be regarded as good management practices. These practices are based on having a clear vision for the school and establishing a set of aims which have been communicated to the school community. They are also based on a real intention to improve the quality of teaching and learning within the school by establishing and maintaining quality assurance procedures that enable teachers continuously to improve what they do for the benefit of their pupils. The vision, the aims and the monitoring of the quality of teaching and learning in the school combine to provide the foundation on which the school development plan can be constructed. The school development plan must be manageable and realistic with time scales and resources allocated. It must be clear to everyone where the responsibility rests for each aspect of the plan. Everyone must understand how the plan affects them and what they do in their classrooms. It is this strategic plan that provides the framework for the continued improvement of the school and enables the activities of all of the members of the school community to be harmonised and coordinated towards achieving a set of agreed and understood common goals.

Chapter 3

The central position of the school development plan

When budgets were delegated to governing bodies under the local management of schools (LMS) provisions of the 1988 Education Act, genuine authority and the right to make local decisions which went with it, was transferred from the LEA to the school, and was invested in the governing body. This new authority, coupled with the governors' direct accountability to parents at the annual meeting and the introduction of the National Curriculum, encouraged schools to make fundamental changes in their internal planning processes, and created the need for a single working document around which all major decision-making was focused. The document had to encapsulate, in a manageable form, a statement of the school's unique purpose, and set out how the financial resource now delegated to the governors would be deployed to ensure the successful achievement of the educational, professional and philosophical aims of the school. This document became known as the school development plan. Its centrality and importance has been recognised by OFSTED, whose inspectors are required to make a judgement on the quality of the school development plan, its usefulness as an instrument for change and improvement, its realism and the achievement of any priorities set. (OFSTED 1993)

THE PREREQUISITES OF SCHOOL DEVELOPMENT PLANNING

Schools have been writing development plans for a number of years, and have adopted styles and layouts which suit their particular circumstances. Certain key features need to be established and in place before the school starts its annual revision of the plan. This chapter will use the example of Madison School to illustrate these features. This is but one model, and the version chosen and developed by each school must be unique and individual to that school. There are, however, certain prerequisites for sound development planning which will need to be present in all schools before development planning can succeed.

Prerequisite 1: quality of leadership

The single factor most likely to enable, or obstruct, the school in its ambition to be effective and to achieve its ambition for its children is the quality of leadership shown by the headteacher. As we discuss in Chapter 7, without that particular vision and leadership, even the most professional and loyal of staff will lose their motivation. With it, staff will rise above themselves, and the mass of external and internal difficulties that seek to deter them. Staff and governors will have a long-term view of where the school should be heading. Expectations will be high and there will be shared values and norms about learning, behaviour and relationships. Headteacher appraisal, discussed in detail in Chapter 4, provides an excellent opportunity for professional or informed colleagues to work with the headteacher, focusing on particular aspects of management. OFSTED, HMI and LEA internal inspections will also review the headteacher's management style, and assess how this contributes to the efficiency of the school. There are several excellent commercially published questionnaire style formats such as GRIDS (SCDC 1988) which can be completed by the headteacher and senior staff, or by the staff as a whole, and which give a clear profile of the current management systems and style which exist in the school. Several benefit by being administered by an external neutral facilitator. Additionally, many LEAs, universities and commercial training agencies offer a range of management courses for headteachers and senior staff. Some are specifically targeted towards experienced headteachers.

In Madison School, the management section of the development plan sets the following objectives in order to improve the quality of the leadership of the senior management team:

- to involve staff and governors in the review and development of management policies, ensuring commitment to their successful implementation;
- to introduce a three-year cycle of review for all management areas using national documents and OFSTED criteria, in preparation for future inspections;
- to use a three-year cycle spread sheet to identify termly targets/actions for the headteacher and senior management team.

Prerequisite 2: the aim statement

The school will have already expressed its shared understanding of its basic purpose in the school aim statement. The desire to achieve the aim statement drives the development planning process. When the governors, headteacher and staff reaffirm their commitment to the aim statement by putting it at the start of the written plan, they are demonstrating that all the decisions and actions which are detailed in the plan stem from their determination to achieve that aim. The words themselves may appear fairly bland and predictable, but behind them, and explored in detail in the discussion which took place during the writing, will be the expression of the uniqueness of the vision that the providers have for the children. Parents should be invited to share and support the statement.

Governors must understand the principles expressed in the aim statement, regard it as their own, and use it as the reference point for their decision-making. The framework for Inspection makes it clear that the evidence on which inspectors will assess the efficiency of the school, in terms of the strategic management of resources, will be found in the minutes of governors' meetings and documents outlining school policies, and will show the extent of governors' involvement. The inspectors will also assess whether spending priorities have matched the educational priorities laid down in the school development plan, and the extent to which both reflect the school's aims.

The aim statement should be free of jargon, clear and understandable by all who will have occasion to read it, and brief enough to be remembered. It should be a lucid statement of what the school is seeking to achieve, focused on agreed priorities, a reference point for future decision-making, a reflection of the values, beliefs and philosophy of the school and a reflection of achievable standards.

The Madison School aim statement says that the school 'aims to provide a stimulating and interesting environment in which all children are encouraged to reach their full potential in all areas of the curriculum, as members of a happy and caring community'.

Prerequisite 3: a shared understanding of the school philosophy

The third prerequisite is a common understanding, and a belief in, the school's philosophy and value system. *The Handbook for the Inspection of Schools* makes it clear that schools are expected to address the children's spiritual, moral, social and cultural needs as well as the requirements of the National Curriculum and for RE. If the aim statement is to be achieved and the school development plan is to be meaningful, the ethos in which the school exists must be right. Pupils will show through their actions that they know what constitutes appropriate behaviour, that they understand what is expected of them, and that they respond accordingly.

> They are considerate, courteous and relate well to each other and to adults. (They) take responsibility for their own actions, appropriate to their age and maturity. They develop self-esteem, self-discipline and adhere to high standards of behaviour which contribute to effective learning.
>
> (OFSTED 1993: Part 4, section 5.1)

If there is a need for change, these changes and the resources they will need in order to be successful, must be identified when the plan is revised and updated.

Prerequisite 4: an understanding of need

A further prerequisite for effective planning is an understanding of the various needs of all who come into contact with the school: the children, parents, governors and staff. The needs of the children will be paramount, but if the school is to achieve its aim for them, it will recognise in its development planning that parents, governors and staff also have their own unique and important development requirements. The needs of parents are well catalogued: quality information about the organisation of the school, the curriculum, their own individual children's place and achievements within it, free and friendly access to those who work with their children, and a confidence in a partnership with the school which recognises and values their role as parents. The governors need a clear understanding of their responsibilities in law, and their particular and individual responsibilities within the life of the school; to be internal, not external, to its processes, successes and challenges; to understand what they see in classrooms, and to be valued as partners as they strive to deploy the delegated budget in order to achieve the aim statement. The staff need to be valued and resourced as the prime movers in the learning and growing processes in the school, to be supported through professional training and advice, praised for success and supported through difficulties.

Prerequisite 5: up-to-date job descriptions

Accurate and up-to-date job descriptions are essential if each member of staff is to know what his/her responsibilities are and how these will contribute to any subsequent planning process. The alternative to the job description is the job assumption. Job assumptions can lead to gaps in provision, duplication of effort, exclusion, and considerable stress in working relationships.

Prerequisite 6: an understanding of role

The development plan must be written against the background of a clear understanding of the different roles and responsibilities carried by the headteacher, the governing body as a whole, various governors as individuals, the teaching and non-teaching staff as a whole, and individual members of staff in their own right and as expressed in their job descriptions. It must be clear which tasks each has agreed to undertake, and how and to whom they are accountable. For most staff, apart from the governors, the tasks will be set out in detail in their individual job descriptions. When tasks or responsibilities are delegated to governors, headteacher or staff by the governing body, the minutes of a full governors' meeting must give clear terms of reference in order to avoid any future misunderstandings. This is especially important when either staffing, budgetary or major decision-making functions are delegated. It must also be clearly stated that any decisions can be made only in order to further the agreed aims and objectives laid down in the development plan.

Prerequisite 7: agreement on empowered delegation

Clarity of role and responsibility must carry with it genuine delegated authority empowering the person to whom duties have been delegated to make decisions, to have the time and the money budget to fulfil the tasks, and work to agreed success and completion criteria. If a teacher, governor or any member of the school staff does not feel they own the process, control the resources and have a clear definition of the task they have agreed to undertake, then the delegation is hollow, and success unlikely. An effective school is characterised by staff and governors who undertake responsibilities and tasks knowing the parameters in which they are to work, who are aware of the support and advice available, and who have a sense of being trusted to achieve success. If things do go wrong, such schools are able to support their colleague and recognise that inability to achieve success is not necessarily always the fault of the person charged with its achievement.

Prerequisite 8: a cyclical process

Development planning is a cyclical programme of review, prioritisation, resourcing, implementation, evaluation and review. Some parts of the annual cycle are external to the school. The size of the delegated budget is an external decision. The plan cannot disregard financial constraints, and must work within them. This will be explored in full in Chapter 8.

Prerequisite 9: systematic review

Effective planning cannot take place without first conducting a structured analysis of the existing situation. Clearly the school cannot review the detail of every aspect of its life every year, and should first list all of the aspects of the school which will have to be reviewed within the cycle. The list should be as broad as possible, from curriculum to premises, from contact with the community to the use of stationery, from discipline to equality of opportunity. Some categories will have to been broken down into smaller sub-sets. The curriculum should be subdivided into subject areas. Priorities will have been agreed with the governors, and set out in the medium- and long-term planning sections of earlier development plans. The headteacher's role is central in ensuring that firm arrangements for period review exist. It is important that the implementation of plans is monitored, problems are identified early and finance is efficiently managed and focused on clear priorities for the provision of resources. Some aspects of the school might need to be reviewed every year, others will take their turn in a cyclical process. However, nothing must be omitted. A manageable group should be identified within the development plan for detailed audit in the forthcoming year.

A typical list from which the selection could be made could include:

- assessment and recording;
- teaching and learning styles;
- responsibilities of the teaching staff;
- the premises;
- differentiation;
- community links;
- school management and organisation;
- relationships with parents;
- links with other schools and educational establishments;
- school, LEA and national documents.

(adapted from Hargreaves et al. 1989)

Hargreaves also suggests that the following must appear every year, although one facet of each might be identified for specific investigation:

- *The curriculum*   The curriculum should be reviewed on a regular basis, one core subject each year and three other subject areas. The coordinator should take a lead role and consider among other things: the relevance of current policies and documents, standards achieved at each key stage, assessment and record-keeping, test results where known, currency of current staff INSET (inservice education and training), levels and appropriateness of stock and materials and recommended future actions. The result of this audit should be used to inform school forward planning, and the priority rating of the subject area within the development plan.
- *School resources*   School resources should be reviewed as part of a three-year cycle. Suitable areas for regular scrutiny include the library, artefacts and subject specific resources, use of the building itself, display and art materials and policies.

An analysis of the OFSTED Framework for Inspection suggests that schools should also review the following on a regular basis:

- the spiritual, moral, social and cultural development of pupils;
- standards of achievement within the school, both in relation to national norms, and to their own capability;
- the quality of learning;
- the quality of teaching;
- the efficiency of the school;
- behaviour and discipline;
- attendance;
- assessment, recording and reporting;
- curriculum content;

- use of teaching and non-teaching staff;
- resources for learning;
- accommodation;
- provision for pupils with special educational needs.

At the end of the audit, the school will have identified its current position and strengths, identified areas for development, demonstrated how children will benefit, quantified the resources available and be ready to write its revised development plan. The Madison School plan includes a brief record of the results of its most recent reviews clearly demonstrating how their current position informs the next three years of development. For example, in the curriculum section:

Assessment

- All targets met. Considerable developments in internal assessment procedures have enabled a consistent approach to teacher assessment, used to enhance pupil development.
- Approaches to records of achievement have been piloted and adjusted. The most successful will become our policy and printed for introduction in September.
- Coordinators have begun to develop moderation folders. Throughout the next year further examples of work will be collected and added by the coordinators. They will be used to agree internal standards and National Curriculum levels.

Development of curriculum areas

- All targets met except mathematics, where the INSET has been delayed due to a change in postholders.
- Coordinators have worked hard to develop their curriculum areas, support colleagues, purchase and allocate resources and liaise with inspectors and advisory teachers. The role of the coordinators has been the subject of a school review and resulted in revised job descriptions and the three-year cycle of curriculum development.
- A request for additional, regular non-contact time has been added to the resource priorities for the next three years.
- The need for a specific science coordinator remains a priority when staffing changes occur.

THE STATUS OF THE DEVELOPMENT PLAN

The DFE expects that schools will produce an annual development plan, and as was seen in Chapter 2, OFSTED Inspectors list it high on their agenda of documents requested at the start of an inspection. Development plans, however, must not be written merely in order to satisfy an externally imposed requirement. The purpose and status of the plan is clear. It is an internal document, agreed by all involved in the development of the institution, and regarded by them as the mainspring for all that happens in the school. It is the reference point for governors, the headteacher and staff, whenever any major decision is made. It will be revised and annotated many times during the school year as events unfold, and targets are met. It will be regarded by staff, governors and parents alike as the agreed route to be followed by the school in the achievement of its aim statement. Therefore, the status, purpose and validity of the development plan must be agreed by staff and governors as their first step in drawing it together.

Essentially, the school development plan states how the school plans to evolve in order to become more effective, and how it will increase the likelihood of achieving its aim. It explains how the achievement of objectives will add up to the vision. The budget, the business element, will be the engine for the eventual plan. Limited resources will act as a constraint, but however constrained and cut back the budget, the plan must still be in charge. The management of the conflict between what is needed and what the money is sufficient to buy, will be explored in greater detail in Chapter 7.

The concept of business plan is becoming more common in education, and with it the misconception that the act of writing a business plan in some ways solves all the problems automatically and that success is guaranteed. Business plans also carry the implication that the plan will be successful if financial targets are achieved. A carry forward, or profit, at the end of the trading period means that the aim of the organisation has been met. This is not the business of schools, but schools have delegated budgets and have to be businesslike in their conduct. The governors are accountable at the annual meeting for the dispersal of their budget, and the LEA can remove their delegated powers if gross financial mismanagement is proved. The delicacy of the governing body's task is to ensure that the aim of the school, which has nothing to do with finance, is met by careful deployment of the budget in order to achieve that aim. This will require systems which ensure equity, a sophisticated audit of current levels of achievement and resource, and an agreement on the prioritisation process if differing bids are competing for limited funds. This, in turn, will require an open, understood and balanced decision-making forum.

THE STRUCTURE OF THE DEVELOPMENT PLAN

The development plan should be written and organised in a structured way so that it is easily accessed, and presents its sections in a logical order. Figure 3.1 lists the constituent parts likely to be included.

1 The aim or mission statement
2 An introduction stating the purpose, status, audience and authority of the plan
3 The objectives, with priorities agreed
4 The tasks which need to be completed to achieve each objective
5 The responsibilities allocated to named individuals
6 The resources, including money, time, staffing and accommodation, needed to achieve each objective
7 Staff development needs identified, planned for and resourced
8 The governors' own professional development plan
9 The premises development plan
10 Success criteria specified
11 Monitoring and evaluating strategies agreed
12 Appendices

Figure 3.1 The structure of the development plan

The aim statement

As we noted earlier in this chapter, the aim statement is the key reference point for all that follows in the plan and its inclusion at the start of the document reinforces the assumption that everyone involved in the plan understands and supports the philosophy and value statements which lie behind it. There will also be an assumption that the school and the governors formally revisit the aim statement on a regular basis to ensure that it continues to reflect their current thinking, and that new colleagues on the governing body or school staff understand and share its rationale. There has to be the understanding that it is the reference point when all major decisions are made, that the governors stand firmly and publicly with it at the annual meeting with parents, and that the parents and children understand and support it as the agreed purpose of their school. Its language may be generalised, but the thinking behind it will be deep, and reflect belief and commitment.

Madison School chose to develop its main aim statement with a number of current aims which would be subject to annual review and revision. These include:

- the development of a lively enquiring mind through an environment which fosters enthusiasm, curiosity, the ability to observe, question and discuss;
- the acquisition and application of the basic skills of language in listening, speaking, reading and writing; and similar aims for all the other curriculum areas;
- the development of awareness of values and social skills, shared concern for other people, self-discipline, acceptable behaviour, and positive attitudes towards themselves and others;

- the development of respect and understanding for religious beliefs and moral values, and valuing people of other races, religions and ways of life.

The introduction

The introduction will make clear that the development plan has the full understanding and support of staff and governors, whose representatives, the chair and headteacher, will sign it after major revisions. The signatures are not just an administrative mechanism, but a clear affirmation of their partnership in setting out, jointly, to achieve the aim and objectives agreed for the school through the strategies outlined in the plan. The Introduction should clarify that the development plan is a working document, and although the document which follows will not contain all the detail of all the planning, it will make very clear what the priorities for the coming year will be, how they will be achieved, by whom, by when, what resources will be required, and how the outcomes will be evaluated. It will be made clear that the objectives which have been set are a result of a rolling programme of review of where the school is currently placed and where it is striving to be. Although the development plan is an internal working document, its readership should go beyond those who are its authors. The plan is a statement of how the governors and school will deploy the public money allocated to them to maximise the learning opportunities for the children in the school. Therefore, it should be written in language which is jargon-free and readily understood by non-specialists.

Madison School introduces its development plan by reminding its readers that it is designed to:

- assist the school to fulfil its aims;
- link the management, financial, curriculum and staff development plans of the school;
- recognise the involvement of all staff in the school's development;
- strengthen the partnership between staff and governors in order to develop and enhance children's learning.

The objectives

Each objective, and the tasks which arise from it, will probably need a section of the development plan to itself. Madison School sets separate groups of objectives for management, curriculum, governors and premises. It is important that those who have to achieve the objectives are part of the team which write them, so that the eventual form of words is understood and owned. Different objectives might need to be written in slightly different ways, but certain features are common to all:

- a clear statement of the objective;
- clarity that the definition of the objective is based on a sound appraisal of the current situation which it seeks to develop;
- a statement of its priority in relation to other objectives;
- clarity that the achievement of the objective is central to achievement of the aim statement.

The tasks

Tasks can only be achieved if they are set within an understood framework. Each will be different according to the task itself, and the skills and resources available to achieve it.

Certain common features will apply to all:

- a clear understanding of what the task is;
- a specific focus;
- knowledge that the definition of the task is based on a sound appraisal of the current situation it seeks to develop;
- a statement of its priority;
- understanding that the achievement of the task is central to the achievement of the aim statement;
- a named key worker, and a reporting line;
- a definition of the authority of the key worker, including clarity on the level of delegated powers of decision-making;
- an action plan showing how each task will be achieved;
- a time scale;
- the names of other governors or staff involved, and how;
- an agreed allocation of resource of time, money, or staff;
- agreed professional development, if required;
- an agreed statement setting out how completion or success will be known and evaluated.

The Madison School development plan section on curriculum sets five objectives:

- to implement a three-year cycle of policy making, monitoring and evaluation which provide a framework for the school's approach to sustained curriculum development;
- to review and develop all curriculum areas over three years, using OFSTED criteria;
- to produce curriculum policies which aid the realisation of the school's aims for pupil's learning and achievement;
- to develop the role of the curriculum coordinators enabling them to fulfil the responsibilities agreed in their job descriptions;
- to identify priorities and make effective use of available resources.

These are then linked to each area of the curriculum, a place in the three-year cycle, and a status report which shows whether the curriculum area concerned is under *review*, is rewriting its *policy* as a result of the review, or is in a consolidation phase *monitored* by the coordinator. This process appears in the development plan in a simple tabular form. The following is an illustrative excerpt:

Area	Year 1	Year 2	Year 3
English	Review	Policy revision	Monitor
Music	Monitor	Review	Policy revision
IT	Policy revision	Monitor	Review
Special needs	Review	Policy revision	Monitor

Figure 3.2 Curriculum development within a three-year cycle

Responsibilities

The balance between the overall accountability of the governing body for the dispersal of the budget and the need for them to be involved in the detail of the development plan will differ from school to school. However, when a governing body attempts to go far beyond its responsibility for setting down the broad directions in which the school should go, and seeks to be consulted about and make the smallest of decisions, the result is the weakening of the headteacher's professional position and a cause for concern. Governors, headteacher and staff should be working together, with a clear understanding of their respective roles and responsibilities. It is important that the governing body understands the development plan, feels comfortable about asking questions about it, and receives regular reports and updates on the progress of its implementation. Once the broad objectives have been agreed, the detail of how they will be achieved must be delegated to the headteacher and the staff.

The governors will need to revisit the plan on a regular basis. It is not an annual event, as different prompts during the year will influence its content. The budget-setting process must dictate the number of objectives which can be resourced, but so will other events which will occur at different times: a change in roll profile in September, an increase in the number of children claiming free meals, or a member of staff leaving the school. The importance is that the governors understand, set and support the broad context of the plan, delegating the detail of the planning and the authority to implement, to the headteacher and the staff. If an OFSTED inspection takes place during the year, the governors will be required to produce an action plan in relation to the report's main findings within forty days. The writing of the action plan might well result in mid-cycle revision of planning and the relocation of resources from a priority which has now been superseded.

Specific responsibilities may be allocated to named governors. These should be recorded in the plan, along with the level of responsibility they carry. Many school governing bodies have set up a committee structure to make good use of expertise held by individual governors, and to assist the headteacher and senior staff in carrying the complex responsibilities of a devolved budget. Premises and finance sub-committees are good examples. However, clear terms of reference are essential to avoid misunderstandings or inappropriate practice.

In most cases, the responsibility for the achievement of an objective will lie with the headteacher, a curriculum coordinator or other member of staff. Issues relating to the efficiency or management of the school must be the responsibility of the headteacher. Issues relating to different areas of the curriculum or to key stages, are likely to be the responsibility of specific members of staff.

The headteacher will normally assume overall responsibility for writing the development plan, with the teaching staff as the main contributors. The contribution of others either as, for example, governors writing the section on the fabric of the building, or the caretaker on plans for the refurbishment of the furniture, are equally valid. The chair of the governing body should be seeing drafts and have an opportunity to comment as, ultimately, he or she will have the final responsibility for its resourcing, implementation, and for supporting it at the annual meeting with parents.

Madison School allocates responsibility to the coordinators by including their names in the development plan table (Figure 3.3):

Area	Coordinator	Year 1	Year 2	Year 3
English	Mary Smith	Review	Policy	Monitor
Music	Peter Jeffrey	Monitor	Review	Policy
IT	Emily Danby	Policy	Monitor	Review
Special needs	Kamaljit Singh	Review	Policy	Monitor

Figure 3.3 Curriculum development within a three-year cycle with responsibilities attached

The resources

The development plan is about the allocation of resources in order to achieve objectives. We explore this in greater detail in Chapter 8, but the development plan is meaningless without the allocation of quantified sums of money, time and staffing to each objective. There never will be enough money to meet all the demands. Governors, as the ultimate arbitrators, must be clear in setting priorities against known criteria and explaining why some objectives have to slip down the list in times of budget constraint. Priorities will normally be set within the context of the basic philosophy of the school. For example, in what ways should the money gained under the socio-economic part of the formula be used? Reference to the school aim statement will be needed to inform the decision.

Madison School records that the implementation of the school development plan will be supported by the efficient and effective use of various resources:

- the delegated budget, which is set out in detail as an appendix to the plan;
- grants for education, training and support (GEST) set out in detail as an appendix to the plan (see Figure 3.5);
- donations from the PTA, to be spent on a prioritised list of curriculum resources agreed by the parents and staff set out in detail as an appendix to the plan.

Resources from within the delegated budget will need to be allocated to specific objectives and tasks. Figure 3.4 illustrates how the two figures 3.2 and 3.3 can be expanded to summarise the allocation of the key resources of time and money.

Area	Coordinator	Year 1	Resources (in year 1)	Year 2	Year 3
English	Mary Smith	Review	a) cover £450 b) library £1,000 c) professional development £200	Policy	Monitor
Music	Peter Jeffrey	Monitor	Cover £200	Review	Policy
IT	Emily Danby	Policy	a) secretary, 4 days £100	Monitor	Review
Special needs	Kamaljit Singh	Review	a) 3 days, advisory teacher £900	Policy	Monitor

Figure 3.4 Curriculum development within a three-year cycle with responsibilities and resources attached

Staff development

The development plan must identify the staff development needs which are integral to the achievement of any of the objectives. Additionally, planned staff development for all teaching and non-teaching staff, and the governing body, should be a resourced objective in its own right.

There are important links between the development plan, teacher appraisal and staff professional development. The development plan should include the allocation of resources, financial and time, for staff development. In order to avoid raising false expectations among staff during teacher appraisal interviews, it is essential that professional development takes place within its own established and agreed policy. It is pointless to raise expectations among teachers that their professional development needs will be met, if time and money cannot be allocated within the development plan. The status of inservice education and training (INSET) or professional development coordinators, and whether they actually hold the cash INSET budgets, are the best indicators of the priority a school development plan places on professional development. It is pointless to name the deputy headteacher as professional development coordinator, and then refuse to allow him or her to control, in practical terms, how the budget is deployed. In carrying out their analyses of the professional development needs of schools, professional development coordinators will have to weigh up several potentially conflicting or competing factors. The needs of the school itself, revealed through the audit process, might, in their turn, be considerably influenced by externally imposed requirements. The National Curriculum forced some schools and teachers to examine the balance of their curriculum content, and some were found wanting. The needs of the individual teacher, probably identified during the appraisal discussion, might not always mirror the needs of the school. A teacher may want to build on an existing curriculum strength, while the needs of the children might be better met if the teacher's curriculum insecurities were addressed. This can be a difficult situation to manage, particularly if certain undertakings were given during the appraisal interview. This reinforces the need for a clear and public INSET policy as the first essential of any programme of professional development. The analysis of the school's and the individual's needs will then be measured against clear criteria, the school purpose as expressed in the aim statement, and the governors' practical commitment to the principles of staff development. The prioritisation of valid bids against a cash- or time-limited budget will be against the same criteria.

The governors should identify a professional development budget when they decided on the dispersal of the delegated GEST and LEA funds. Their commitment to the concept of development will lead them to identifying a resource which is at least 2 per cent of the gross salary budget within the school. Whether this is spent on delegate fees for courses, the purchase of

	Objective	Link to SDP or post-OFSTED action plan	Activity	Time scale	GEST £
1	English review	Item 4	a) Cover for coordinator to spend half day with each class	Summer	450
			b) LEA course AAA123	July 20	50
			c) Half-day support from SLS	May 17	200
2	Fewer behaviour problems at lunchtime	Item 7b	LEA course A765×4 places	Nov.	140
3	Increased use of IT at KS2	post-OFSTED action plan item 4	a) Purchase of hardware	Jan.	500
			b) LEA IT course A45	17 Feb.	75
			c) LEA TA two days	20, 21 Feb.	590
			d) Sec. support for new policy	Apr.	100
			e) Cover for [b] + follow up	Feb.	230

Figure 3.5 The allocation of GEST funds

supply cover, professional development books and materials, travel, or fees for advisory teachers, inspectors and other external consultants, will be the internal business of the school. What is of major importance is that the final package is seen as central to the effective delivery of the development plan in its pressure for excellence and the achievement of the aim statement, and is driven by the identified needs of the school. The governors will also wish to maximise their entitlement to government GEST grants, and are required to submit outline plans to their LEAs by the end of the previous financial year so that the necessary approval can be given. The governors of Madison School work within a simple proforma which is attached to the development plan.

The governors' own plan

The governors should have their own development plan, and this should form part of the overall school development plan. They too should assess their developmental needs in a structured way, and plan to meet them over a sensible time scale. The budget available for governor training should be used to meet those objectives. Despite the constraints on their time, governors usually take on their role wishing to bring a high quality of application to their responsibilities. Individual governors will have their own developmental and training needs, and the school will be looking for specific types of support from governors. The two elements should not conflict, but form a unified strand of development within the plan.

The objectives set for the governors of Madison School include:

- to be involved in agreeing and setting the policies which underpin the school development plan;
- to enable new governors to attend relevant courses on the governing of schools;
- to implement a policy of visiting the school during the school working day;
- to further develop the direction and purpose of the work of the various sub-committees;
- To form part of the review of school management systems using OFSTED criteria.

The premises

The premises section of the report must also reflect the needs of the building and will be assessed and resourced on a regular basis. Most schools plan over a three-year period. As will be seen in Chapter 8, the proposals are likely to have been brought to the governing body by a premises sub-committee. They will have inspected the fabric of the building on a regular basis, and will be aware of the staff's concerns and plans to make the building an appropriate environment for the children's learning. Likely headings for their review of the fabric will include plumbing, internal decoration, furniture, and the school grounds. When their costed proposals have the governors' approval, the sub-committee's proposals can appear in the development plan in tabular form: In the case of Madison School the plan would be laid out as in Figure 3.6.

Success criteria

Each objective within the development plan should include a statement setting out how success will be evaluated. Whenever possible this should be in measurable terms. For example, the criteria for the successful introduction of a whole school policy on assessment could be the writing and circulation of the guideline document by a certain date, and actual implementation within classrooms by a second agreed date. The success criteria for the introduction of a parents' newsletter might be an agreed number printed and circulated by an agreed date, and a predetermined number of favourable comments logged within three weeks of publication. The basic question is always: I know that I have completed the task, but how do I know if it has been successful?

Area	Year 1	Year 2	Year 3
Plumbing Pupil toilets Classroom sinks	replace cisterns £570	replace 4 £640	replace 4 £700
Decoration Classrooms Reception	classroom 1 £450 £400	classrooms 2–5 £1,800	classrooms 6–8 £1,400
Furniture Pupil tables Pupil chairs Carpet	£800	£600	classroom 1 £300
Grounds			paving, main entrance £500
Other			

Figure 3.6 The premises section summary within the development plan

If we take the examples set out in Figure 3.5 on page 58, success criteria should be added as a further negotiated column. The negotiation is between the member of staff responsible for achieving the task, and the person to whom they report. Figure 3.7 includes a success criteria column. Behind this summary lies discussion about what was required, and what would be achievable given the constraints of time, budget and the nature of the task itself.

Monitoring and evaluating strategies agreed

Evaluation is the natural extension of the previous section. Once the school knows that an objective has been successfully achieved, its impact must be evaluated and reviewed. The school needs to know whether the investment of time, money and other resources has been justified and whether there has been an impact on the learning achieved by children. The success of the objective to introduce a new maths scheme might be measured by recording that the scheme had arrived, the supportive INSET had taken place, parents had attended a workshop and the scheme had been introduced into the classrooms. The evaluation of the impact its introduction has on the mathematical achievement of the children could take a year. The review will dictate the next set of objectives. Having successfully introduced the new scheme, what next? Too many mistakes were made in the past when the achievement of

Objective	Link to SDP or post-OFSTED action plan	Activity	When complete	Success criteria	£
1 English. To review the effectiveness of the teaching of English at KS1 and KS2.	Key Objective 4	a) NC progress analysis. Cover for coordinator to spend half day with each class	July	a) Mary to produce analysis of each class's achievement in relation to current Eng. policy & NC requirements.	450
		b) LEA course AAA123: 'Recent OFSTED reports on KS1 & 2 English'	July 20	b) Course attended, evaluated, report to staff meeting, and implications discussed with HT by Oct. 1.	50
		c) Half day support from SLS for PD day on library	May 17	c) Action plan for library drawn up and implemented as a result of SLS input.	200
Re-energise the use of the school library					
2 Fewer behaviour problems at lunch time	Item 7b	LEA course A765 × 4 places 'Managing stress in the playground'	Nov.	Number of chn reported to DHT reduced from 15 per week to 6.	140
3 Increased use of IT at KS2	post-OFSTED action plan item 4	a) Purchase of hardware b) LEA IT course A45 c) LEA TA two days	Jan. 17 Feb. 20, 21 Feb.	a) Purchase complete b) c) New machines in use, staff confident as a result of AT input.	500 75
		d) Cover for [b] + follow up	Feb.	Policy typed and circulated.	230
		e) Sec support for new policy	Apr.		100

Figure 3.7 The allocation of GEST funds

the task was seen to be sufficient evaluation in itself. Effective evaluation is only achieved when someone stands back and takes an objective view of the impact the achievement has had on children in classrooms. It should form the basis of a report to governors. Having evaluated success, the review stage indicates what happens next.

The Madison School development plan section on monitoring and evaluation opens by defining monitoring as the process of looking at what is being done in order to support, develop and improve. Reviewing is looking at what has been done. Evaluating is making judgements about what has been achieved, based on previously identified criteria. The school includes monitoring and evaluation in its plan so that it can sustain commitment, check progress, identify and overcome problems, recognise achievement, inform parents, achieve objectives and assist future plans and achievements. The school identifies four levels of evaluation:

- Curriculum coordinators and members of the senior management team record termly progress and evaluate annually using previously agreed and negotiated success criteria.
- Discussions, formal and informal meetings and classroom visits enable the headteacher and deputy to monitor individual progress, support staff and evaluate the effect of policy implementation on pupil learning.
- Governors will be involved through visits to the school and classrooms, presentations and reports to governors' meetings. They will aim to ensure that finances are efficiently managed and focused clearly on the provision of resources to support objectives detailed in the development plan.
- The school recognises the external role of the LEA and OFSTED.

Appendices

Appendices are useful ways in which to include complex information without overloading the main body of the text. Appendices could include:

- staffing information in terms of staffing lists and the management structure;
- the budget details;
- cost centre finances in detail;
- staff meeting and professional development programmes;
- contracts with LEA or external suppliers and consultants.

THE FINAL DOCUMENT

The final document will be brief and summative. The first page will start with the aim statement and set out the purpose, status, audience and authority of the plan which follows (Figure 3.8). Subsequent pages will address, in outline, what each objective is, and how it will be achieved (Figure 3.9, or as Figures 3.4, 3.6 or 3.7). Appendices will provide supporting material.

Figure 3.9 sets out how the objectives relating to English might appear in the development plan. The coordinator must be prepared to explain the detail behind the summary. For example, what form the analysis will take and why, and what is meant by 'successful'. Tables similar to Figures 3.4, 3.6 or 3.7 might also be included. Appendices will provide supporting material.

Madison School

The agreed aim of this school is to achieve for all pupils:

- the development of a lively enquiring mind through an environment which fosters enthusiasm, curiosity, the ability to observe, question and discuss;
- the acquisition and application of the basic skills of language, numeracy and science as part of the achievement of a broad and balanced curriculum;
- the development of awareness of values and social skills, sharing concern for other people, while developing self-discipline, acceptable behaviour, and positive attitudes towards themselves and others;
- the development of respect and understanding for religious beliefs and moral values, and valuing people of other races, religions and ways of life.

This development plan has the full understanding and support of staff and governors and sets out how they will work together to achieve the aim and objectives agreed for the school. It is a working document, and although it does not contain all of the detail, it sets out the priorities for the coming year, how they will be achieved, by whom, by when, what resources will be required, and how the results will be evaluated. It is based on a clear understanding of where the school is currently placed and where it is striving to be. It links the management, financial, curriculum and staff development plans of the school, and recognises the involvement of all staff in the school's development in order to increase and enhance children's learning.

Figure 3.8 Page 1 of the development plan

REVIEWING THE SCHOOL DEVELOPMENT PLAN ITSELF

Once the plan is written, it should be reviewed as the basis for moving forward.

Reviewing the plan: 1

Was the writing process open and understood? The headteacher, governors and staff will have to come to an agreement on the process itself. If everyone sees every draft, and everyone else has the right to veto, then the plan will

	Main task	Resource implications, including staffing	Key worker	Time scale	Success criteria	£
4a	To produced analysis of each class's achievement in relation to current Eng. policy and National Curriculum requirements	a) Time for work alongside each teacher; non-contact time fo analysis	Mary Smith	By July 20	Analysis and recommend-ations presented to HT	450
	To evaluate outcomes and implications of Language co-ordinator's course on 'Recent OFSTED reports on KS1 & KS2 English'	b) Cover by HT		Meet HT Oct. 1		50
	To formulate and present plans for the revisions to the current English policy	Time		Oct. 1	Policy rewritten on basis of sound analysis	
4b	To re-energise the use of the school library	a) Half day PD for whole staff. Buy in of SLS advice b) New money for library stock and support IT	Mary Smith	Summer	a) Successful PD morning b) Book stock pruned c) New stock and budget identified	a) 200 b) 1,000

Figure 3.9 Madison School: Key Objective 4
(a) To review the effectiveness of the teaching of English at KS1 and KS2
(b) To re-energise the use of the school library

never be written. Responsibility has to be placed with named, key people. All those likely to be affected by the plan should be kept up to date through a periodic involvement and manageable consultation process. Total ignorance of the plan, and the absence of any opportunity to comment at the draft stages, will result in staff disillusionment. Consultation has to be genuine, and not solely for effect. Consultation has to be genuine in order to respect the various strengths and starting points of the writing team, and to ensure ownership of the final version. A special staff meeting and governors' meeting might need to examine the final version, with clear editorial rights given to the headteacher to revise and amend as the plan rolls forward.

Reviewing the plan: 2

Is it a *school* development plan, or a curriculum development plan? If it is solely a curriculum development plan, then it is ignoring the reality of LMS (local management of schools), and the need to identify how the total delegated budget will be deployed in order to achieve the purpose of the school. This requires planning and allocation of resources far beyond the detail of the curriculum, as it involves and includes decisions on the number and grading of the staff, and the physical environment in which they, and the children, come to learn. The curriculum must stand at the centre of the plan, as its *raison d'être*, but within the context of other facets of the school.

Reviewing the plan: 3

Does the development plan relate to the aim statement? If the relationship is tenuous, or non-existent, then either the aim statement, or the plan, is in need of urgent revision. If the aim statement needs revision, this should be addressed by the governors and staff as their most urgent priority. No decisions or plans can be made if those involved are uncertain about what the purpose of the organisation is. If the aim statement is a correct summary of what the school is striving to achieve, but subsequent plans appear to be unrelated or even in opposition, then they must be ruthlessly rewritten until there is uniformity of direction and purpose.

Reviewing the plan: 4

Does the plan identify the principle objectives and priorities for the coming period? The plan must identify the main objectives for the deployment of the budget during the following year, including the allocation of the quality time which will be needed in order that action plans can be implemented. Some plans will have priorities which reappear over several years, other objectives will be time limited, others will have to take their turn in subsequent years. By making this clear, the plan will demonstrate the developmental nature of its middle- and long-term planning, and highlight the importance of all concerned being involved in the consultation processes and understanding how decisions were made. Examples could include a rolling programme of internal decoration, the phased replacement of classroom computers, or a programme of curriculum review. The four-yearly cycle of OFSTED inspections will produce their own agenda, and may well cause the school to reassess its priorities.

Reviewing the plan: 5

Is the final written version set out in the way which is most helpful to those who have to implement it? Many local authorities sought to assist their schools in writing their early plans by sending out models or requiring that the finished products were expressed in a common format set by the LEA. Many schools found this a constraint and reworked otherwise perfectly acceptable plans in order to make them fit into the LEA format. Each school should seek to refine the way its plan is organised so that it is presented in the most suitable format for the school itself. Key elements like the aim statement must be included, but the fundamental design should reflect the fact that the plan is a working document and that its prime users are the governors and staff of the school itself. It may suit the school which has, for example, identified five main priorities for the forthcoming year, to set out the objectives, tasks and action plans arising from those priorities on five separate sheets of A4. Another school may decide to plan in sections relating to staffing, finance, curriculum and premises. The model we suggest in Figure 3.9 should only be used if it meets the needs of the user school. The best plans are designed by the school in the light of its own experience.

Reviewing the plan: 6

The final check list. Whatever the format, the plan must:

- be clearly organised;
- be written in plain English;
- have budget implications of the plan properly explored;
- be based on achievable objectives;
- say who will do what by when, and how task completion will be evaluated;
- enable OFSTED inspectors to make a judgement on the quality of the school development plan, its usefulness as an instrument for change and improvement, its realism and the achievement of any priorities set.

The adults who work in schools in order to achieve its aims for pupils, are learners themselves. If the school can recognise that it is a learning society, it will also recognise that the professional development of its staff is central to its success. This is the focus for the following chapter.

Chapter 4

Managing the curriculum

The complexity and breadth of the requirements of the National Curriculum, and the assessment procedures that accompany it, remain daunting. While decisions concerning the core content of National Curriculum subjects, and what should be covered at each key stage, are not the responsibility of individual schools, how the work is structured, organised and delivered clearly is. The introduction of the National Curriculum highlighted the complexity of the work of the primary teacher, and challenged the 'long-held assumptions . . . that the generalist class teacher can cope, almost unaided, with the contained nature of much primary teaching'. (OFSTED 1994a: 7) The streamlining process proposed by Dearing (1994), aimed to make the curriculum orders less prescriptive by dividing the content into *statutory core* and *optional material,* and by indicating the amount of time available for each key stage in each subject. Schools became accountable to their governing bodies for the way they used the time released and had to record their decisions about this and make them available for inspection. The intention was that teachers' workloads would be cut through the simplification of the National Curriculum and reduced testing and recording requirements, but the actual delivery of the curriculum remains challenging, and its implementation requires advanced and complex management skills.

The headteacher's overall responsibility is to ensure that the curriculum is managed effectively through appropriate delegation to colleagues. The responsibility of the governors is to ensure that the delegated budget is deployed to enable this to happen. The responsibility of the staff is to understand the curriculum, pass on that knowledge to the children at a level appropriate to their age and ability, and assess their standards of achievement and quality of work. The management of the curriculum, therefore, clearly is a shared task within a defined structure which identifies the curriculum role and responsibilities of the headteacher, the deputy headteacher and other senior staff, subject coordinators and other members of staff. This chapter will examine the separate but interlocking responsibilities of the headteacher, senior staff including the deputy headteacher, subject coordinators, the special needs coordinator, class teachers and governors. The cycle is completed by a re-emphasis on the responsibilities and accountability of the headteacher.

The start point for the management of the curriculum is a curriculum statement. This is a succinct statement of the school's overall curriculum aims and objectives. The curriculum statement will generate and give authority and context to the individual curriculum policies for each of the National Curriculum subjects and for religious education. These subject policies, in turn, will generate the individual subject schemes of work which the teachers will use for their termly and weekly lesson plans. Figure 4.1 sets out the inter-related levels of curriculum planning.

THE HEADTEACHER AS OVERALL CURRICULUM MANAGER

The formal responsibility of the headteacher is to manage and direct the content of the core and foundation subjects of the National Curriculum, and of religious education where appropriate. The headteacher must ensure that assessment, recording and reporting procedures are effectively in place, and that the needs of pupils in groups, classes or as individuals are fully met. In order to fulfil this responsibility and manage the curriculum successfully, the headteacher will need to demonstrate leadership and a clarity of vision concerning teaching and learning styles, classroom management, equality of opportunity and staff professional development and support. There is also a management responsibility for the school's policy documents, the levels of subject specialisation, the marking and record-keeping policies, levels and forms of parental involvement, resource management, and the planning, decision-making and evaluation processes. This will involve the headteacher in a great deal of focused discussion with colleagues: leading, and contributing to, staff and team meetings; developing and reviewing policies; analysing assessment data and children's work; observing children and teachers at work; consulting members of the governing body and others with a concern for the work; keeping up to date with local and national documentation; and, very importantly, finding the time to reflect on progress and the direction of the work.

The delivery of the school's curriculum will be judged by the extent to which its content, structure, organisation and implementation: contribute to the achievement of high standards and to quality in learning; comply with statutory requirements, reflect the school's aims, provide equality of access for all groups of pupils, and is enhanced by extra-curricular provision. We have already proposed that this will be expressed in succinct terms in the form of a curriculum statement which sets out the school's aims and objectives for the whole curriculum. The statement will be unique to the school, but fully compliant with the requirements of the National Curriculum and related legislation, broad and balanced, and sensitive to the guidance and requirements

Level	Content
The curriculum statement	A statement of the school's aims and objectives for the whole curriculum. It will be unique to the school, but fully within the requirements of the National Curriculum and related legislation, broad and balanced, and sensitive to the guidance and requirements of the LEA. Although probably written by the headteacher, it will be equally owned, supported and understood by all the staff and governors. Accountability is to the governing body.
The curriculum policies	Statements of the school's aims and objectives for each of the core and foundation subjects of the National Curriculum and for RE. Each will be unique to the school, recognising its particular needs and strengths. Each will link specifically to the school's curriculum statement and the achievement of the aims of the school as set down in the development plan. Appropriate account will be taken of cross-curricular issues. Although probably written by the appropriate subject coordinator, it will be equally owned, supported and understood by all the staff and governors. Accountability will be to the headteacher.
Schemes of work	The school's unique plans for the detailed delivery of each part of the National Curriculum and RE. They will ensure continuity and progression between and within key stages. Component parts will consist of work planned for each year group and form the basis for individual teachers' termly and weekly planning. Although written by the appropriate subject coordinator, it will be equally owned, supported and understood by all the staff, and open to governors. Accountability will be to the headteacher.
Teacher's individual plans, weekly and termly	Each teachers' unique plans for the detailed delivery of each part of the National Curriculum and for RE. They will ensure continuity and progression, and appropriate differentiation, for all pupils. Component parts will consist of work planned for each child or group, and form the basis for individual teachers' termly and weekly planning and assessment procedures. Although written by each teacher as an individual, they will form a cohesive whole within subjects, within year groups and key stages, and within the single aim to achieve the objectives laid down in the school's curriculum statement. Overall accountability will be to the headteacher, with a professional accountability to the appropriate subject and year group coordinators.

Figure 4.1 The levels of curriculum planning

of the LEA. It will be equally owned, supported and understood by all the staff and governors, who will have been fully involved in its compilation. Although accountability is to the governing body, the headteacher has the overall responsibility for the delivery of the curriculum statement in terms of its management, coordination and monitoring and evaluation. The headteacher is also responsible for the delegation of appropriate curriculum responsibility, the creation of effective decision-making processes, thorough planning and the maintaining of a proper balance of taught time between the various subjects. These aspects of the headteacher's management responsibility need to be examined in separation, but are intrinsically inseparable.

THE HEADTEACHER AS CURRICULUM COORDINATOR

The staff, parents and governors will look to the headteacher for a clear view of the school's own curriculum, and how it relates to the National Curriculum. The headteacher will seek to achieve the objectives of the curriculum statement through the coordination of the delegated responsibilities given to the subject coordinators. The staff will expect the headteacher to give them clear guidance on the time allocated to each of the core and foundation subjects, and how they are to meet the requirements of the National Curriculum and fulfil the wider aim of the 1988 Education Reform Act that the curriculum should be broad and balanced. While it is clearly the responsibility of each subject coordinator to write the individual subject policies and schemes of work, it is the headteacher's coordinating role to see that the several parts come together into a coherent whole which meets the objectives laid down in the curriculum statement. The headteacher's overall sense of direction for the curriculum should also be self-evident from the public support given to all the various curriculum policies and statements, and how these are presented to parents as complementary sections of the whole. If there is pressure from some parents seeking, for example, a greater emphasis on basic skills and a reduction of time allocated to the arts and humanities, the headteacher's ability to lead, inform, persuade and adhere to the agreed principles, will be a clear indication of commitment to the curriculum statement and the principles which underlie it. It is the headteacher's responsibility as coordinator to identify the processes which will bring together the various curriculum policies and schemes of work and set out the ways in which curriculum decisions are made and communicated. The cohesion of the curriculum will also be evident from the way in which it is presented by the headteacher in the termly report to governors and in the school development plan. Overall, it is the headteacher's management responsibility to organise the curriculum to ensure that it seeks to achieve the aims of the school, meets statutory requirements and promotes the individual learning opportunities offered to each child.

THE HEADTEACHER AS MONITOR
OF THE CURRICULUM

The headteacher should monitor the teachers' planning and preparation in order to ensure that there is appropriate cover of all of the various attainment targets and programmes of study within the statutory curriculum, and of all of the aspects of the school's own unique agreed curriculum. It is necessary also to monitor the work undertaken in the classrooms in order to see how the work which has been planned and prepared is actually transacted and assessed. This must be done openly and professionally and with the full understanding of the processes by the staff concerned. If lessons are to be observed or children's work examined, the teachers should understand what is being observed, why and how, and that the monitoring takes place within a context of professional feedback and support. Judgements should be based on the specific and concrete, rather than the general and abstract. The discussions should focus on the present rather than the past, with an exchange of information rather than advice. The advance of teacher appraisal and an acceptance and understanding of accountability have made teachers more receptive to colleagues observing them at work. Great sensitivity is still necessary, but even if teachers are resistant to the concept of observation, possibly through their own insecurity in the curriculum area being taught, the headteacher must persist. The identification of an area of professional insecurity is the identification of an area for professional development and support from colleagues. If the school chooses to overlook the fact that an area of the curriculum is being taught inadequately, for whatever reason, it is condoning a reduction in the children's entitlement to learning.

THE HEADTEACHER AS CURRICULUM EVALUATOR

Within the context of the OFSTED Framework for Inspection, headteachers should evaluate the whole curriculum using the criteria of breadth, balance, continuity, progression, coherence and compliance with National Curriculum requirements. They should evaluate: the teaching techniques and organisational strategies employed, using the criterion of fitness for purpose; the standards and progress achieved by individuals and groups and looking for trends and patterns of achievement; the overall quality of the education provided, including extra-curricular activities; and the standards achieved and the quality of education provided.

This is an extensive list, and the headteacher may decide to delegate some parts of it to the deputy headteacher or subject coordinators. This does not remove the headteacher's ultimate accountability, and should only occur as part of an agreed process which is understood by all the staff. A school may decide to look at the list as their focus for a training day and work out a series of strategies which could be used under the direction of the headteacher to evaluate various aspects of the curriculum in their own school. In Chapter 3 we suggested a triennial cycle of review as a means of redefining the needs of the school. Evaluation of the existing curriculum is the same task. The staff should discuss how the triennial review of 'where are we now, where do we need to be, and how will we get there?' should be carried out. This will assist the headteacher in the formation of an objective view of, say, various teaching techniques used in the subject under review. It should be agreed what the headteacher should do, and what should be the responsibility of the coordinators. The time available will be limited and any tasks identified must be achievable. If classroom observation or an analysis of children's books agreed as an appropriate strategy, the staff need to know who will do what, why and by when, and how the information is to be used and presented. Reassurances need to be given that if 'problems' are found, they will be addressed professionally and in the context of staff development and that any report will not identify individual teachers by name.

THE HEADTEACHER AS CURRICULUM DELEGATER

It is impossible for headteachers to carry out all their responsibilities, and manage by themselves all areas of the curriculum in the detail outlined above. Most schools will appoint specialist staff to assist the headteacher in the detail of curriculum management, without detracting from or lessening the headteacher's ultimate accountability. The role of the coordinator will be discussed in greater detail later in this chapter. The headteacher must be seen to delegate genuine responsibility to coordinators, together with the authority to act which must go with it. If it is proposed that coordinators should, as part of an agreed process, monitor the teaching, learning and assessment taking place in their subject area in classes other than their own, it must be recognised that this will have to take place within the teaching day and will require the allocation of sufficient non-contact time. This, in turn, will require that the headteacher works with coordinators in a review of how existing non-contact time is used, or allocates additional time at those points in the triennial-annual review when the extra time is needed. Delegation to coordinators should be part of the headteacher's management policy, endorsed by the governing body and set within a professional climate which recognises teachers' individual strengths.

The headteacher may wish to delegate assessment to an appropriate member of staff. In managing the curriculum, headteachers have a responsibility to ensure that the arrangements for assessment, recording and reporting to parents:

> result in an accurate and comprehensive picture of the achievements of individual pupils in relation to National Curriculum attainment targets. The operation and outcomes of assessment arrangements should

be manageable, constructive and helpful to teachers, parents, employers and pupils and should inform subsequent work.

(OFSTED 1993: 12)

Although headteachers should have delegated genuine authority and responsibility to subject coordinators, they will still need to make regular and structured judgements themselves on the quality of assessment, recording and reporting in their schools. They will need to evaluate the extent to which the school's arrangements result in accurate and comprehensive records of the achievements of individual children in relation to National Curriculum attainment targets and against other objectives. They will need to check regularly that the school's arrangements for assessment are manageable, and that the outcomes are constructive and helpful to pupils, teachers and parents, also that subsequent work is informed by these outcomes. If parts of this monitoring role are also to be delegated, the coordinator must be given a clear statement of what the delegated responsibilities entail, the resources that will be used to support them and a statement of the authority within which the coordinator will work with other members of staff. The statement should take its authority from the staff meeting which agreed the processes which would be used to monitor the curriculum, and be quite specific in its detail. For example, as the headteacher of Madison School informed her staff: 'Following the agreement at the staff meeting on 15 July, I will be taking Mary's class on four Wednesday mornings in October. This will enable her to spend a morning in each of the Key Stage 2 classes, hear six children read in each class (two above average, two average and two below average), and assess the children's ability in speaking and listening according to the criteria agreed at the staff meeting. Mary will be discussing her conclusions with me and the four teachers concerned on 4 November. The agreed outcomes of our discussion will form the basis for any revision of the current scheme of work, and provide the focus for our training day on 4 January.' The absence of such a brief will make the coordinator's job almost impossible, and lead to misunderstanding, confusion and a failure to achieve the objective. Delegation without an explicit definition of authority is a waste of time. There must also be a clear understanding of how and with what regularity the coordinator will inform the headteacher of the outcomes of the monitoring.

The headteacher as curriculum decision-maker

There will be occasions when the headteacher has to make decisions about the curriculum. The amount of money available for resources will never be enough and, on occasion, the headteacher will have to decide between equally valid claims for financial support. If the school development plan has been based on an accurate assessment of need, such occasions of choice should be rare as the priorities will already have been established and agreed. On other occasions there will be proper and healthy professional debate about teaching styles and the content of schemes of work. The headteacher will have to weigh the arguments, match them against the objectives in the development plan and the aim statement which drives it and make firm decisions. The decision-making process must be seen to be public and equitable. It should be influenced by the needs of the children rather than the competing aspirations of individual members of staff. It should be set within an understood set of priorities, rather than bowing to the fashion of the moment. As we demonstrated in Chapter 3, a fully thought through and costed development plan, which has the overall understanding and support of the staff and governing body, will give a clear unambiguous route forward. Discussions on teaching style and programmes of study should be addressed by all the staff affected, and are an appropriate agenda for a teacher training day. The headteacher must ensure that if there has been a divided opinion among the staff, all members have a proper opportunity for a calm and constructive exploration of the various options for finding an agreed way forward. However, once a decision has been made, all must follow the agreed route, even if it would not have been their own preferred professional choice.

The headteacher as curriculum planner

If the headteacher tries to manage the curriculum without a plan, the school will have no sense of direction, no framework for decision-making and no context for management action. The headteacher has the overview of the school as a whole, and the way in which it will need to develop in the medium- and long-term. As a curriculum planner, the headteacher will oversee the curriculum renewal and revision programmes outlined in Chapter 3 and ensure that all areas of work taught are subject to evaluation, review and policy revision on a regular three-year basis. The headteacher will also balance the knowledge of the numbers of children entering the school each autumn and leaving each summer against the budget available and the consequence of this for the size and number of classes and teaching groups. Significant changes in the size of the school roll will affect the size of the delegated budget, and either squeeze or increase existing financial and physical resources. School rolls seldom divide comfortably into class blocks and many schools have to group children vertically. The usual rationale used is age, with the older children in one year being included with the children in the next year group. This will require careful planning by the class teacher who will have to differentiate the curriculum so that each child is fully and appropriately challenged. The headteacher must ensure that schemes of work and policies are written in such a way that teachers using them to plan the work for mixed age groups can do so easily. As we discuss in Chapter 8, the headteacher will also plan the curriculum within the physical constraints of the building, the number of classrooms, the availability of space for PE and drama and the accessibility of resources. There is seldom an exact match between the number of children and the number of teaching spaces available. Schools are very creative in finding ways in which surplus accommodation can be used to improve children's learning opportunities, as resource bases, library or IT areas. Accommodation in overcrowded schools is more difficult, but children must never be taught in unsafe or inappropriate conditions.

The headteacher as the curriculum manager

The headteacher as curriculum manager will consider the school staff. What is the size and expertise of the existing staff, and how are they deployed? What are their curriculum strengths and weaknesses? Are they teaching appropriate year groups? Do they stay predominately with their own classes? Using the answers to these questions, the headteacher will seek to make the best possible staff dispositions in order to maximise the benefits for the children. Many schools try to see the combined expertise of the staff as a school wide curriculum resource, and will use the ability of a teacher able to offer specialist teaching in a subject such as music to the benefit of a number of classes. Other specialists may act as lead teachers in collaborative or team teaching sessions for history or geography focused topic work. The headteacher, in managing the staffing to the greatest benefit for the children, will balance the belief that the strength of primary education lies in the close relationship between a class and a single teacher, with the recognition that very few teachers are equally competent in all areas of the National Curriculum. Any deficiencies in the curriculum provision offered by individual teachers can also be strengthened by appropriate staff development both within the school itself, or through relevant external experience. Chapter 5 contains several examples of in-house professional development which can be implemented within the professional development element of the school development plan. There will be other organisational, financial and professional issues raised in the staffing audit. The headteacher, governors and senior staff will need to work together to resolve them and include their plans in the revised school development plan. There will be no easy answers, and sensitive issues must be tackled openly and honestly. For example, if KS2 history were an area of concern, the headteacher should analyse the reasons and work closely with the coordinator to ensure that the position is improved. The coordinator may not always be the best person to lead in this area and alternatives may need to be found, the subject given a higher profile achieved through an INSET day, or the level of resources re-examined and the current list of priorities in the development plan challenged. The headteacher's management skills of negotiation and persuasion will have to be deployed in making these decisions, ensuring the effective implementation of the curriculum and assessment requirements and checking that the needs of all children are addressed. In the longer term, the headteacher should seek to achieve a balance of appropriate staff expertise by using any staffing vacancy as an opportunity to make an appointment which meets the needs of the school as identified in the development plan. The end of an academic year should also be used as an opportunity to redeploy staff so that appropriate experience and excellence are moved around the school to the benefit of all.

The headteacher as a curriculum time manager

The headteacher has the ultimate responsibility for the management of the content of the school day and school week. Decisions on time allocation are usually shared and have led to many imaginative solutions including the 'ten-day week' and the 'Continental day'. The aim must be to allocate sufficient class teaching time to each and every part of the National Curriculum, while respecting the needs of the core curriculum and the wider whole school curriculum. Fundamental questions have to be asked which challenge the basic ways in which learning is organised. Is it necessary for each child in Year 1 to read to the teacher every day? Should it be the policy that every Year 6 child, not just those with reading difficulties, can expect to read to an adult in school on a regular basis? Should subjects be taught separately, or thematically, through topic work? How much planned physical activity should each child have each day or each week? What is a reasonable balance of time between the needs of the catering staff to set up and clear away dinner tables, and the needs of class teachers to have maximum access to the school hall for dance, drama and PE? Positive outcomes are best achieved when both parties are fully aware of the other's problems. If, in the example given above, the relevant teaching staff, the caretaker and the cook in charge sit down together to discuss the problem, a compromise should be achievable. The worse that can happen is that all parties understand the tension, the best that can happen is an arrangement which maximises opportunities for the children both as eaters and learners. Figure 4.2 sets out the headteacher's responsibilities for the curriculum plan. The headteacher will *originate* the curriculum statement, *commission* subject coordinators to write policies and schemes of work for those areas over which they have responsibility, and *monitor* the effectiveness of what happens to children in classrooms. This is expanded in subsequent figures in this chapter to show how all staff have interrelating roles and responsibilities in the management and implementation of the curriculum.

We have demonstrated that in order to fulfil the obligation to offer the children a well-managed, broad and balanced curriculum, the headteacher is accountable as a curriculum manager, monitor, evaluator, delegator, decision-maker and planner. Above all, the headteacher is the strategist. The deputy headteacher and other senior staff take the strategy and make it work at the operational level.

Curriculum plan	Role of headteacher	Actions by headteacher
Curriculum statement	Originator	Writes the draft statement, consults with staff and governors. Produces final version and implements.
Curriculum policies	Commissioner Monitor	Requires curriculum policies to be written by subject coordinators. Monitors quality and ensures cross-curricular links and implementation.
Schemes of work	Commissioner Monitor	Requires schemes of work to be written by subject coordinators. Monitors quality and ensures cross-curricular links and implementation.
Termly plans	Monitor	Oversees. Ensures continuity and progression.
Weekly plans	Monitor	Oversees. Ensures continuity and progression from week to week.
Assessment/SN	Commissioner	Requires policies to be written by coordinators. Monitors quality and implementation.
Evaluation	Monitor	Supports and monitors work in classrooms.
Review/revision	Monitor	Requires coordinators to review and revise on a regular pattern.

Figure 4.2 The headteacher's responsiblities for the curriculum plan

THE ROLE OF THE DEPUTY HEADTEACHER AND SENIOR STAFF IN THE MANAGEMENT OF THE CURRICULUM

The deputy headteacher and senior staff will work together to manage the curriculum in partnership with the headteacher, both as leaders and partners in setting the strategy, and as exemplars of good classroom practice in turning the strategy into operational reality. As members of the staffroom, taking part in its conversations, and working alongside their colleagues in classrooms, they will be aware of the distinctive styles of individual teachers and should aim to balance this within the requirements of the school. A variety of teaching styles enriches the learning environment within the school, but must fit within agreed parameters. The teaching in the school must be purposeful, must create and sustain interest and motivation and cater for the abilities and needs of all the children in each class. The teachers' expectation must be appropriate for all pupils, lessons should be planned in ways that ensure an efficient and orderly approach to teaching and learning, and an effective interaction between the teachers and the children. There must be evidence that children's progress is evaluated in order to support, encourage and challenge them. The deputy and senior staff can work closely and informally with colleagues to support them in the achievement of these objectives. They should feel that they share a responsibility in developing and strengthening staff, rather than being there to report on inadequacies. Some support strategies will be identified and resourced during the appraisal process, but a two-year appraisal cycle is far too long to wait for the teacher who has difficulties or the child who is not receiving his entitlement. Senior staff, coordinators and year group leaders should constantly seek ways to lift the overall standards of teaching and learning within the school. Termly discussions of work plans, for example, are appropriate official occasions to raise issues of style and approach, but informal contact over a cup of coffee, the quiet word of praise, the encouragement of good practice, the non-public offer of help with a difficult lesson, all contribute to the overall raising of standards.

The deputy headteacher and senior staff must support the headteacher and governors in their public and unequivocal stance on equality of opportunity in relation to the curriculum. They must ensure that a clear written policy which guarantees equal access to all parts of the curriculum for all children is observed in everyday practice as well as in intent, and that inappropriate customs or messages are rooted out. Stereotypical curriculum assumptions about, for example, girls and technology or boys and dance must be eradicated. Children of both sexes should feel comfortable using any of the school's resources or taking part in any of its activities, be they playing with materials in the reception class, or being selected for sports teams in Year 6. The library stock should be examined critically in order to remove dated or unsuitable materials. Role models used in lessons must be in equal proportion from each gender, and the curriculum must contain a balance of materials which reflect a multicultural world society which values the contributions of all its members. Class registers should be in alphabetical order of surname, and boys should not be listed separately from girls. No one should ask for 'two strong boys' to carry something or refer to the female members of staff as 'the girls'.

Children with special educational needs have equal rights of opportunity, and the curriculum must be managed in order to give them learning opportunities and resources appropriate to their needs. Provision should be made for those with exceptional ability as well as for those with learning difficulties. In some circumstances teachers may need extra resources in order to provide a differentiated curriculum. The headteacher has a responsibility to ensure that the learning opportunities for a whole class are not debilitated because an under-resourced teacher is unable to provide equitably for all the children in her care. The financial, resource and staffing implications surrounding the education of children with special needs are large and should be addressed by the staff as a whole. Teachers need to understand the regulations concerning modification or disapplication from the National Curriculum, how the various support services can be accessed, and the process of statementing. The consequent organisational or curriculum decisions must be understood and endorsed by the governors.

Staff professional development and support are likely to be the responsibility of the deputy or a member of the senior staff. These responsibilities are explored in detail in Chapter 5. However, in considering the management of the curriculum, it must be noted that the headteacher and senior colleagues cannot over emphasise the importance of the professional development needs of the staff. Money must be allocated for in-service training within the school, for the purchase of course places, for 'in house' support, to obtain appropriate support materials, and to bring into the school advisory staff or other agencies who now offer professional development support. Curriculum-related professional development must be seen as an integral part of the development plan, and sufficient time allocated for the training itself and the implementation programme which follows it. It will be a joint curriculum management responsibility of all senior staff to see that there is an understood policy in the school, that resources are provided, that all in-service work is evaluated, properly planned, appropriate to the needs of the school and an integral part of the school development plan.

The deputy and senior staff share a responsibility with the headteacher for the effective use of resources in the management of the curriculum. They will seek to ensure that the resources provided in the school are appropriate and readily available. As is discussed in greater detail in Chapter 5, this will raise financial questions, as those responsible for budgets could be inundated with requests for permanent resources and consumables. In order to adhere to the priorities agreed within the development plan, there should be a publicly understood policy on resources, and an equitable bidding process to which all have access. The agreed spending priorities and cash-limited budgets must be recorded in the development plan, together with the names of those authorised to approve expenditure. Whenever possible this should not be the headteacher, but the appropriate subject coordinator. The teacher responsible for the library, for example, must know within what financial limitations they have to work, but that, within those boundaries, they have final authority and accountability. Some areas of the curriculum – art and maths for example – cannot function without consumable resources. Science, technology, sports and physical education resources must meet health and safety requirements. Care should be taken to ensure that valuable money is not spent on an expensive passing fancy which becomes yesterday's news. All major spending must be to achieve an objective stated in the school development plan. Figure 4.3 sets out the responsibilities of the deputy headteacher and senior staff in relation to the curriculum plan. They act as *advisers* on the strategy encapsulated in the curriculum statement, *support* their colleagues who write the curriculum policies and schemes of work, and *monitor* the ways in which the schemes and policies are implemented.

Curriculum plan	Role of headteacher	Role of senior staff	Actions by deputy headteacher and senior staff
Curriculum statement	Originator	Advisers	Advise the headteacher on the draft statement and supports its implementation.
Curriculum policies	Commissioner Monitor	Supporters	Support and advise on policy implementation.
Schemes of work	Commissioner Monitor	Supporters	Support and advise on implementation of schemes of work.
Termly plans	Monitor	Monitors	Oversee. Ensure continuity and progression.
Weekly plans	Monitor	Monitors	Oversee. Ensure continuity and progression.
Assessment/SN	Commissioner Monitor	Monitors	Monitor quality and implementation.
Evaluation	Monitor	Monitors	Support and monitor work in classrooms.
Review/revision	Monitor	Supporters	Support coordinators.

Figure 4.3 The responsibilities of the deputy headteacher and senior staff in relation to the curriculum plan

It is likely that all senior staff, including the deputy headteacher, will have a curriculum area for which they are responsible. The responsibilities of the coordinator, although part of the intermeshing of accountability, need to be examined in detail.

THE ROLE OF THE COORDINATOR IN THE MANAGEMENT OF THE CURRICULUM

The responsibilities of the curriculum coordinator fall into several main areas, with some inevitable overlap among them. Although all coordinators will pay attention to each aspect of their role, the main emphasis will vary according to the priorities for the school for that particular curriculum area at that particular point in the triennial cycle of policy review, renewal and implementation.

Coordinators should expect to play an important role in the formulation of the curriculum statement, and contribute to the school development plan, ensuring that there is a school policy for their particular curriculum responsibility and that it is properly recognised within the plan. It will be their responsibility to write, and gain approval, for a policy for their curriculum area and to translate the policy into a detailed scheme of work, taking account of the National Curriculum requirements and the particular needs of the school, its children and staff. The coordinator will ensure that the policy and scheme of work is reviewed and revised on a regular basis. The achievement and standards of all the children in the school within that area of the curriculum should be monitored in a structured way to ensure continuity of progression and achievement. All coordinators should be prepared to report to governors on their particular area of the curriculum. This might take the form of a written report, a subsection of the headteacher's report or an oral presentation to a governors' meeting. None of these should give coordinators any concern. They are proper ways through which the governing body can be kept informed on how the allocation of the school budget is being used to the benefit of the children.

All subject coordinators will be responsible for the production, implementation and review of the curriculum policy for their curriculum area. The policy should state what the subject covers, how it relates to the requirements of the National Curriculum, how it will draw on and advance children's experiences, how work will be recorded and assessed, how the subject links to other curriculum areas, how teaching will be staffed, resourced and managed within the classrooms. The schemes of work should set out the school's aims for the subject and the place of the scheme in the whole curriculum. They should identify which aspects of the work are central to the scheme and show how the scheme matches the programme of study and the attainment targets. In organisational terms, schemes of work should show how areas of study can be broken down and sequenced, and how particular aspects might be taught through, for example, group work, discussion, drama, project or problem-solving. Guidance should be given on the amount of time to be allocated to particular areas of study, how the work can be differentiated for more able pupils or for those with learning difficulties, and the opportunities for homework. Links to other parts of the curriculum should be made and resources identified. There should be a clear statement to confirm who has responsibility for reviewing and monitoring each part of the scheme. The scheme should also set out the strategies which will be used for assessment, how assessments might be related to levels of achievement, what records and evidence could be kept for both internal and external moderation. A scheme of work should always be regarded as a working document. It will be subject to regular revision as new or improved ideas are identified. Figure 4.4 sets out a sequence of stages which a curriculum coordinator might use in creating or revising a scheme of work.

CURRICULUM COORDINATORS AND COLLEAGUES

If the school is to be truly effective and meet the needs of children and staff, means must be found so that each curriculum coordinator can support the work of colleagues during the teaching day. Practical solutions include sensible use of the headteacher's own time, unless the headteacher has a full-time class commitment, the planned use of the whole staff's non-contact time, and the purchase of cover. Subject coordinators cannot possibly carry out all of their responsibilities at lunch times or after school. It is essential that they have regular opportunities to work alongside colleagues in their classrooms, advising and supporting them. This heightens the importance of a structured plan for regular curriculum review, spread over a number of years, as the school's resources will never be enough to release every coordinator every term. The development plan must set out the cycle of review. When a particular subject's turn comes up, time and money should be available within the budget to make sure that proper support is available. In the years when that particular curriculum area is not the priority, the particular coordinator should not expect to be resourced at the same level and should be ready to support colleagues whose time of focus it is. Whatever the stage in the cycle of review, revision and implementation, coordinators must be prepared to find sufficient time to help colleagues develop and share teaching materials, provide relevant teaching materials when needed, work with other staff in the establishment of appropriate styles of teaching and assessment and to keep the headteacher, governors and colleagues fully informed of current and relevant developments.

CURRICULUM COORDINATORS AND
PROFESSIONAL DEVELOPMENT

Curriculum coordinators must expect to work closely with the professional development coordinator in their school in the arrangement and provision

Stage 1	Read the appropriate programmes of study and get to know the main ideas.
Stage 2	Compare the areas of study in the school's current scheme of work to the programme of study for the appropriate key stage. Note any inconsistencies.
Stage 3	Consider each area of study in detail and decide which attainment targets the activities match. Within the range of levels, identify which statements of attainment are covered by the area of study. Identify links between areas of study to decide the sequence in which they might be taught.
Stage 4	Check that sufficient and varied activities have been identified in each area of study to ensure that the able and those with learning difficulties are challenged at an appropriate level. Check that all ATs are sufficiently covered. Identify cross-curricular links.
Stage 5	Evaluate the scheme of work so far. Check that the scheme has an overall shape, balance and consistency. Check that continuity and progression have been included within each key stage, and from year to year.
Stage 6	Check the validity and appropriateness of the teaching strategies suggested for each key stage.
Stage 7	Identify opportunities for assessment as a normal part of the teaching and learning process.
Stage 8	Produce draft scheme, introduce to staff at staff meeting and circulate for comment within an agreed time frame. Revise where necessary.
Stage 9	Agree a timetable for implementation, any supportive professional development, supplementary staff briefing sessions and the process for reviewing the scheme. Agree presentation for governing body.

Figure 4.4 Producing a new or revised scheme of work

of school based INSET. They should monitor the in-service provision and its effectiveness for their area of responsibility. They should be prepared to take part in relevant INSET and professional development offered outside the school and use the knowledge gained to influence subsequent developments in the school. They should attend briefings, up-dates and coordinators' meetings offered by their LEAs or other creditable professional bodies in their areas. All of these aspects are examined in detail in Chapter 5. The coordinator should feel encouraged to attend exhibitions which touch on their area of work, and deal directly with trade representatives who may visit the school.

CURRICULUM COORDINATORS AND THE MANAGEMENT OF RESOURCES

Coordinators have a year-round responsibility for ensuring that the resources available enable the curriculum policy and schemes of work to be delivered. They should ensure that their colleagues are aware of the resources available and how to make best use of them. They should make sure that resources are replaced when appropriate and that the number of heavily used items is increased to ensure their reasonable availability. They should keep up-to-date with new resources and inform the headteacher, governors and colleagues of opportunities and developments which could enhance children's learning in their own school.

CURRICULUM COORDINATORS AND EXTERNAL ACTIVITIES

Coordinators' job descriptions are likely to require them to liaise with their counterparts in other schools. This will include networking with colleagues in neighbouring schools catering for the same age range, and with feeder or receiving schools where unruffled transfer must be safeguarded to minimise the effects on the children. This will require detailed discussion on teaching styles and records. The school should not compromise its own right to decide what is best for its children, but will want to work closely with receiving schools to ensure continuity and progression. Coordinators should also link directly with relevant subject inspectors in the LEA, advisory colleagues and members of external high quality training and support agencies. They should keep up to date with local and national curriculum developments through their reading, attendance at area support groups and appropriate courses and conferences. They should monitor and evaluate external curriculum developments and inform colleagues appropriately.

Curriculum coordinators in each subject area should work closely with the headteacher in order to develop an agreed view of what constitutes an appropriate curriculum in their particular subject. They know how it relates to the National Curriculum, and will be able to share this understanding with colleagues, governors and parents. They should work with colleagues to ensure that the curriculum comes together into a balanced whole in order to achieve the aims of the school and the required coverage of the statutory curriculum. The work of the special needs coordinator will permeate all the schemes of work and policies, and influence their content, in order to promote the educational achievement of all pupils.

THE ROLE OF SPECIAL NEEDS COORDINATOR AS A CURRICULUM MANAGER

The special needs coordinator must ensure that the curriculum is planned so that the particular educational needs of all children who have learning difficulties and/or disabilities are positively recognised. This should be encapsulated within a school policy on special needs, coordinated and monitored by the coordinator, and the subject of regular reports to the governing body and parents. The policy should recognise that all pupils share the right to a broad and balanced curriculum, including the National Curriculum. The policy should be within the context of the LEA's statutory requirement to have regard to any parental preference to place a child with special needs in a mainstream school provided that the child's particular needs can be met, there is no educational disadvantage to other children with whom the child is educated, and this is compatible with the efficient use of resources.

The special needs coordinator should work with the governing body when they monitor the security of the National Curriculum within the school. They will be looking to see that proper provision is made for any registered pupil who has special educational needs (SEN), that all teachers are informed when the LEA notifies a responsible person (usually the headteacher or special educational needs coordinator), that a child has special educational needs, and that teachers are aware of the importance of identifying and providing for such pupils. The 1993 Education Act also requires governors to have and publish a special needs policy, make available to parents and the LEA details of the SEN staffing arrangements, the qualifications of SEN staff and broad details of the teaching techniques and methods used with SEN pupils within the school. The governors may welcome the support of the coordinator in the production of an annual report for parents on SEN matters within the school, and in any consultation with the LEA or funding agency.

The special needs coordinator should write the school special needs policy and make sure that it is an identifiable strand within the development plan which sets out how the policy will be implemented and developed, and will work to ensure that the school allocates sufficient resources to provide support for pupils with special needs at levels 1, 2 and 3, with individual programmes of work and clear records of their effectiveness. The staff timetable should be constructed to allow the coordinator sufficient time to work with external agencies in order to meet the needs of statemented pupils, and consult fully with parents. The SEN budget should be allocated equitably in order to meet the needs of all pupils with SEN, whether or not they are subject to a statement. SEN funding can be allocated towards the salary costs of appropriate staff, books, equipment or materials, or to a contingency fund for short-term individual pupil support.

THE COORDINATOR'S SELF-REVIEW

From time to time coordinators should review their role and place within the school. The outcomes might well feature in an appraisal interview or progress chasing meeting. A negative response to any of the following questions should not be seen as a negative comment, but as an indication that the school and coordinator have identified an area for future professional development and support. Review questions might include:

- Do I hold any specific qualifications in the subject for which I am responsible?
- What recent training/external support have I received in this curriculum area?
- Does my job description set out clearly what my responsibilities are as coordinator?
- Are the staff and governors aware of my responsibilities?
- Is the school doing well in my area of curriculum responsibility?
- What developments in my area of responsibility have I been encouraging over the past year?
- What are my priorities for the medium- and short-term and how are these integrated into the school development plan in terms of curriculum update, curriculum policy review and revision, and resources?
- Is my current programme of professional development supporting my area of curriculum responsibility? Is there more that could be done?
- Do I have any concerns about my area of curriculum responsibility?
- How do I monitor and evaluate the teaching and learning in my curriculum area across the school?
- How do I use my non-contact time to develop my role?
- What is my budget and how has it been deployed?

Figure 4.5 sets out the responsibilities of the subject coordinators in relation to the curriculum plan. They will advise the headteacher and other senior staff in the writing of the curriculum statement, write the policy and scheme of work and support class teachers in the implementation of their termly and weekly plans.

THE ROLE OF THE CLASS TEACHER AS CURRICULUM MANAGER

Although the headteacher has the overview of the complete curriculum, and curriculum coordinators the day-to-day management responsibility for its several parts, the burden of the management of the delivery of the curriculum falls on class teachers in the primary school. However plentiful the resources and offers of support, putting theory into practice in terms of skilled planning can only be done by the class teacher. Teachers have become skilled in the

Curriculum plan	Role of headteacher	Role of senior staff	Role of subject coordinators	Actions by subject coordinators
Curriculum statement	Originator	Advisers	Adviser	Advises headteacher on the draft statement and ensures implementation.
Curriculum policies	Commissioner Monitor	Supporters	Writer	Write policies and support staff in their implemtation. Advises headteacher and governors on progress.
Schemes of work	Commissioner Monitor	Supporters	Writer	Supports and advises on implementation of schemes of work. Advises headteacher.
Termly plans	Monitor	Monitors	Supporter	Support staff when they write their termly plans.
Weekly plans	Monitor	Monitors	Supporter	Support staff when they write their weekly plans.
Assessment/SN	Commissioner Monitor	Monitors	Writer Supporter	Supports and advises on implementation of policies.
Evaluation	Monitor	Monitors	Supporter	Supports and monitors work in classrooms.
Review/revision	Monitor	Supporters	Writer	Reviews and revises.

Figure 4.5 Role of the subject coordinator in the management of the curriculum

translation of principles into practice. They recognise that the planning process for each part of the curriculum is cyclical and within a context of the long-, medium- and short-term. It is cyclical in that it starts by each teacher reviewing where the children are currently in each curriculum area, what their needs are as a group and what the span of their need is. The programmes of study and the school's own internal policies and schemes will establish how the work is planned. The use of resources – by the whole class, groups and individual activities – will need to be planned and thought through in advance. The teacher will assess progress and complete the cycle by asking again: 'Where are the children now? What are their needs?' The long-term planning – ensuring that all the subjects in the National Curriculum and RE are properly covered, that there is progression in each subject at each key stage, that there is a balance within and across subjects in each year of each key stage, that there is coherence within and between subjects, appropriate allocation of time, appropriate cross subject links and continuity between key stages – will be the responsibility of the headteacher and whole staff. The development of the key stage plan for a particular year into a detailed sequence of subject specific and linked units of work, is the responsibility of the class teacher supported by the subject coordinators. The balance between different types of activity and learning style, differentiation, appropriate pace, constructive feedback to learners, time for teacher assessment and monitoring and evaluation of progress, is the responsibility of the class teacher. In order to achieve the aims expressed on the school's curriculum statement, there must be a broad framework for each year of the key stage which reflects the school's overall curriculum aims and objectives. It should state the content of each subject, organise the content into manageable and coherent units of work, allocate time to each unit of work, sequence the work and identify links between aspects of different subjects. The medium-term plan should be a specification of each unit of work, setting out specific learning objectives and the depth of treatment they will receive, identifying the resources required, linking and referencing to other units of work, setting out the nature of the tasks and activities the children will follow, suggesting teaching and grouping strategies, demonstrating how differentiation will be achieved, and indicating assessment opportunities. The responsibility for daily or weekly lesson plans, and associated records which ensure effective day-to-day teaching and inform future planning, lies with individual class teachers.

In managing the curriculum, class teachers should bear in mind the conclusions of OFSTED (1994a) that the factors associated with high standards of achievement within the curriculum include teachers having satisfactory or good knowledge of the subject they are teaching, that children achieve high standards when teachers demonstrate good questioning skills to assess pupils' knowledge and challenge their thinking, and that in better lessons, teachers make effective use of exposition, instruction and direct teaching. Inspectors also noted that in better lessons teachers used a good balance of grouping strategies, including whole class, small group and individual work, that they used ability groups effectively and had clear objectives for lessons, good time management, used other adults effectively, used an appropriate range of assessment techniques and had well established classroom techniques providing minimal disruption to tasks and teaching, good classroom organisation of resources and materials, and were effective planners of children's work.

In unsatisfactory lessons OFSTED (1994a) noted that no actual teaching was done by the teacher, who acted mainly as a supervisor of, or service to, individuals or groups, that there was poor management and use of time in lessons, often with no deadlines being set and/or wastage at the beginning and ends of sessions, that there was an overuse of undifferentiated worksheets. They also noted that the tasks set to the children were insufficiently challenging or dull, often as a result of poor management and control of pupils, that there was poor organisation and management of resources, and that the aims and objectives set for the lessons were unclear, often leading to unsuitable tasks for the children. Figure 4.6 sets out the responsibilities of the class teachers in relation to the curriculum plan as the writers of termly and weekly plans, and the implementers of the curriculum.

THE ROLE OF THE GOVERNING BODY IN THE MANAGEMENT OF THE CURRICULUM

The governors have the ultimate responsibility for the effective management of the curriculum, and this must be the focus for their disposition of the budget. The detail of the management of the curriculum is a task that they should delegate to the professional managers in the school. This delegation does not weaken their accountability nor the importance of their role as monitors. The governing body has every right to expect to be kept fully up to date by subject coordinators on the main National Curriculum debates and how these will affect the particular school for which they are responsible. They should be given regular reports in plain English or factually based oral presentations which make them aware of the standards of achievement within the school, and how the staff will be working to increase them. A critical or complimentary comment on the curriculum from OFSTED should not come as a surprise. Governors should be encouraged to gain a greater understanding of the school's curriculum, either by taking a close interest in a specific subject area or key stage and working alongside staff on a curriculum sub-committee, or by joining staff working groups which are reviewing or revising policies and schemes of work. This will enable them to understand how the curriculum needs of the school should be dictating the disposition of the budget, and not the reverse. Governors have statutory responsibilities for religious education and sex education policies. Their stance should be based on careful consideration of parental and teachers' views but should result in

Curriculum plan	Headteacher	Senior staff	Subject coordinator	Class teacher	Actions by class teachers
Curriculum statement	Originator	Advisers	Adviser	Supporter	Supports and implements.
Curriculum policies	Commissioner Monitor	Supporter	Writer	Implementor	Supports and implements.
Schemes of work	Commissioner Monitor	Supporter	Writer	Implementor	Supports and implements.
Termly plans	Monitor	Monitor	Supporter	Implementor	Writes.
Weekly plans	Monitor	Monitor	Supporter	Implementor	Writes.
Assessment/SN	Commissioner Monitor	Monitor	Writer supporter	Implementor	Supports and implements agreed school policies.
Evaluation	Monitor	Monitor	Supporter	Information giver	Informs coordinators and headteacher on levels achievement.
Review/revision	Monitor	Supporter	Writer	Information giver	Informs and work with coordinators to improve scheme.

Figure 4.6 Classroom teachers as managers of the curriculum

Curriculum plan	Headteacher	Senior staff	subject coordinator	Class teacher	Governors	Actions by governors
Curriculum statement	Originator	Advisers	Adviser	Supporter	Mandate giver Reporter	Support and authorise. Allocate/delegate the budget. Report to annual meeting.
Curriculum policies	Commissioner Monitor	Supporter	Writer	Implementer	Supporter	Support and resource via development plan.
Schemes of work	Commissioner Monitor	Supporter	Writer	Implementer	Supporter	Support and resource via development plan.
Termly plans	Monitor	Monitor	Supporter	Implementer	Supporter	Aware of.
Weekly plans	Monitor	Monitor	Supporter	Implementer	Supporter	Can see.
Assessment/SN	Commissioner Monitor	Monitor	Writer Supporter	Implementer	Supporter	Support and resource via development plan.
Evaluation	Monitor	Monitor	Supporter	Information giver	Monitor	Support and resource via development plan.
Review/revision	Monitor	Supporter	Writer	Information giver	Monitor	Support and resource via development plan.

Figure 4.7 The responsibilities of governors for the management of the curriculum

clear policies for implementation. Figure 4.7 sets out the responsibilities of the governors in relation to the curriculum plan and indicates how the partnership between school and governing body will enable them to carry out their responsibilities and understand and support the philosophy which lies behind the curriculum statement.

THE CURRICULUM MANAGER: THE HEADTEACHER

The headteacher provides the vision and leadership needed to ensure the delivery of the curriculum. To do this, headteachers must be involved 'directly and centrally, in the planning, transaction and evaluation of the curriculum. ... Headship is leadership in quality assessment and assurance, and this will assume even greater importance as the National Curriculum and the Parent's Charter take full effect.' (Alexander, *et al.* 1992) Headteachers are the originators and the inspiration for the curriculum statement, they commission the policies and schemes which flow from it and monitor what actually happens in classrooms in terms of learning objectives achieved. The role of the headteacher is also to give firm leadership in:

- the construction of an entitlement curriculum for all pupils which has balance, continuity, progression and relevance, which is differentiated according to need, and is linked through cross-curricular initiatives;
- working with fellow teachers in the process of developing the curriculum and the formulation of a policy for teaching and learning;
- applying the professional skills of observation to identify evidence with which to answer the question: Does the school do what it says it does in ways which are mutually supportive?;
- communicating what the school does, how it does it, how staff monitor curriculum progression and how assessments are made about the quality of the teaching and learning.

Headteachers may find that the size of the school, or the uneven curriculum strengths of the staff, may require them to lead on the detail of a particular area of the curriculum. This must not deflect them from carrying out the responsibilities discussed earlier in the chapter. The headteacher's commitment to the overarching principles of the secure delivery of the complete curriculum, as expressed in the curriculum statement, is essential to its success. The management of the curriculum is the prime responsibility of all the staff and the governing body. It is essentially a partnership where roles and responsibilities are understood and acted upon. It is the central focus for which all decisions are made and where each penny of the budget is allocated for the greatest benefit of the children. It is the headteacher's greatest management challenge.

Chapter 5

Professional development and teacher appraisal

Professional development in a primary school is the responsibility of the school's professional development coordinators (PDC), or of the headteacher acting in that capacity. Whoever has this responsibility will need to work closely with colleagues and to liaise effectively with senior staff and governors. Professional development coordinators will also have three other significant roles in relation to the professional development of colleagues. These are:

- To be an exemplar of good practice themselves, to demonstrate appropriate attitudes, acceptable behaviour and commitment to colleagues and to show a concern for their own professional development as well as for that of all other members of the school staff.
- To initiate many of the individual programmes of professional development and in-service training within the school. This does not necessarily mean that coordinators will deliver the training, but they will be responsible and accountable for organising it and evaluating its effects.
- To act as a facilitator who enables professional development (for all members of staff, both teaching and non-teaching), to take place whether this involves in-school or out of school provision.

Just as the whole-school role of the curriculum coordinator has five main parts, as we saw in Chapter 4, so does that of the professional development coordinator. These are:

- **Policy formation** Contributing to and advising on the writing of the school development plan and professional development policy, ensuring that the policy is monitored, evaluated and revised as necessary, and helping to identify the professional development needs at whole school level and for individual members of staff.
- **Policy implementation** Working alongside colleagues and advising and supporting them as they seek to identify and meet their own professional development needs.
- **In-service training** Establishing and maintaining an overall view of the school's in-service provision and ensuring that each member of staff has a

suitable professional development programme. This will also involve the identification of appropriate professional development activities, doing the necessary administration, obtaining reports on courses and giving feedback to colleagues, including the headteacher and governors.

- **Managing resources** Managing the delegation of the GEST budget and submitting GEST spending proposals to the LEA and being able to demonstrate that value for money is obtained, ensuring that colleagues are aware of and benefit from the available professional development opportunities.
- **External activities** Liaising with other schools, in conjunction with the headteacher, to collaborate on professional development activities, and keeping up to date with professional development opportunities.

The professional development coordinator does not work in isolation. Everybody in the school has a contribution to make to professional development. The governors are responsible for planning the resource allocation on which much professional development depends for its success. They must also ensure that there is a school professional development policy and participate in its formulation, give approval for programmes, receive feedback and monitor the implementation of the policy, especially the value for money aspect.

The headteacher has overall responsibility for establishing and maintaining the professional development policy, for initiating and conducting staff appraisals and, through the professional development coordinator, for the identification of whole school professional development needs. The headteacher should also monitor the implementation of the programme and evaluate its outcomes, especially the extent to which they constitute value for money and contribute to the aims of the school development plan. Many headteachers will wish to involve the whole of their senior management team in this work.

All staff in primary schools have a part to play in professional development. They must conduct self-evaluations and seek to identify their own professional development needs relevant to their position in the school. Each person should have an up-to-date professional development record showing the professional development activities undertaken and their outcomes. Staff who have attended courses should write an evaluation report for the professional development coordinator and retain a copy in their portfolios. All staff also have a part to play in the professional development of colleagues.

Professional development, therefore, involves all staff in the primary school. It is part of an annual cycle of school development and may result in relatively short-term developmental activities based on the identification of professional development needs. Much of what the coordinator does will depend on the needs that have been identified within the school. Many of these will be derived from the school development plan, but individual needs are also likely to be identified by processes of staff appraisal and professional review.

TEACHER AND HEADTEACHER APPRAISAL

Staff appraisal is both an integral part of professional development in primary schools and, at the same time, separate from it. Professional development is linked to the annual cycle of school development planning while appraisal has its own two-year cycle. Appraisal identifies strengths and weaknesses, reviews job performance and results in specific targets between the appraiser and the appraisee that are confidential. Professional development has a whole-school focus and its activities are relatively public. Nevertheless, appraisal has a contribution to the success of wider professional development within the primary school.

Appraisal is a sensitive issue. It has to be carried out diplomatically and with staff cooperation. All staff should be involved in the initial discussions about the proposed procedures and should be given an opportunity to respond openly and to express their natural fears and reservations. The same is true once a system is implemented. It should be reviewed after the first cycle of appraisal and modified where necessary. After that the headteacher and the staff development coordinator should be aware of how well appraisal is working in the school and can consult the staff about the need to make adjustments from time to time.

Teacher appraisal can be carried out in a number of different ways. The National Steering Group on Teacher Appraisal suggested that a good appraisal scheme would have the following features:

- appraisal should take place within a national framework, comprising regulations and guidance from the DES;
- responsibility for implementing appraisal for all LEA maintained and voluntary aided schools should rest with the LEA;
- appraisal should focus on facilitating professional growth and development and should not be related to pay;
- appraisal should respect and promote equal opportunities;
- the headteacher should decide who should appraise each teacher in the school;
- headteachers should have two appraisers, one of whom must have relevant experience as a headteacher;
- appraisal should be conducted against a background of sound educational criteria;
- all appraisers should receive training;
- access to the resulting appraisal statement should be restricted to the appraiser, the appraisee, the headteacher of the school and the Chief Education Officer (CEO) or a nominated representative.

These recommendations were embodied in the *Education (School Teacher Appraisal) Regulations* (DES 1991) and the supporting *Circular 12/91 School Teacher Appraisal* (DES 1991b) which were sent to all schools. In addition, the regulations determined that appraisal should take place on a two-yearly cycle and that each appraisal programme should have the components identified in Figure 5.1.

Year One
- an initial meeting between the appraiser(s) and the appraisee to clarify the purpose and to identify areas of work on which the appraisal might concentrate
- self appraisal by the appraisee
- classroom observation for teachers on at least two separate occasions and either a classroom or a task observation for headteachers
- review of other relevant information, work with pupils, information about duties outside the classroom
- an appraisal interview, providing an opportunity for genuine dialogue between the appraisee and the appraiser
- the preparation of an appraisal statement recording the conclusions of the interview, including agreed targets for future action/professional development

Year Two
- a planned programme of development activities to enable the appraisee to achieve targets
- a follow-up meeting or meetings to review progress in the second year of the cycle and to make amendments to targets and professional development activities if necessary
- a formal review meeting to assess progress towards achieving targets, to make changes in the appraisal statement if necessary and to identify any further support that might be needed

---

Figure 5.1 The Appraisal two-yearly cycle

Headteacher appraisal is somewhat different from that of other teachers because two appraisers are involved and because the process may not be classroom based. Of the two appraisers, one must be a headteacher. In some LEAs headteachers are allowed to exert considerable influence over the choice of this professional colleague. In others, the choice is made by the chief education officer. In either case three criteria should operate. First, the headteacher chosen should have current experience of headship in a school of similar size, type and intake to that of the appraisee. Second, the schools should not be in the same area and, therefore, in competition for pupils. Third, the appraising headteacher should have at least two years' experience of headship.

One way of choosing a first appraiser is for the headteacher to identify a number of colleagues who would be acceptable and for the person responsible within the LEA to make the final choice. Another approach is for the LEA to second a group of suitably experienced and trained headteachers to act as appraisers for a limited period. Headteacher colleagues will be able to chose an appraiser from this group. The second appraiser may be appointed by the LEA and will need to have:

- knowledge of the school and the community which it serves;
- knowledge of national and local policies which apply to that school;
- knowledge of the LEA where relevant.

The choice of second appraiser often gives rise to concern, especially if a school is grant maintained or the LEA does not make specific recommendations. Some headteachers are inviting ex-headteachers working as educational consultants to become familiar with the school and to act as a second appraiser. Others are using colleagues who have been members of Her Majesty's Inspectorate, while others are being appraised by the chair of the governing body. It is essential that whoever is chosen as an appraiser is able to take the appropriate professional stance on the work of the headteacher and to make sound recommendations about further professional development. This professional credibility is a necessary quality for anyone involved in the appraisal of headteachers.

The appraisal of headteachers is unique within schools since, however much they have devolved responsibility to their colleagues, they are the only members of school staff who are wholly accountable to the governing body and to the LEA for what they do. Their appraisal must look both inward at how they manage and lead their schools, and outward at their relationships with LEAs, parents and the community (Poster and Poster 1991). Those involved in headteacher appraisal are also more likely to experience some difficulty in identifying a specific focus for the appraisal because the role of the headteacher is so large and diffuse. Care needs to be taken to agree a set of clearly defined areas, up to a maximum of three, that will be appraised and to collect data related to those areas. Appraisal in this context may not look at the whole job. It may rather be a sampling procedure which, over a period of time, will encompass all responsibilities.

Much the same may be true of teacher appraisal, although here the range of responsibilities will be narrower and must include work in the classroom. For both headteachers and their colleagues a well-structured appraisal process affords the opportunity to take stock of performance over the previous two years, to examine how far agreed targets have been achieved and to identify new targets where appropriate. Appraisal is not an opportunity to criticise the appraisee, to discuss the appraisee's colleagues or to apportion blame. It should concentrate solely on the individual teacher's own performance within the school. It provides an opportunity for a professional dialogue between an appraisee and an experienced, senior and supportive professional colleague, although not always the headteacher. Ideally a teacher should have only one appraiser at any time, although there must be an appeal system in which a second person can become involved in the case of serious, unresolved disagreement between the appraiser and the appraisee. The appraiser may change for each two-year cycle, although it is advisable to keep such changes to a minimum. Many small primary schools have adopted a system by which staff are appraised by the headteacher in one cycle, and by another member of the senior staff in the next cycle.

Dialogue will be based on shared factual information and may explore such issues as:

- the accuracy of the teacher's current job description;
- how well the teacher is performing;
- the celebration of success and the giving of praise;
- the recognition of disappointments;
- discussing whether performance could be improved in any areas;
- what actions are necessary to improve performance;
- who should initiate those actions;
- what potential does the teacher have for taking on more responsibility;
- what actions might be taken to develop new skills;
- what the teacher's views are about the job;
- what ambitions and aspirations the teacher has.

If these areas are to be explored then information has to be collected. One source of information that is built into the DES regulations on appraisal is classroom observation (DES 1991a).

CLASSROOM OBSERVATION IN TEACHER APPRAISAL

Any method of classroom observation will need to be valid and reliable, free from subjectivity and bias, and based on agreed criteria. It must focus on good classroom practice. Good teaching is notoriously difficult to define. OFSTED defines it as follows:

Where teaching is good, pupils acquire knowledge, skills and understanding progressively. The lessons have clear aims and purposes. They cater appropriately for the learning of pupils with differing abilities and interests, and ensure the full participation of all. The teaching methods suit the topic or subject as well as the pupils; the conduct of the lessons signals high expectations of all pupils and sets high but attainable challenges. There is regular feedback which helps pupils to make progress, both through marking and discussion of work with pupils.

Relationships are positive and promote pupils' motivation. The National Curriculum Attainment Targets and Programmes of Study are taken fully into account.

(OFSTED 1993: Part 4: 48)

Any appraiser observing a teacher at work with children in the classroom must be able to recognise the distinction between performance and competence. A teacher's competence is made up of the skills, abilities, knowledge and beliefs that are relevant to the process of teaching and that the teacher brings to the classroom. These tend to be relatively consistent and stable over time. Teacher performance is the behaviour of teachers in the classroom at any given time as they plan, teach and evaluate their work. The appraiser observes pupil responses and behaviour, management and organisation skills, and takes note of personal and social factors. Teachers may perform better with one group of children than with another and performance might vary from time to time.

Teaching and learning are part of the same process. It follows, therefore, that when a procedure for classroom observation is being considered within a primary school for appraisal or other purposes, this discussion should focus on factors in the classroom which foster pupil learning. HMI have found that effective pupil learning takes place in classrooms where teachers:

- establish and maintain a good classroom ethos in which pupils are motivated to learn;
- plan, prepare and organise lessons well and ensure that pupils are clear about what they have to learn and why they are doing a particular task;
- recognise the need for good classroom organisation including the organisation of resources;
- set a good example, and foster good relationships with pupils;
- have high, but attainable, expectations of pupils in respect of both academic performance and behaviour;
- provide tasks which are well-matched to the needs, aptitudes and prior knowledge of individual pupils;
- understand the role of language;
- ensure that pupils acquire knowledge, understanding and skills, are encouraged to become independent, resourceful and responsible and are able to work purposefully on their own and with others;
- check that learning has taken place by ensuring that assessment is an integral part of classroom work and provides diagnostic information on pupil progress and information that can be used to evaluate their teaching and to inform parents;
- support classroom learning with work done at home where this is appropriate and in accordance with school policy.

(adapted from Scottish Education Department 1989)

Even where such relatively clear criteria are used as a basis for classroom observation as part of teacher appraisal, a sequence of observations is likely to be of more value to the appraisee than a single one. This is time-consuming but it ensures that the observation element of teacher appraisal is developmental rather than judgemental. Any classroom observation must be based on agreed criteria, recorded in a cooperative way and have a specific focus which will change from year to year. Such a focus might be narrow, concentrating on the learning of small groups of children within a series of lessons, or the development of a particular aspect on the National Curriculum, or the use of a specific teaching strategy. It might be broader, looking at a range of factors such as:

- planning and preparation of the lesson;
- beginnings, endings and transitions between activities;
- selection and presentation of materials;
- appropriateness of content and teaching strategies;
- communication, including verbal and non-verbal skills;
- progression within a subject area over time;
- pace of the lesson and work of the children;
- differentiation within teaching, learning and tasks;
- discipline and control;
- use of equipment;
- assessment of pupils' work;
- record-keeping and use of records to plan work.

Another approach to observing teachers at work in the classroom is to pose a series of questions about the teaching that is being observed. Such a list might include:

- **Understanding Objectives**   How well does the teacher understand and describe the objectives of the lesson? How sound is the understanding of the pupils in respect of what they are doing and why they are doing it?
- **Preparation and Organisation**   Is the work thoroughly prepared and are teaching materials and activities chosen effectively? Is the lesson well-structured with a clear start, with well-planned transitions and a specific end? Is it clear what the children should have learned or be able to do at the end of the lesson? Does the single lesson contribute to a continuum of planned and progressive learning outcomes?
- **Teaching Skills**   Which teaching styles are used and to what effect? Are a variety of styles employed? How well are pupils catered for as individuals, in groups and as a whole class? How well is questioning used and how effectively are pupils helped and guided?
- **Pupils' Work and Assessment**   How satisfactory, given their age and ability, is the quality of pupils work? Does it challenge their ability? How does the quality of the learning match the age and ability of the pupils?

Is it displayed or otherwise used for the benefit of others? How is it marked, assessed and followed up with individual pupils? How effectively does the teacher record the progress of each pupil? How is this information used to plan future work?

- **Evaluation**   How well does the teacher assess relative strengths and weaknesses of different teaching strategies, given the age and ability of the pupils? How is such evaluation used to plan future work?

A similar approach might be based on a series of statements describing the ideal state which teachers would wish to achieve in their teaching. The observer in this case would comment on the extent to which each intention had been met as part of the appraisal process. It is important that in each primary school, staff should establish its own set of such statements, although any list will need to take into account the OFSTED criteria for effective teaching and good classroom organisation that were discussed in Chapter 2. A list of statements could be agreed from the following examples:

- **Clarity of objectives**   The purposes of the lesson are clear to teacher and pupils.
- **Appropriateness of objectives**   The objectives lead to tasks that are neither too easy nor too difficult for the pupils. They are appropriate to and understood by the pupils.
- **Organisation of the lesson**   The individual parts of the lesson are clearly related to each other in a suitable way. The total structure of the lesson facilitates learning.
- **Selection of content**   The content is appropriate for the age and ability of the pupils, for the objectives of the lesson, and for the teaching methods used.
- **Selection of teaching methods**   The teaching methods used are suitable for the age, ability and numbers of pupils in the group and will enable the lesson objectives to be achieved by the pupils. Pupils will experience individual, group and whole-class teaching across a series of lessons.
- **Selection of materials**   The materials and human resources used are clearly related to the content of the lesson and complement teaching methods.
- **Beginning the lesson**   Pupils come quickly to attention and direct themselves to the task to be accomplished.
- **Clarity of presentation**   The content of the lesson is presented so that it is understandable to the pupils. Different points of view and specific illustrations are used when appropriate.
- **Pacing of lessons**   The movement from one part of the lesson to the next is governed by the pupils' achievement. The teacher stays with the class and adjusts the tempo accordingly.
- **Pupil participation and attention**   The class is attentive. When appropriate the pupils actively participate in the lesson.
- **Ending the lesson**   The lesson is ended when the pupils have achieved the aims of instruction. There is a deliberate attempt to tie together the

planned and chance events of the lesson and relate them to the immediate objectives and longer-term aims of the teaching.

- **Teacher–pupil relationship**   The personal relationships between teacher and pupil are harmonious and conducive to productive work.
- **Variety of evaluative procedures**   The teacher devises and uses an adequate variety of procedures, both formal and informal, to evaluate progress in all the objectives of the lesson.
- **Uses of evaluation to improve teaching**   The results of evaluation are carefully reviewed by teacher and pupils for purposes of improving teaching and learning.

This list is rather long but can be used to structure classroom observation. It consists of a series of performance indicators that can help teachers to organise their work in classrooms. It can also help to clarify the focus of the observations that take place as part of the appraisal process.

Yet another possible approach is for the observation to be based on some measure of performance on an agreed scale. Figure 5.2 provides an example of this approach. This is based on the scale adopted by school inspectors (OFSTED 1993), and gives a feeling of objectivity. Its accuracy and reliability depends on how thoroughly anybody applying the scale understands the criteria used to make the judgement about the scores to be awarded, since the weakness of this approach is in the possible variations in interpretation. One observer's 'good' may be another's 'average'. It does, however, enable comparisons to be made across lessons and between teachers.

All attempts to structure classroom observations have their weaknesses and are subject to interpretation. It is important that everyone involved understands and agrees with the methods to be adopted and knows what the criteria are and how they should be interpreted. Participants also need to know how the data that is collected will be used, who will have access to it and how it will inform the appraisal interview. Difficulties associated with classroom observations can best be overcome by agreeing a particular focus for each of the two observations that are required. It may be that the appraisee identifies the first focus and the appraiser the second. These can then be discussed in the meeting following the classroom observation as well as contributing to the main appraisal interview.

THE APPRAISAL INTERVIEW

Appraisal interviews should have a standard structure. It is important to treat all appraisees in the same way. This is done by ensuring that the sequence of questioning and responses follow a similar pattern. A short, workable sequence can be based on the following questions which relate to the period since a teacher's last appraisal:

- Is the job description up-to-date?

	5 Very poor	4 Weak	3 Sound	2 Good	1 Very Good
Purpose/intended outcome					
Preparation of materials					
Relevant pupil activities					
Individual differences					
Intial motivation					
Communication					
Questioning					
Class control					
Guiding/advising					
Conclusion of lesson					
Marking/assessing					
Recording					
Evaluation					

Figure 5.2 A checklist for observing teachers' classroom performance

- What are the key aspects of the teacher's role?
- What are her strengths – what has she done well?
- What are the main difficulties that have been encountered?
- What needs to be done in order to minimise or eliminate these difficulties in future?
- What are her staff training and development needs?
- What should be done in order to meet these needs?
- How do these fit with the overall development needs of the school?

These points are aimed to examine teachers' performance in their present posts and should be discussed in the context of teachers' job descriptions. Interviews conducted in this way will lead to the listing of further training needs and to the agreeing of improvement targets for the individual. Such an interview can be conducted in about one hour. If an appraisal interview is to explore future career development then this will take more time. The following questions can be incorporated:

- What abilities and interests are not being fully used in the present job?
- What new tasks or roles could be taken on in the coming year?
- What is the best way to develop new skills?

If it is intended to check on job satisfaction during the interview, the following points could be included:

- What aspects of the job give the most satisfaction?
- What caused any dissatisfaction?
- What steps can be taken to minimise dissatisfaction?

Guidelines for both the appraisee and the appraiser have to be established to enable them to prepare for the interview (See Figure 5.3). All those involved should be briefed about their responsibilities for preparation. A pre-appraisal form is useful for self-review and for appraisees and appraisers to make some notes about the forthcoming discussion, incorporating information collected from the classroom observations and other sources where relevant.

Many primary schools have found it helpful for appraisees and appraisers to respond in writing in advance of the interview under six headings:

- **Performance** Think back over the period since your last appraisal interview. Comment on your most important or satisfying achievements. Itemise particular results and successes with which you have been involved. Have there been changes in your role that might need to be reflected in your job description?
- **Disappointments** Think back over the period since your last appraisal and comment on any disappointments with respect to your own responsibilities.
- **Obstacles** What factors outside your control hindered you in achieving a better performance. What could be done to minimise their effects?
- **Training and new experience** What training or new planned experience did you undergo last year? In what ways have these helped you? What have been the changes which have take place as a result of these experiences?
- **Increased knowledge or skill** What part of your present job might benefit if you received additional training or new planned experience?
- **List of training needs** As a result of completing the whole form, list the areas of professional development, training or new planned experience that would further develop your professional expertise and help you to carry out your responsibilities even more effectively.

It is helpful to both parties if the appraiser has a copy of the appraisee's responses to these questions in advance of the interview. She is then able to read carefully through those responses and identify areas of agreement and omission. The appraiser is then better equipped to concentrate on what has

- Make arrangements

- Set a date, time and place for the appraisal interview

- Allow at least 60 minutes for the interview

- Give at least two weeks notice of the interview to the member of staff, to allow time to prepare, and carry out self-appraisal

Also brief the appraisee on how to prepare, running through the interview outline.

Appraiser's preparation	Appraisee's preparation
Before the interview go through each interview question, noting important points, using all relevant information including that from classroom observations and other agreed data. Concentrate on training and development needs, and ways to satisfy these needs. Provisionally decide realistic training and/or development aims for the next year. Consider whether any problems might arise during the interview and plan how to handle them.	Concentration on: - things that have gone well; - problems; - training and development; - aims for the next year. Think of realistic training and/or development aims for the next year. Think of ways to achieve improvement aims with guidance or support.

Figure 5.3 Preparation for staff appraisal

gone well and to identify areas in which positive and realistic improvement and development targets for the future can be set and support given.

Each interview must be planned in detail, basing the approach on two principles. First, the appraiser asks the appraisee to comment fully on each area before discussing specific issues and making additional points. The appraiser must be well prepared for this and able to give praise and positive comments as well as making suggestions for improvement. Second, the appraiser concentrates on the appraisee's strengths and positive contributions before examining areas where improvement might be necessary. The interview should finish with a list of agreed actions to improve performance and to ensure further professional development. The list of professional development activities will normally include much that can be done inside the school and within existing resources. The activities must be consistent with the school's overall professional development policy and the school development plan.

The list should show who will do what, by when and identify the resource implications. These actions form the appraisal statement which is written by the appraiser, agreed and signed by both parties.

The appraisal statement is confidential to the appraisee and the appraiser and both should have a copy of it. The headteacher has access to it. The governors also receive a general report on the appraisal cycle but must not embark on discussion of individual teachers. It is important that decisions about confidentiality are taken at school level. For example, should the appraisal statement be hand written or should it be word processed? If the latter, who should do this? These decisions are best made by the individuals likely to be affected by them.

A thoroughly planned and well-conducted appraisal interview will enhance the professional performance of all teachers in primary schools and help them to meet the many demands placed upon them by recent and forthcoming educational changes. Such an approach to teacher appraisal will also make a significant contribution to professional development throughout the whole school.

Its central purpose is the identification of the professional development needs of the appraisee by a process of discussion with a senior colleague. These will fall into three main areas: the future development of the teacher as an individual, the future development of the teacher within the context of the job description and the development of the teacher within the context of the overall development of the school.

In practical terms, the appraisee and appraiser could well have identified, for example:

- That the teacher will follow a particular Open University Management Course. (The professional development of the individual teacher in order to improve job performance.)
- That the same teacher, who has responsibility for Humanities as part of her job description, should attend a number of course sessions on Key Stage 1 history advertised by the LEA. (The future development of the teacher within the context of the job description and to help meet the needs of the school.)
- That the same teacher should be part of the team planning a professional development day for the local schools' cluster on the effective use of libraries and, in preparation, should work with the Schools Library Service adviser looking at the school library. (The development of the teacher within the context of overall school development.)

Individual and school needs cannot exist in isolation. The professional development coordinator should work with the headteacher, governors and senior staff to ensure that the pattern of needs forms part of a coherent, consistent and equitable professional development programme and appears as a fully resourced and integrated part of the development plan. Audit procedures will have identified the principal developmental needs of the institution as a whole and set a timetable for their achievement. The agreements reached in appraisal interviews will have to fit into the overall plan. The staff will have cooperatively agreed the priorities for the short-, medium- and long-term development of the school and these will have been set out in the development plan. The overall needs of the school and its agreed priorities have to take precedence in the allocation of money and time. It is unfortunate that limited resources might mean that individual professional development needs sometimes have to be dropped, postponed or accommodated in a different way. It is essential that appraisers work within the framework of priorities set out in the development plan and do not raise false expectations during the appraisal interview.

Chapter 6

The management of professional development

Once the school has agreed its professional development profile and programme, it will seek ways to meet it. Successful professional development is not limited to off-site course attendance. Much can take place within the school itself, managed largely by those who work there. This can include:

- **Use of training days** Whole or half days organised by members of the school's own staff, under the overall direction of the professional development coordinator, can be part of staff development. Alternatively, the school might decide that its needs would be best met by bringing in appropriate external expertise. All the costs of such days can be set against GEST funding
- **Mentoring** Staff with appropriate expertise can work alongside other colleagues who wish to develop their own expertise in that area. This can take place at any suitable time of the school year and could be the direct result of targets set within the appraisal programme. The mentor's normal activities could be covered by a supply teacher costed against GEST funding. The impact of the mentor will be far more effective if it takes place within a well-planned and structured programme of support, rather than on a casual basis.
- **Collaborative teaching** Staff with appropriate expertise can operate in partnership on a work-share basis with colleagues who wish to develop their own expertise in that area, or as part of a team teaching approach where the teacher with the particular interest or responsibility conducts a lead lesson attended by several classes or groups, who then go away to work under the direction of their own teacher. This is an especially effective way of helping colleagues who feel insecure in curriculum areas or key stages where they have not taught for some time.
- **Staff exchanges** Staff exchange with colleagues in a teacher's own or a cluster school can be organised in order to spread good practice, offer complementary skills or gain additional experience. This is especially important in areas where there are a number of very small schools, or where two schools (Infant and Junior, for example) share the same site.

The exchanges might be for a half day a week, but could continue for a whole term or year. It is important that the exchanges form part of the overall professional development plans of all the schools concerned, as well as of the individual plans of the teachers concerned. Some school clusters publish a cluster development plan as an appendix to that of their own individual schools.

- **Use of staff meetings**   Professional development items may be included on staff meeting agenda and, given sufficient time to ensure successful outcomes, can form part of a rolling programme of staff development and revision. Adequate time must be allocated in order to ensure that the professional development items do not get squeezed by business or organisational items.
- **Working parties**   Relevant and representative staff can work together in order to achieve a specific objective within an agreed time frame. These will include policy revision working parties as well as those addressing new initiatives. Membership can include governors, non-teaching staff and parents and can contribute to the wider agenda of professional development.

PLANNING A PROFESSIONAL DEVELOPMENT OR INSET SESSION

Professional development coordinators have a key role to play in ensuring that whatever strategy is adopted, it is properly planned resourced and delivered to a high professional standard. They should work closely with the colleague responsible for the event to assure its quality. Knowledge of one's subject area is not in itself a sufficient qualification for being able to run an effective INSET day or after school session.

Imagine that the school library is much as it was five years ago when the former class libraries were brought together into an unwanted classroom. Non-fiction is grouped according to topics. A team of Year 6 children keep the room tidy. There is no catalogue. About half the fiction stock still carries the colour banding used six years ago when reading books were coded into 'readability' groupings. Several teachers have started to set up libraries in their own class again. The PTA has said that it would like to use the money raised at the annual summer fête to breath new life into the library. You are the deputy head. There are twelve on the staff including the headteacher and yourself. The headteacher has asked you to use the morning of the next staff development day to decide how the library and the rest of the book resources should be organised in the future. Your objective is to lead a staff review of the current library stock and the way it is used and agree proposals for its future development. Plan the three hour session.

It is an essential discipline to work to a set of questions when planning the session:

Planning question 1. What is the purpose of the session?

Many INSET sessions are planned with only the vaguest of briefs. The session organiser must have a clear understanding of the purpose of the session. It is good practice to start the planning with the sentence 'As a result of the session on—, colleagues will be able to—.' This defines the learning objective in unequivocal terms. If the coordinator is uncertain exactly what the headteacher as commissioner foresees as outcomes, this must be clarified before any further planning is undertaken. Following clarification, the brief for our example would now read: 'Agreed aim: by the end of the morning the teaching staff will have reviewed the current contents of the library and the way they are used, and agreed proposals for future development.' The coordinator or session leader can now plan in confidence.

Planning question 2. Who will be there?

The audience must be defined in terms of what they already know and can do and what they need to know because of their role or responsibilities within the school. On some occasions it will be necessary that all the staff are there, including the part-timers. On other occasions, the work of the school would benefit from the presence of the general assistants and nursery nurses, or a few members of the governing body. It is usually essential that the headteacher attends. The absence of the headteacher, especially if for a low priority reason, will devalue the session. Any decisions and suggestions which might arise will lose their strength and immediacy if the headteacher is not there to hear them. There could be a possibility that suggestions might be over-ruled or ignored. The inclusion of governors can reinforce the concept of partnership, and give them a greater understanding of the evolving professional strengths within the school.

Planning question 3. What will those who will be there already know?

The content of the session will be determined by the pre-session knowledge of those attending. On most occasions, there is likely to be a 'mixed ability' audience. The organiser must take careful account of the group's pre-knowledge, especially if there is likely to be considerable understanding of the topic already, or if some of those attending are likely to feel threatened by the content. A simple check sheet could be given out before the detailed planning takes place, identifing the main topics identified for the session and inviting colleagues to tick against each one whether they have considerable, average or slight knowledge of each heading. It is important to ensure that everyone reaches a common start point as early as possible. This can also be achieved through a short briefing paper, circulated with the outline plan for the session some days before it takes place.

Planning question 4. Where will the session take place?

Not all staff rooms are ideal for professional development or INSET sessions. Although comfort is important, the session leader needs to have good eye contact with all the participants. Moving comfortable chairs into a bigger space ought to be considered, especially if any practical or small group sessions are anticipated. Seating should be in an open horse-shoe shape and with sufficient space to allow chairs to be moved into small discussion groups when needed. Some activities will require tables, and chairs comfortable for adults, not always easy in an infant school! If an overhead projector and screen are to be used, the cable must be safely secured to the floor and the screen placed where people can see it. All too often the overhead projector itself is allowed to obscure the screen. Overheads must be neat, legible and carry the minimum of text. High quality transparencies can be produced quickly on many word processors, and give a professional feel to the session. A flip chart or pad of A1 paper on an easel is useful for running notes or noting action points.

Planning question 5. How is the detailed planning done?

The session leader starts to plan, based on who the audience will be and their likely present state of knowledge of the subject, with a clear understanding of the required outcome for the session in mind. The next stage will be to brainstorm the main points which will need to be covered if the required outcome is to be reached. These should be kept as relevant and to as few as possible. There is a great danger in trying to include too much. Once the main areas of focus have been identified, and ordered into a progression, detailed planning can begin.

The detail of each focal point will depend on the subject to be addressed. The planning must include a decision about the method whereby each point will be covered. Generally speaking, teachers value being given practical help and quality information in plain English. They like to have opportunities for discussion and to feel that there are relevant practical outcomes at the end of the session. Teachers abhor artificiality, time wasting, and 'trainer techniques' which serve no obvious purpose. Writing down issues on large sheets of paper, for example, should only be done if it is the best way to achieve the objective.

Planning question 6. Is timing important?

'Invisible' timing is one of the best ways to make professional development successful. A carefully constructed private timetable will ensure that the session moves forward at a sensible pace and reaches its conclusion at the advertised time. Colleagues have commitments and responsibilities beyond the school day and an INSET session which seriously over-runs its advertised time has been badly planned. In order to run to time, inputs and practical activities need to be thought through and timed with as great a care as they would be in the classroom. The audience is one's colleagues, and therefore one's greatest critics (see Figure 6.1).

Colleagues who are going to attend the session will be wondering what it will be about and what the planned outcomes are. The session is far more likely to be successful if they are given an information sheet before the event which sets out the objectives, gives timings and heightens their expectation that the planned activities are relevant to them and their situations (see Figure 6.2).

The plan for the day is very straightforward. It will address the central issue, carry the reluctant by peer group pressure, involve genuine consultation and ensure real outcomes. Careful planning and timing, an appropriate mix of informed input, activity and genuine decision making by those most likely to use the library, ensures success. The more the staff seem unaware of the *process itself*, but feel purposeful about the outcomes, the more satisfied the session organiser can feel.

PROFESSIONAL DEVELOPMENT THROUGH VISITING ANOTHER SCHOOL

Visiting another school can be an extremely stimulating form of professional development. To illustrate the value of observing another school, imagine that your school is considering restructuring its management team by giving increased responsibility to key stage and subject coordinators. To maximise the benefits of a visit to Madison school where this already happens, it would be advisable to:

- Decide on a single main focus for the visit. This should either arise out of an objective identified in a teacher's own appraisal discussion, or as part of an agreed strategy to meet a school priority identified in the school development plan. In our example, this would be to understand the role of subject coordinators in – Madison School.
- Break this down into things you want to have achieved by the end of the visit. It is essential that the visiting teacher and receiving school has a clear agenda for the day. In our example this would be:

By the end of the visit I will have . . .

1 talked to the headteacher about their perception of the role of coordinator;
2 seen copies of a coordinator's job description;
3 talked to the English and KS 1 coordinators;
4 developed an understanding of coordinators' responsibilities in relation to: writing policies, monitoring policy implementation and quality assurance; ability to allocate resources; consultation with staff; opportunities to be in colleagues' classrooms during lessons; professional development; links

THE EXAMPLE IN PRACTICE: FACILITATOR'S COPY
Plan for INSET half day based on the school library

AIM
By the end of the morning the teaching staff will have reviewed the current contents of the library and the way they are used, and agreed proposals for future development.

METHOD

08.30 onwards Coffee in staffroom. Opportunity to meet representative from School Library Service.

08.50 Session starts. Briefing on morning: reminder of purpose of morning, broad outline of programme. First exercise explained.

09.00 Task one: 'Teacher raid on library'.
Staff are given list of differing requirements (a spooky story, something on a 'green' issue, India, puberty, a map of Central Europe, something about their locality) and sent to find them.

09.15 Task two: Discussion in the library in threes.
(Prewritten questions and predetermined groups) Did you find the books? Was it easy? How did you go about it? What do you think about the books now you have them? (Back up copies for distribution to groups who didn't manage to find all the books.) Consider the condition of the books, date of publication. Is there any imbalance between what you have found and the school's policy on equal opportunities? (Gender, race)

09.35 Input from Schools Library Service Adviser: 'The place of the library in the primary school.'

09.50 Questions and discussion.

10.00 Input from Schools Library Service Adviser: 'Ways to organise the school library.'

10.15 Task three: Group discussion.
Match the efficiency/appropriateness of our library against our own experiences this morning and some of the models we have heard described. If you see the need for change, ignore the resource and implementation implications, and describe the ideal which would meet the particular needs of this school.

10.30 Coffee and cakes available.

10.45 Group report back.
DHT to make notes on a flop chart of major recommendations as the ideal picture emerges. The sheet is divided into comments on improving ORGANISATION and STOCK.

11.15 Task four: Group discussion.
If that's the ideal, draw up a school action plan spread over three years in order to achieve it.

11.30 Groups asked to write main points on sheets of A1 paper.

11.45 Groups pin up outline plans, and move round room to read and discuss the various suggestions. Free flow is encouraged.

12.00 Plenary session: DHT takes consensus views on the key points. Action team of two or three staff selected to work with SLS and PTA to get the action plan moving. DHT or professional development coordinator leads discussion to establish success criteria and a review period. Example: book loans up by 40%; stock 'weeding' complete by half-term; staff to review the library provision, relevance and usage in one year, etc.

12.20 Lunch.

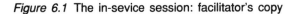

Figure 6.1 The in-sevice session: facilitator's copy

with appraisal; involvement in cross-curricular/cross-phase planning; links to appropriate support outside the school.

- Recognise that the list is the *ideal*, and that you may have to compromise in some areas of research.
- Have a preliminary discussion with the headteacher and key contacts you will be meeting during the day to confirm the following: that the school is comfortable with your agenda; when it will be convenient for you to arrive/leave the school; arrangements for lunch; who you can see and when; how your visit will be explained to the staff who *must* understand why you are visiting; what school documents you can take away, and how they can be used or copied; what confidences you will be required to observe if you are to visit classrooms during the day; and exactly what you will be observing and why.
- Draw up a timetable for your visit. Allow time during the day for reflection and writing up notes. Be prepared for emergencies which might mean the teacher you had hoped to spend 30 minutes with at lunchtime, now has to cover a colleague. Leave sufficient time at the end of the visit to thank people. Leave sufficient time at the end of the day (at least an hour) to think back over the day, and put your notes into some sort of shape.
- Let the headteacher and key contacts have an advance copy of your outline programme and aims for the day. This can be circulated to the staff you are going to meet.

PROFESSIONAL DEVELOPMENT DAYS IN SUMMARY

Well-structured staff training days will:

- encourage better staff cooperation by recognising complementary strengths and skills, fostering the concept of 'team', and enabling colleagues to feel confident about working collaboratively.
- encourage better use of facilities by enabling staff to see the building as a resource for them *all*, with opportunities for everyone to benefit. The result is whole-school thinking and planning. Our example earlier in the chapter shows how the effective use of the library becomes a joint responsibility rather than that of a named post-holder.
- lead to improved strategies for all school systems by developing the staff into a cohesive and mutually supportive team accustomed to addressing whole-school issues, resulting in the improvement of the learning of all the children in the school, and not just those in their own classes.
- provide time to exchange ideas by creating a forum where ideas can be exchanged and talked through without the pressure of an after-school staff meeting, where other competing items loom on the agenda, or a busy lunch time break where the bell cuts across the time needed for professional discussion.

THE EXAMPLE IN PRACTICE: PARTICIPANT'S COPY
Professional development morning – The School Library

AIM
by the end of the morning we will have reviewed the current contents of
the library and the way they are used and agreed proposals for future
development.

PROGRAMME

08.30 onwards Coffee in staffroom, with an opportunity to meet John
Robinson from the School Library Service.

08.50 First session (in the library) Welcome. Explanation of the
programme (Mary Smith).

Teachers raid on library
'The place of the library in the primary school, and how it can be
organised (talk by John Robinson).
Opportunity for questions and discussion.
Group discussions in order to evaluate the efficiency/appropriateness of
our library, our own experiences in the 'raid', and compare its organisation with some of the models we have heard described. To make
recommendations.

10.30 Coffee and cakes available.

10.45 Session two   The different groups report back to the complete
staff. We will consider future requirements and how we will work to
achieve them.

12.20 Lunch

Figure 6.2 The in-service session: participant's copy

- create opportunities to visit colleagues, liaise and share good practice by
  enabling teachers to enjoy seeing the success of others in their own or
  other schools, and to discuss common or shared problems with time for
  fruitful discussion.
- help to develop school policies by being part of the process and able to
  shape the policy, rather than being the passive and unconsulted recipient
  of a policy written by someone else who may not have sufficient understanding of the needs of the person receiving the policy.
- help to highlight specific needs by creating a structure which encourages
  all members of staff to contribute to the planning of professional development days and ensures that they are part of the school development
  plan contributing towards the successful achievement of its aims.

(based on Cowan and Wright 1990: 117)

Training days that are not well planned will:

- fail to match the needs of the school as a whole because they are not
  part of a clearly defined and previously agreed programme of professional

development focused on needs identified as priorities in the development plan.

- fail to meet individual needs because insufficient time and effort was given to establishing exactly what the needs of individual staff were, and ensuring that this drove the subsequent planning.
- occur at times which are inappropriate or unhelpful for immediate follow up. Days which create an enthusiasm for subsequent action or change but take place when this is impossible, because of other considerations, can only generate frustration. They are likely to make staff think that future similar days will not be a productive use of their precious time.
- not support the long-term professional development plan for the school because they have been planned outside the context of the agreed plan, are unlikely to attract any resources and are seen as peripheral to the main thrust of the school's work. Those staff with plans which are central to the achievement of the school development plan are unlikely to be enthusiastic about the loss of precious professional development opportunities.
- have themes that occurred in isolation and without regard for previous or subsequent activities. Staff will view them as peripheral, intrusive and a waste of their most precious resource : their non-contact time.
- not be properly evaluated, and therefore, will not improve or foster the long-term commitment of staff.

(adapted from Cowan and Wright 1990: 117)

EVALUATION AND VALUE FOR MONEY

Teachers are familiar with the evaluation sheets which are given out at the end of many courses. Internal school-based INSET and professional development should be evaluated with equal rigour by the professional development coordinator. Governors will be expecting to receive a balance sheet at the end of the year showing how the money allocated for professional development has been used. The balance sheet should be accompanied by a report which lists all the in-service activities which have taken place, both externally and internally, evaluates their success and shows clearly how they fitted within the objectives of the school development plan. Examples should be given which illustrate that changes had occurred in classrooms, and that children's learning had been enhanced. Governors and staff will be expecting to see evidence of value for money. Increased delegation of central LEA funding for professional development services places a responsibility on governors for the allocation of sufficient funding for training and support. The same money could be spent on staffing, books or materials. Unless professional development is seen to be value for money and of sufficiently high priority to push other competing calls on the budget further down the priority list, it will become squeezed out. This will not happen if it is seen as an integral and essential strand within the development plan, and central to its success. The senior staff and professional

- Name of colleague running or attending a course/event

- Nature, date and venue of course/event

- What were the costs, and how will they be recovered?

- What were the objectives?

- Were they achieved?

- If yes, how?

- How did attendance at the event/course contribute to the achievement of the school development plan?

- What happens next? Include the names of key workers, resource implications, dates and time scales.

- Summary of event/course and subsequent benefits for the children (for inclusion in report to governors).

Figure 6.3 A form for reporting on a professional development activity

development coordinator should discuss success criteria with staff and governors, show how it can be monitored in terms of change and improvement and ensure that a consistent policy is followed. If standards within the school are to stay high, the professional development coordinator must take the initiative in supporting colleagues who undertake in-service responsibilities or who attend courses and should make sure that their personal achievements and new knowledge contribute back into the achievement and enhanced knowledge within the whole school. The school policy should include a structure, in written form (see Figure 6.3), which sets out the context in which individual professional development has taken place.

The proforma provides a discipline for the professional development coordinator. It serves as an important reminder that all professional development activities undertaken within the school must be seen as a contribution to the overall aims of the development plan, and are value for money. They will form a useful body of data for OFSTED inspectors, linkages to individual targets in appraisal outcomes, and for GEST returns.

Using our example from earlier in the chapter, Figure 6.4 illustrates a completed form.

OTHER FORMS OF PROFESSIONAL DEVELOPMENT

A great deal of effective school based in-service work takes place in classrooms with *teachers working alongside teachers*. Often this will be another teacher

Madison School

- Name of colleague running or attending a course/event
  Mary Smith
- Nature, date and venue of course/event
  PD half-day 26 May School-based
- What were the costs and how will they be recovered?
  £200 fees payable to School Library Service: code to GEST 1 School Effectiveness
- What were the objectives?
  1 To review the existing library book stock
  2 To evaluate current book stock usage
  3 To formulate future development
- Were they achieved?   *Yes*
- If yes, how?

  Objective 1 All the staff took part in the book stock evaluation. Serious deficiencies were noted in humanities and in fiction suitable for able readers in KS2
  Objective 2 John Robinson, the School Library Service adviser, led the discussion on the place and organisation of a primary school library. Library records provided data on usage.
  Objective 3 An action plan was agreed (see below).
- How did attendance at the event/course contribute to the achievement of the school development plan?
  Revitalisation of the library is part of objective 4 in the SDP (to review and develop school-based resources).
- What happens next? Include the names of key workers, resource implications, dates and time scales.

  1 Jim and Baljit to be the library working party, reporting progress to Mary Smith at monthly intervals
  2 Agreed tasks:
  2.1 Jim to work with John Robinson (SLS) to compile costed proposals for new humanities and fiction stock by 30 June. Mary to take proposals to SDP review meeting in September for budget approval. Note draft SDP allocated £1,000 to the library.
  2.2 Baljit to bring proposals for improved 'opening hours' and simplified loans system to July staff meeting, for implementation in September.
  2.3 School Library Service commissioned to spend three days (no cost due to school being a subscribing member of SLS) weeding book stock.To be complete by 20 July.
  2.4 Mary to bring proposals to PTA for funding to purchase a free standing PC and SIMS library software.
  2.5 Mary to take costed proposals to the budget sub-committee for 10 hours per week clerical assistance for period Jan.–March for cataloguing book stock (reliant on 2.4 being achieved).
  2.6 Sam Locket to evaluate improvements in book stock and usage and report to governors on 20 March.
- Summary of event/course and subsequent benefits for the children [For inclusion in report to Governors]

Sam Locket report see above 2.6

Figure 6.4 The completed report form

from the same school who has an expertise in the particular curriculum area or year group where another colleague needs support. In order to make the support effective, the school will have analysed the strengths and weaknesses of all the members of staff, including non-teaching staff. A grid with the names of the staff down one side and the curriculum areas, classroom management, teaching style and so on, across the other axis, will provide a simple mechanism for the headteacher to identify the strengths and needs of individual teachers. Many of these will be identified through the appraisal process. If the grid indicates that one area of the curriculum is a need for many staff, then support might be needed through a training day. If the need is only felt by one or a few staff and another member of staff is a competent leader in the field, then a mentoring or collaborative teaching approach will be the best solution. Time spent with another teacher means that the supporting teacher is not with their own class. Careful management will be needed to ensure that the support teacher's own class does not suffer and that sufficient cover from the headteacher or elsewhere allows the absent teacher to give his or her whole mind to the support, and not feel worried about what is happening back in their own classroom.

On some occasions the school will decide to buy in support from an advisory teacher. This ensures that a variety of practice is brought into the school which otherwise could become very sterile if it only relied on internal expertise. Advisory teachers have a significant role to play when working alongside teachers in classrooms. Newly qualified and recently qualified teachers benefit from this type of friendly non-threatening professional support, as do colleagues who have been many years in the profession and welcome the opportunity to build on their skills and abilities. The school and the advisory teacher will want to ensure that there is a proper briefing before the support starts. Many advisory teachers will suggest that the school first quantifies its need in writing. The advisory teacher then provides a written plan or programme so that the school can ensure that both parties understand the nature of the contract before it starts. The agreement should contain clear objectives for the advisory teacher and for the teacher who is to be supported. It should specify any tasks to be undertaken and identify the dates when the support will be provided. When appropriate, reference should be made to the school development plan or OFSTED report outcomes. Many advisory teachers are now only available as part of an agency charging for its services, or as individual consultants. Schools should be wary of employing agencies or individuals with whom they are unfamiliar, and should always ask for the name of a school where the consultant has worked previously so that references can be taken up. The professional development coordinator should evaluate the work of advisory teachers with the same rigour that is applied to courses or other types of professional development. Governors and senior staff will want to know if the objectives detailed in the contract were achieved and whether changes are evident in children's learning. Were the aims of the school development plan moved forward? Was there value for money?

Smaller schools often cluster together for a variety of reasons, including professional development. There are clear advantages in economies of scale. In many such groups, clusters identify individual curriculum strengths and needs, and interchange teachers on a regular basis so that all parts of the curriculum in all of the schools get a healthy input of expertise. This needs careful management to ensure that the class whose teacher is elsewhere is not disadvantaged. Some school clusters share the salary costs of specialist staff who are timetabled to ensure equality of provision and support in all the schools. Financial savings can be made when school clusters meet together for training days in which an external consultant or advisory teacher is bought in to address a particular issue of concern to the group. Such days also benefit all the staff who can enjoy being part of a wider professional circle where contact on a working daily basis is often with a very few number of other adults.

A POLICY FOR PROFESSIONAL DEVELOPMENT

In a climate of competing claims for scarce resources, professional development must be given status and authority by operating within an agreed and resourced policy statement. This should be written by the professional development coordinator, achieve the backing of the staff and be given authority for implementation by the governors.

The professional development policy should state that every teaching and non-teaching member of staff has an equal entitlement to professional development and that they can expect to focus on future support during their appraisal interviews. The policy should make it clear that professional development is not a strategy brought into play when someone is doing their job badly, but is an entitlement to grow professionally, with support, and without the fear that by undertaking professional development one is some how having a favour. The policy should also recognise that there will be different but equally important professional development needs for different groups of staff. Newly qualified teachers, main professional grade teachers, classroom assistants, nursery nurses, senior staff, and the headteacher, all have their own particular developmental needs if they are to increase the effectiveness of the work they do with children. Training and support for senior staff, especially in management skills, can be expensive. The policy should recognise this, and establish a climate where the costs of individual professional development needs should not make the recipient feel guilty. If senior staff do not advance their own skills, the whole school will be the loser. In the same way, there will be different but equally important professional development needs for governors, clerical and site management staff and lunch time supervisory assistants. The professional development policy will make it clear that it applies equally to all staff whatever their role.

Professional development must not appear to be in isolation from the mainstream thrust embodied in the current agreed priorities for the school as set down in the school development plan. The needs it seeks to service will be those already identified as important to the achievement of the aims of the school. They will be key strategies in the drive to maximise learning opportunities for children, or to increase the effectiveness of individual teachers. The professional development policy should require that all professional development programmes are adequately resourced, not only at the time of the course or event, but subsequently to an agreed level, to ensure time for reflection, promulgation and implementation.

Therefore, when the professional development coordinator and staff are considering development opportunities, courses and events, they need to ensure that:

- the course aims, objectives and content are appropriate to the needs of the school and proposed participant;
- the course meets needs identified in the school development plan;
- the costs, both financial and in time, have a secure budget;
- the course information is clear, including the name and status of the lead tutor and guest speakers;
- the course participant knows what she or he and the school are expected to gain from the course;
- the course participant knows how the benefits of the course will be used by the participant him/herself and passed onto colleagues.

The professional development policy should make clear that all teachers attending courses, briefings or other events should be well aware before they go of what they are expected to do back in the school as a result of being on the course. They might, for example, be asked to produce an action plan, to make arrangements to apply new skills in their classrooms or within the school, or to provide an in-house, in-service briefing based on their expertise. Everyone attending a training session of any kind should provide feedback and an evaluation of the course in terms of its usefulness to them as individuals, to the school in general. Only by so doing can it be shown that resources are being effectively and efficiently used, that value for money is being obtained.

The professional development policy should clarify the role of all involved: the governing body as the publicly accountable body responsible for the school, the headteacher as the mainspring for all the activities which take place in the school, the professional development coordinator as the person charged with the management of professional development of the staff, and the staff themselves as partners in a process designed to enable them to build on their skills and expertise and maximise learning opportunities for their children.

The role of the governing body is to participate in policy formation by agreeing the content and philosophy which underpins the idea of professional development and empowers the policy which seeks to achieve it. The governors should publicly support the concept of professional development by delegating a sufficient budget to the coordinator, ensuring that devolved government grants are used to the greatest effect, and actively undertaking their own programme for professional development. They should give general approval to the overall programme proposed by the school staff, showing a positive interest in its purpose and outcomes, and ensure that professional development is an integral part of the school development plan. Their continuing interest and affirmation of the importance they place on professional development can be achieved through regular termly reports from the coordinator. This will enable them to observe actual outcomes, assess value for money and be able to defend the principles of professional development to anyone who might challenge the priority they place on it. Many governors participate actively in school training days and attend after-school sessions. Schools will want to extend this process by inviting governors into schools to see the actual changes in classroom practice or experiences which have resulted from the professional development of the staff.

The role of the headteacher should be to initiate the identification of whole-school needs by ensuring that all aspects of the life of the school, its curriculum, organisation and management structures are subject to regular review. The headteacher's insistence on a regular programme of review, analysis and identification of need, provision of support, implementation of agreed actions, periods of consolidation and then further review, will ensure a healthy organisation where the professional development of all of the staff is seen as a high priority, attracting adequate resourcing. It is also the headteacher's responsibility to see that job descriptions are regularly revised, reflect the current agreed responsibilities of the postholder and link into the professional development strand of the development plan. The future professional development needs of appraisees are a fundamental element of appraisal discussions and agreed outcomes. The headteacher carries the responsibility of ensuring that these are relevant to the post-holder, the agreed needs of the school, and that once negotiated, are implemented. The headteacher should also monitor professional development programmes organised within the school and the various courses and events attended by staff beyond the school. Governors will be expecting to see value for money, that the time spent on professional development is part of a cohesive plan, with the ultimate aim of benefiting children in classrooms.

Senior staff should review provision of professional development on a termly basis:

- What professional development has taken place this term?
- What have been the positive outcomes?
- What concrete evidence exists to support this assumption?
- If the experience was not satisfactory, what steps have been taken to redress the balance?

- Are the outcomes on track with the objectives set within the development plan?

The answers will form the basis for the headteacher's, or professional development coordinator's, termly report to the governors and will provide OFSTED inspectors with factual evidence by which to measure the efficiency of the school and to check that planned professional development is an integral part of the school development plan.

The role of the professional development coordinator is to identify staff development needs arising in appraisal outcome statements, within regular audit and review cycles of the curriculum, or as a result of the introduction of a specific initiative agreed by the school as a priority. The subsequent planning should be done on an annual basis, within the constraints of the budget and the priorities set by the school, and should form an integral part of the development plan. Once the overall plan has been agreed, the coordinator should design and publish an annual programme so that all the staff can see how the various activities fit together to further the agreed aims for the next twelve months. The plan should be broken down into individual staff professional development programmes, and match the agreed outcomes of their appraisal discussions. If there is a mismatch, the reasons for this (lack of finance, lower priority need) must be explained to the staff member concerned. The coordinator has a dual responsibility to individual members of staff, not only in including them in the current programmes of development, but also in supporting them in personal and career development. This has implications for the coordinator's own professional development, as high order interpersonal and counselling skills will be required. As a manager, the coordinator must establish and maintain an overview of school INSET provision by ensuring that there is a plan, that it has short-, medium- and long-term objectives, that it recognises the needs of individuals as well as the school as a whole and that it is adequately resourced and recognised within the development plan. The coordinator should expect to have complete delegated authority from the governors to manage the INSET and GEST budgets, to obtain course reports from those who attend them, and to organise their appropriate dissemination. The coordinator will work with the headteacher in evaluating the effects of external and internal staff development and INSET programmes, by measuring and quantifying the outcomes in classrooms which can be attributed to professional development.

The staff have a shared responsibility to self-evaluate and establish their own personal needs as individuals, while playing their full part in the collaborate process of agreeing the needs of the school. It is an individual's own responsibility to keep their own staff development record, portfolio or profile up to date, ensure that their job descriptions refer to current responsibilities and support colleagues in their own development. On occasion this will have to mean that the particular needs of one individual might be met in the medium-term rather than the short-term, as the overall priorities the school must be met first.

In summary, the staff development policy should recognise the entitlement of each member of staff, teaching and support, to a well-planned and properly resourced programme of personal development. It should focus on individual, group, team and whole-school needs. It should form an integral part of the annual cycle of school development, and must be recognised as a priority within the development plan. The climate of the school should be totally supportive of the concept of professional development. The governors must understand the importance of professional development, that considerable attention to this aspect of school management will be paid by OFSTED inspectors and that to be successful it must be properly resourced in financial terms. Whatever the level of government grant allocated to the school, governors should aim to ensure that the budget allocated for professional development is driven by the needs of the school and is not an arbitrary allocation. However, as a general guideline, a budget equal to at least 2 per cent of the total staff salary bill would be about right. Budgets are finite and hard decisions will have to be made between competing bids for the same funds, but an institution which chooses to neglect the professional development of its staff is failing to invest in itself and its future. Most schools use their in-service funds to buy teacher cover to enable staff to attend courses during the working day and to give them time back in school after the course so that they can develop what they have learned and benefit the school as a whole. This is an expensive way to use limited resources, but essential if the school is to ensure that external professional development is not just for the benefit of the individual teacher, but part of the overall learning experience and development of the whole school. This will only happen if it is thoroughly planned and part of an integrated whole school professional development programme which balances the proper needs of the individual with the overarching needs of the school as a whole and is resourced to an appropriate level.

The positive attitude of the headteacher is also of paramount importance. By virtue of their appointment, headteachers play a key role in the appraisal of staff and will know the principal training and support needs which have been identified among the staff. In many primary schools, headteachers place such a high value on professional development that they, or the deputy, carry the role of professional development coordinator themselves. The headteacher should also be regarded as an exemplar of good practice, perhaps in a specific area of the curriculum, but certainly in terms of management or educational philosophy. If the commitment of the headteacher to the concept of professional development is not apparent for all to see, then it will cease to be a priority in the eyes of the governors and the staff and will not attract the necessary commitment or resources of time and money.

Although the senior staff must be publicly committed to professional development, the start point has to be an assumption that the school has an agreed written policy on the place and importance of professional development. The written policy will give the professional development coordinator the delegated responsibility for the analysis of developmental needs. Some of these will have been identified through individual interviews with staff, as part of their profession review, or the appraisal programme. The general needs of the school may have been identified through a structured audit. The development needs of the school, as a result of an externally imposed requirement will also have to be considered. As a result of the analysis, and subsequent discussion with senior members of staff, the coordinator will be able to prioritise needs, balancing the requirements of the school and the needs of individuals. Governors policies towards professional development or areas of the curriculum, and the school's aim statement, will inform the process. For example, the fact that the governors have stated that one particular area of the curriculum had to be seen as a priority because of critical comments in an OFSTED inspection report, and part of their consequent action plan, would be a powerful factor in deciding between competing bids.

The written professional development policy will recognise that the teaching staff of a school are its most important resource and that their professional development has to be regarded as one of the school's highest priorities. No organisation, however constrained its budget, can afford to defer its training, appraisal and supportive structures for staff professional development. It is of equal importance that the professional development which does take place is planned, and forms an integral, cross referenced and resourced section of the school development plan, giving clear indications of who will be doing what, by when and why, the resources required and the evaluation strategies which will measure whether the objectives have been reached. The plan will address the developmental needs of all staff, teaching and non-teaching, from those who are well-established within the school to those whose professional development is actually their induction on appointment.

Chapter 7

Selecting and appointing staff

In any primary school the implementation of the school development plan depends, to a greater or lesser degree, on teachers carrying out their duties and responsibilities in their classrooms and throughout the school as a whole. The inspection process examines how effective each individual teacher is and makes judgements about the extent to which the individual members of staff are blended into a coherent group with a shared sense of purpose and direction. Creating this common vision of where the school is going is the direct responsibility of the headteacher, although all staff, especially those in senior positions, have an important part to play. This shared view will inform all the work of the school and especially the selection and appointment of staff.

Staff selection in primary schools is a relatively intermittent process. It requires, therefore, a clear structure in order to make it work effectively. This is especially important since 1988 because the Education Reform Act gave responsibility to the governing body for all appointments under LMS although all or part of this responsibility may be delegated to the headteacher or to a small group of governors or to the headteacher and a group of governors acting together. It is worth recognising that while governors select staff, the LEA appoints them, although LEAs must accept the recommendations of the governing body unless the candidate fails to meet the criteria with respect to:

- qualifications;
- health and physical capacity;
- fitness on educational grounds or other respects.

Staff selection is best regarded as a partnership between governors and the headteacher. This allows the governors and the headteacher jointly to be involved with, and accept responsibility for, the consequences of selection decisions. Headteachers and governors together need to identify the main features of an effective staff selection procedure. The procedure should be agreed in advance of it being needed so that it is ready when a vacancy occurs. There is not always time to debate a process which is not already in place.

Any procedure must comply with education legislation and with employment law. It must be workable within the resource constraints of time and budget, yet it must enable the school to attract applications from a number of suitable candidates and thus allow real choices to be made. It should ensure that prospective candidates have sufficient information about the school and the post to enable them to decide if they suit the job and if the job suits them. It should provide reliable, consistent and objective ways of judging candidates' abilities and aptitudes and must treat all applicants fairly.

Staff appointments do not take place in isolation although they are often treated as if they do. The starting points for all appointments are the aims of the school and the school development plan. Unless the school knows what its aims are and how it intends to achieve them then the only basis on which to make decisions about staffing is the existing situation. With a well thought out development plan, however, those responsible for selecting staff will have much of the information required to enable them to take an informed and sensible choice as to whether there is a vacancy and, if there is, the nature of that vacancy. The audit of the staff and curriculum, carried out as part of the development planning process, will have identified the curricular strengths of the staff, the areas in which there is a lack of expertise and the priorities for development. All of this information is necessary in order to ensure that when an appointment is made the decision is going to do more than merely replace the colleague who is leaving. The key to good staff selection is in knowing what it is that the person to be appointed will be required to do, what qualifications, experience and expertise are necessary and how these might be recognised. This begins with the job description.

JOB DESCRIPTIONS AND PERSON SPECIFICATIONS

Job descriptions are an important instrument for the effective management of all primary schools and can help staff to fulfil their professional duties effectively. A good job description will detail the range of responsibilities that a particular teacher may have and thus enable that teacher to allocate time and effort in a considered way. It will also clarify the relationships between colleagues and be an essential document in the appraisal process. When attached to a vacant post it will enable potential applicants to have a clear view of the challenges of the post, its place in the overall structure of the school and the extent to which it will offer job satisfaction and career progression.

Job descriptions do not just emerge. They must be negotiated by the headteacher or a senior member of staff with the postholders when these are current members of the staff. Governors should be informed of the content of the job descriptions of the staff of the school for which they are responsible. Job descriptions must match both the expectations and the practice of the postholder, especially at the selection stage. Nothing is more calculated to be a constant source of conflict and irritation than a significant mismatch between the job description and the teacher's expectations. A teacher who comes to a school expecting to play a major part in the development of mathematics at Key Stage 2 across the primary curriculum, but who finds that timetable constraints prevent this from happening may, with some justification, feel aggrieved at those who made the appointment. The same can be said of teachers who are presented with job descriptions that have only a passing resemblance to what they actually do or which contain significant changes for which agreement has not been sought. Job descriptions, therefore, are practical and rooted in practice.

A good job description will concentrate on the what of the job rather than on the how, although how is important for identifying the criteria to be used for filling the post. By focusing on what the job entails it is possible to be precise about what the postholder will and will not be expected to do. This gives both a set of guidelines and some protection about unrealistic expectations. Thus, a job description needs to be sufficiently clear to enable the postholder, or potential applicant, to have a clear view about the principal responsibilities of the post and the tasks that arise from those responsibilities. It must be sufficiently detailed to avoid misunderstandings between the postholder and other staff and should make clear the position of the postholder within the school's management structure. It does not need to spell out all the duties required of a teacher under the Pay and Conditions of Service Legislation (DFE 1994a), but can contain a reference to those duties. It must, however, define the particular duties required in relation to the specific post to which the job description refers.

The job description in Figure 7.1 makes a distinction between the main function, the main duties and the responsibilities. The main function is the overall statement of what the job entails. The main duties expand upon this, drawing attention to what it is that the teacher is required to do in order to carry out the main function. The responsibilities are not necessarily actions which need to be taken by the holder of this post, but may require supervision and monitoring of the activities of others by that person. The use of words like 'prepare', 'assist', 'identify' and 'organise' help to keep the job description concise and indicate the extent of the involvement of the postholder in the tasks listed.

If the job description is about the 'what' of the post then the person specification in Figure 7.2 is about the 'who' and the 'how' of it. On the basis of the person specification it is possible to identify the expertise, experience and qualifications of the person who would best be able to do the job defined in the job description. This is extremely useful when seeking to make a staff appointment to a particular post and it is also useful for identifying the professional development needs of existing staff. It would be unfair to appoint a candidate to a post for which she is not qualified, but it is even more unfair to expect a teacher to carry out duties for which her qualifications, experience and expertise do not prepare her.

Job title
Standard scale teacher with incentive allowance A for mathematics across the primary school curriculum.

Main functions
To act as class teacher for a Year 6 class and to be responsible for mathematics throughout the school.

To carry out those duties and responsibilities contained within the 'School Teachers' Pay and Conditions' document

Main duties
To be the class teacher in Year 6.

To prepare a new scheme of work in mathematics.

To provide guidance and support to all colleagues in implementing the scheme.

To monitor work in mathematics throughout the school including record keeping and progress assessment.

To assist colleagues in diagnosing children's learning difficulties in mathematics.

To identify support strategies to improve the performance of children with learning difficulties in mathematics.

To arrange school-based INSET in mathematics for colleagues.

To liaise with head of mathematics at Willingham High School over work done in final year of the primary school

To organise necessary resources for mathematics and to inform colleagues of what is available and how it might best be used.

Responsible to
The headteacher

Responsible for
The work of all colleagues in mathematics.

School-based INSET in mathematics.

Providing support for children with learning difficulties in mathematics.

Advising the headteacher and governors on new developments in mathematics.

Resources
Two hours of non-contact time each week.

The resources to fund a new mathematics scheme up to £2,500 over two years.

The equivalent of half a day of secretarial time to help with preparing material.

Two hours of classroom helper time each week for one year to help provide materials in the infant department.

Figure 7.1 Job description

The person specification must refer to and be derived from the job description. The two are closely interrelated. The job description will certainly define the minimum qualifications and indicate the required nature and length of previous experience. It will also give some guidance as to the aptitudes and expertise that a postholder may need to possess. Parts of the specification, for both existing and newly appointed staff, may indicate where further training and development are necessary or desirable. When being used to make an appointment both the job description and the person specification must be written in the light of the current needs of the school. They must

Job Title
Standard scale teacher with incentive allowance A for mathematics across the primary school curriculum.

Qualifications in primary education
B.Ed. or equivalent with mathematics as a specialism or PGCE in primary education with mathematics as a specialism.

Evidence of attending INSET courses in primary school mathematics.

Experience
At least five years as class teacher in a primary school.

Recent experience of teaching Years 5 and 6.

Experience of involvement in curriculum change in mathematics.

Experience of coordinating the work of colleagues.

Experience in providing school-based INSET in mathematics.

Aptitudes
Evidence of successful class teaching.

Evidence of ability to work with colleagues and to provide curriculum leadership.

Evidence of ability to diagnose learning difficulties and to identify strategies to cope with them.

Evidence of ability to communicate with colleagues in other schools.

Evidence of ability to keep up-to-date with developments in primary school mathematics teaching.

Physical
Must pass LEA medical examination.

Interests
Must be interested in and committed to multi-cultural education.

Interest in PE and games would be an advantage.

Figure 7.2 Person specification

also conform with equal opportunity legislation and should not imply or state that the post can only be carried out by an able bodied person, or a person of a certain racial group or gender. Job titles must also be gender neutral. Similarly, descriptions of tasks or details of specifications should not give the impression that applicants of one sex would be more likely to be appointed. Such points are easily overlooked especially where the description and specification are based on those that were negotiated with the previous postholder. The existence of a sound person specification and a clear job description is a necessary part of the staff selection process but, in itself, is not sufficient to ensure that the process is effective. Now that most schools have delegated budgets, far more of the responsibility for establishing a workable selection procedure rests with the headteacher, senior staff and governors of a school. Schools may wish, however, to involve the LEA in all or part of the process. For example, the LEA's facilities to advertise the vacancy are likely to be used. The school may wish to consider possible candidates from among those teachers that are being redeployed within the LEA or to receive LEA advice as part of the selection process. Of course, grant maintained schools will not have access to such support and will need to organise the selection procedure for themselves.

THE MAIN STAGES IN STAFF SELECTION

Under LMS much greater responsibility for decision-making in respect of staff appointments now falls upon governors. It is important, therefore, that they are fully involved in all the main stages of selection. Since all the stages of the selection procedure are closely linked it is bad practice to have somebody playing a key role in the interview who has not been party to the discussions about job descriptions, person specifications and selection criteria which precede that interview. Some governors may wish to delegate the authority for making appointments to all but the most senior posts to the headteacher and senior staff of the school. Others may wish to take a full part in the selection of all teaching and support staff. While governors can delegate authority, they cannot delegate responsibility. They must account for the selection procedures and for their management of the school's resources. They must, therefore, be involved in taking the initial decisions about the appointment.

The initial decisions

Every vacancy presents the headteacher and governors with a series of decisions that have to be made. Does the post have to be filled in its present form or at all? The only post that governors are obliged to fill is that of the headteacher. Are there other ways of filling the vacancy apart from a full-time appointment? A series of part-time appointments, or job sharing, might provide more flexibility. Is this an opportunity to bring in different skills to the school? Are there teachers on the existing staff who could fill the vacant post or who could be trained to do so? What are the likely implications of considering an internal appointment and how should this be managed? The selection procedure must ensure that all members of staff feel that they have had an opportunity to be considered for the post if they so wish. Internal and external candidates should, as far as possible, be treated in the same way.

The school's development plan provides a context within which such decisions may be considered. The headteacher may wish to consult staff in the school about the choices to be made. They will bring a valuable perspective to the decision-making. This might be supplemented by an exit interview with the departing colleague. A well-conducted exit interview enables the headteacher to establish exactly how the incumbent carried out her duties; to explore privately her reasons for leaving; and to identify those areas of the school organisation that might need to be improved (see Figure 7.3). At the same time an exit interview can produce a valuable discussion about ways in which the existing post might be changed and the skills,

PURPOSE

- To thank the person for her contribution to the life of the school
- To discuss the person's reasons for leaving the school with a view to taking any remedial action, if necessary, in respect of:

  Poor recruitment
  Inadequate staff development
  Poor management of supervision
  School policy
  Selection

- To secure the member of staff's goodwill and the school's reputation
- To identify the main elements of the job which is being vacated and to amend the job description if necessary
- To seek advice about the qualities required in a person appointed to the post

PREPARATION

- Check resignation letter – reason stated
- Check staff records
- Where appropriate check with other members of staff
- Ensure privacy and no interruptions
- Allow adequate time

CONDUCT

- Put at ease
- State purpose of interview
- Encourage and allow member of staff to talk freely about the job, the school and the people
- Listen and observe, be alert for clues to underlying reason
- Thank member of staff for services rendered and wish her well

FOLLOW UP

Decide if any action is necessary in the light of information gained and implement accordingly

Figure 7.3 Exit interview – checklist

experience and qualifications that are now necessary to do the job well. The job description and person specification can then be modified before the job is advertised. The selection panel should be formed at this stage so that it can consider or, at the very least, be informed about these details.

Forming the selection panel

The selection panel is the group of people who will conduct the interview part of the selection process. Since effective selection consists of a number of closely related stages, a good selection panel will do much more than this. Members of the panel ought to be involved in finalising the details of the post to be filled and the advertisement to be used, examining the applications, long-listing and short-listing, conducting the interview and recommending to the LEA the making of an appointment or not, as the case may be.

The panel need not, indeed should not, be too large. A large number of people conducting an interview tends to intimidate candidates. Various interests may have to be represented on the panel. This will help to establish both its size and composition. The headteacher and representatives of the governors are likely to be present and the LEA may be included. Where appropriate, senior members of staff may also be involved. Beckett *et al.* (1991) suggest that five or six people is the optimum size for a selection panel while Hume (1990), writing for governors, suggests that three governors should be involved in most appointments. He also reminds us that it is important to ensure that both men and women are represented on the panel. Similar consideration might also be given to members of minority groups, depending on the nature of the school's community.

Selection is a time-consuming process. This may limit the extent to which certain members of a governing body can take part. Some schools establish an appointment board from which governors and staff are identified to form a panel when a vacancy occurs. This has the advantage that members of this group have the opportunity to develop an expertise in interviewing. It has the disadvantages that such groups can become distanced from their parent body, from the needs of the school, and may be dominated by a very few individuals. A rota system which calls upon governors in turn to be part of the selection process provides an alternative method of sharing out the duties and responsibilities of staff selection.

However the appointing panel is formed, all of its choices and decisions must be taken according to agreed, relevant and specific criteria. A wise panel will ensure that written records are kept about how and why decisions were made and how the criteria were applied. The decisions of a selection panel may be subject to question. Candidates who are not short-listed or selected may wish to know why. There is no reason why such information should not be given to them. The full governing body may wish to receive a report on the selection process at its next meeting. The selection may, in rare cases, be subject to a formal grievance or industrial tribunal. All decisions taken in such cases need to be justified and justifiable. The selection panel as a whole is responsible for ensuring that its decisions are fair and reasonable, but it is likely that much of the weight of that responsibility will fall on the headteacher and his or her colleagues.

In order to carry out its duties the selection panel will need a core of essential information. This will include the job description, the person specification, agreed procedures and practices for fair selection and a timetable for carrying out the appointment procedures. The combination of job description and person specification provides a detailed definition of the post to be filled and a list of criteria according to which the appointment will be made. The basic job description of all teachers is now enshrined in the *School Teachers' Pay and Conditions Document* (see DFE 1994a) which is updated annually. This must be drawn to the attention of the appointing panel.

The panel should have an initial meeting before the post is advertised to agree on the school's needs, opportunities, the details of the post to be advertised and the method of dealing with applications as they arrive. If the school development plan is in place, if there are up-to-date job descriptions and person specifications, and if an exit interview has been held, then much of the information on which to base these discussions will be readily available. Although the person specification in Figure 7.2 gives a specific set of criteria for making the appointment, further consideration needs to be given to where and how the evidence will be found. Some consideration also has to be given to the precise wording of the advertisement since this is the first indication that potential candidates will have that there is a vacancy.

The advertisement and further information

Any vacancy may be advertised within the school, within the LEA in its own staffing bulletin, in the local or national press, in the educational press or in specialist journals. The location of the advertisement will determine its content, but the general principles for identifying that content remain the same. The advertisement must give sufficient information about the post to enable potential applicants to decide whether or not they may be suitable for the post and how far the post may suit them. They also need to know how, where and by when to apply.

Since the cost of the advertisement is likely to be a factor it should be kept as brief as possible while being as long as necessary. It should contain an outline of the post and the grade at which the successful candidate will be appointed; the name of the school, its LEA and location; the address from which application forms may be obtained; the closing date and the proposed date of appointment. If the job is subject to certain conditions, or is for a limited period, then this should also be stated. If the requirements of the post are quite specific then the advertisement should also be specific, but if the post is a very general one with few precise specifications then the advertisement should convey this.

Arrangements to respond speedily to requests for application forms and further information have to be made well before they start to arrive. Details of the post in the form of the job description and person specification should go to all prospective applicants. They need to know what the job entails and what kind of person is required to fill it. Once they have this information they can decide whether or not they are likely to be suitable and how best to present the details of their application if they decide to apply.

Relevant information about the school, its surroundings and about the LEA should also be included, although if the post is only advertised within the LEA this last item can be excluded. It is not easy to summarise all the information that a prospective candidate may find useful. The purpose of this information is to inform intending applicants about the situation in which the successful candidate will work. The school handbook, while written for parents, should be made available to the short-listed candidates, as should a staff handbook if one exists. The existing members of staff might also be consulted about the information that they think a prospective applicant would find useful.

The following information should be provided to prospective candidates:

- the school and its situation, including the type, group size, numbers on roll over the past few years, site and buildings, features of the catchment area, history and significant events in the life of the school;
- the internal organisation of the school, numbers in each year, method of organisation, arrangements for transfer to and from the school, community involvement, arrangements for teacher appraisal and school inspection;
- staffing establishment and number of permanent teaching staff and support staff in post and their responsibilities, planned changes in the structure, organisation of the management team, distribution of allowances and where this post fits into the staffing structure;
- curriculum, including special needs provision, the strategies adopted to enable the school to cover and assess the relevant key stages of the National Curriculum and details about aspects of the curriculum and its resourcing relevant to the post;
- links with parents, parental involvement in the work of the school, parents' meetings, parents' education meetings, parent-teacher association, expectations about attending such meetings, methods and the timing of reporting to parents;
- support available for professional development including LEA and school-based provision, courses and other activities available at the local teachers' centre and other teacher education centres;
- the composition and organisation of the governing body, including division of responsibilities and, where applicable, special curriculum interests;
- links with the local community, contacts with churches and other agencies and the community use of premises.

All of this information can be used by the prospective candidate to make a decision about applying for the post and to help that person to fill in the application form in such a way as to give the selection panel the information that it requires. These details, especially the job description and the person specification, give clear criteria against which the suitability of the post and the candidate can be judged. They also provide a context within which the initial screening of applications can take place. Much now depends on how

APPLICATION FOR POST OF

FULL NAME:

PRESENT ADDRESS: AGE: DES NUMBER:

TEL NO:

NATIONALITY:

EDUCATION: School/College/University	INSERVICE COURSES:
Dates	Dates
Qualifications	Qualifications
	and any other relevant professional development

DETAILS OF EMPLOYMENT:
Are you currently employed?

YES/NO   If YES
                                                state notice required by your
                                                present employer:

Details of all recognised teaching employment, working back from your
current post or most recent post

From Mth/Yr	To Mth/Yr	Employer's name and address	Position, brief description of post	Reasons for leaving

Details of other professional industrial or commercial, military or research
experience.

From Mth/Yr	To Mth/Yr	Employer's name and address	Position, brief description of post	Reasons for leaving

INTERESTS (Hobbies, Club membership, etc.)

HEALTH RECORD
Give details of any disabilities or any illnesses which have caused you to
be absent from work for more than four weeks:

CRIMINAL CONVICTION
Have you ever been convicted of a criminal offence? If yes give details
below:

NOTE: The Rehabilitation of Offenders Act DOES NOT apply to this
appointment. YOU ARE THEREFORE REQUIRED TO ANSWER.

REFEREES:
Candidates are asked to provide the names of three people to whom
reference may be made concerning their suitability for this post:

Name: Position:
Address:
Relationship to candidate

Name: Position:
Address:
Relationship to candidate

Name: Position:
Address:
Relationship to candidate

FURTHER RELEVANT INFORMATION

Candidates should submit a letter in support of their application of no more
than 1,000 words indicating how they meet the spcifications for this post
(see Job Description and Person Specification). Forms should be typed or
completed in black ink.

Figure 7.4 Example of application form headings

far the application forms themselves enable the selectors to identify and assess relevant information and relate this information to the selection criteria that are derived from the person specification.

The application form, if carefully designed and interpreted, can provide a wealth of information about candidates. It is a way of seeking information by correspondence and should be structured in such a way as to provide evidence as to how far the applicant meets the selection criteria for the post. Standard LEA forms often elicit information which is valuable to the personnel department but is of little use in the selection process. Some schools may wish to design their own application form. The specimen form in Figure 7.4 can be adapted to most posts, although for very senior appointments a more flexible approach may be required to enable candidates to develop their ideas more fully. In such a situation a letter of application must supplement the form. In either case a letter of application is helpful to both applicants and selectors provided that the candidate is given clear guidance about what the letter should include. The standard exhortation to 'write a letter in support of your application' is of little help to either the candidate or the selection panel unless the letter addresses the selection criteria. Candidates might be asked to show how they meet the criteria given in the person specification and to discuss how they would expect to carry out the duties and responsibilities contained in the job description. Even more detailed guidance may be given. For the post carrying an allowance for primary school mathematics, candidates may be asked to provide evidence about:

- their recent inservice activities in mathematics both as a participant and a provider;
- how they would plan, organise and evaluate children's mathematics in their own classroom;
- how they would plan to coordinate mathematics across the curriculum;
- how they would influence the work of colleagues;
- what, in their view, the main functions of a mathematics coordinator are and how would they carry them out.

In this way the letter of application enables the selection panel to obtain information about the candidate that is directly relevant to the post and to differentiate among them on the basis of evidence provided in the letters.

Analysing the evidence

After the closing date for applications the selection panel will have a substantial amount of reading to do. It will need to plan a timetable for carrying out this process, for long- and short-listing and for interviewing. The applications must be acknowledged and the applicants given some idea of when they are likely to be called for interview if they are selected to proceed to the next stage. All too often applicants are left without information and in a state of uncertainty. This is unfair to them and to their present schools.

A wise panel will already have established appointment criteria based on the person specification and identified those criteria which are essential and those which are desirable. For example, for this post the qualifications, the length and nature of experience and involvement in curriculum development in mathematics might have been identified as essential criteria. They can then be used to screen the applications. There is nothing to be gained by spending time on a detailed analysis of a candidate who lacks any of the essential criteria.

An initial reading of the application forms and the letters of application will enable the selection panel to group the remainder of the applicants into two groups, probables and possibles. To do so the panel will have to seek evidence from the documentation for all candidates about how well they meet the essential and desirable criteria. If the probable group is large enough then the possibles group should be re-read and, if appropriate, discarded. This can be a time-consuming task but it has to be carried out promptly. A simple grid with essential criteria along one axis and candidates' names along the other provides a very useful format at this stage. A more detailed analysis may be carried out using the grid in Figure 6.4 on page 118. The panel may wish to delegate this task to some of its members, say the chair and the headteacher, but all members should have the opportunity to read the forms and be told the reasons for discarding applications. A record of the reasons for discarding applications must be kept for six months. Candidates whose applications are not being pursued should be informed at this stage. This enables them to make further career choices.

Once a list of probable candidates exists, all of whom should meet the essential criteria and be appointable to the post, the panel has to decide on the next stage. It can either send for references before inviting candidates to interview with a view to reducing the list still further, or invite all the candidates for interview. The aim should be to interview about five candidates for any post, although it is the practice in some schools, especially for senior posts, to invite up to eight candidates for a morning long-listing selection process which might be a series of short interviews, job-related written tasks, exercises or discussion groups. This number is then reduced to a short-list of three or four who attend a further interview by the whole selection panel in the afternoon. This approach is certainly appropriate for headteacher and deputy headteacher appointments in primary schools but may be too time-consuming and cumbersome for other posts.

An alternative strategy is to ask some candidates to complete a short written task while others are being interviewed. They might be asked, for example, to write no more than two sides of A4 on, 'How to develop cross-curricular themes in Year 6' or, 'Outline the main characteristics of a mathematics policy for this school'. This means that more than one interviewing panel can be used, but their criteria and areas of questioning must be clear. This process provides a format of:

	Candidate			
	A	B	C	D
Time				
9.00–9.45	Interview	Task 1	Interview	Task 2
9.45–1.30	Task 2	Interview	Task 1	Interview

The process can be extended to suit the number of candidates and can allow the same candidate to be interviewed by different groups. The tasks can provide a deeper insight into the candidates' understanding of key issues than may be obtained during the interview.

It is realistic to assume that the short-list will be drawn up on the basis of application forms, letters and references, although the headteacher may wish to visit those candidates on the short-list in their schools to see them at work in order to gain further relevant evidence. If visits do take place then all candidates should be visited and the same criteria applied. References are only as useful as the information contained in them. They can be made more useful by requesting specific kinds of information that are relevant to the post. This might be done by drawing the referee's attention to significant parts of the information about the post, such as the person specification and job description, and asking for comments on how far the candidate meets the specifications. This can give a clear structure to the reference, leaves the referee in no doubt about what is being asked and minimises the risk of receiving a standard reference for a candidate that bears little relationship to the post for which he or she has applied.

Once candidates are short-listed they may wish to visit the school if they are not already familiar with it. The selection panel may wish, as a matter of course, to extend such an invitation to candidates, especially for senior posts. Such visits must be well-planned (see Figure 7.5). It provides an opportunity to see the school in operation, to meet colleagues, to see specialist rooms, books and equipment and to be informed about curriculum, relevant policy documents and the school development plan. There should also be time for a discussion with the headteacher. It would be naïve to assume that such a visit would not form a small part of the selection process but, at this stage, the candidate is likely to be less stressed than at an interview and can make sure that the post would be acceptable if offered.

The interview

The keeping of detailed records of the selection process becomes even more important as the references start to arrive. Compiling a long- or short-list is a complex process and all available evidence will need to be used. If a small group has been delegated the task of long-listing then the whole selection panel should be involved in the short-listing. Again, this requires a careful judgement as to how far each candidate meets the criteria in the person specification. It is easy to allow prejudices to cloud judgement at this stage. Handwriting and general presentation are important but should never be the main criteria for selection, nor should a panel operate a rule of thumb such as 'Never look at a typed application form because the candidate is trying to conceal untidy handwriting'. A checklist such as that in Figure 7.6 should be used by each member of the selection panel for codifying evidence on each candidate at this stage. There is then a basis for a logical and rational debate about the merits of each candidate related to the person specification and the job description. The essence of such a form is to identify clear reasons for making judgements.

Information required
- application form
- job description/person specification
- plan of visit indicating time/place, person or staff responsible for meeting candidate

Structure of visit (headteacher) 9.30–9.45 in headteacher's office
- introduction
- welcome and coffee
- explain structure of visits
- deal with initial questions

Tour of school (headteacher) 9.45–10.30
- general tour
- return to:

  - meet key staff
  - talk to pupils
  - see key areas
  - examine key facilities and equipment

Meet staff (headteacher in staff room) 10.30–11.15 coffee prepared
- meet all staff
- meet present holder of post
- meet other key staff again

General discussion (headteacher in office) 11.15–12.15 with deputy and key staff
- answer candidates questions
- provide more relevant information
- give candidates a summary sheet of each school policy
- information including plan of school
- depart for lunch

Figure 7.5 A structure for the candidate's visit

Once the short-listed candidates are identified they need to be informed and invited to the interview. They should be given the following information:

- where and when the interview will be held;
- travel, parking and, if appropriate, accommodation arrangements;
- the exact time and approximate duration of the interview or, if appropriate, the structure of the selection programme;
- names and status of the selection panel;
- other details including catering arrangements, meetings with staff and opportunities to see the school if arranged;
- how to submit expenses claims and the appropriate rates;
- how and when decisions will be made and candidates notified;
- a request that candidates reply in writing stating that they will attend, indicating approximate time of arrival and any special arrangements that may be necessary.

On the day of the interview the candidates should be met and welcomed, refreshments made available and a suitable area in which to wait provided. Sitting in the staff room at coffee time is hardly the best way to prepare for an interview. The selection panel will also need to prepare. Each member of the panel will require copies of the letter of application, application form and references for each candidate, as well as the job description, person specification and programme for the day. Some panels may prefer to consider references after the interview. The panel should agree on how information about each candidate will be identified, recorded and discussed. There will also need to be an agreement that different members of the panel will concentrate on different areas of the person specification and on the length of time that each panel member will have to ask questions. Each candidate must be asked the same basic questions but follow-up questions should reflect the initial answers. Notes should be kept. Sufficient time will have to be allowed to ensure that each candidate is given a fair interview. Thirty minutes is probably not enough time for five people to interview one candidate. It is better to allow slightly too long for each interview than to allocate too little time. After all, an important decision is being made.

The selection panel will contain those people who did the short-listing, so a partially shared view already exists about the candidates as they appeared from their applications. The panel now has to ensure that this view is either confirmed or challenged by seeking evidence through the selection process. The interview, and any other approach to selection that might be used, should be structured in such a way as to help the panel to identify, and the candidate to provide, relevant evidence. The key to this is asking the right questions and making judgements about the quality of the answers.

Interviewing involves a number of specific skills that enable a dialogue to take place between the selection panel and the candidate in which the

CHECKLIST FOR ANALYSING APPLICATIONS	Name of candidate and present post	Name of candidate and present post	Name of candidate and present post	Name of candidate and present post
Qualifications				
Teaching Certificate				
B.Ed. or similar first degree				
PGCE				
Higher Degree				
Other advanced qualification				
INSET courses				
Experience				
Infant				
Junior				
Other				
Involvement in curriculum				
Change in				
Coordinating work of colleagues				
Providing school-based				
INSET in				
Aptitudes				
Successful class teaching				
Providing curriculum leadership				
Organising resources				
Diagnosing learning difficulties and identifying strategies to cope with them				
Communication with colleagues in other schools				
Communication with parents				
Knowledge of recent developments				
Interests				
Commitment to multi-cultural education				
PE/Games				
Other comments				
Physical				
Any indication of ill health				
Rank order of candidates				
Final rank order of candidates after discussion				
List of those invited for interview				

Figure 7.6 Checklist for analysing applications

candidate does almost all of the talking and the panel most of the listening. Listening takes place on three levels:

- making sense of the response being given;
- relating that response to what has gone before;
- forming judgements about the accuracy, relevance, validity and weight of the response with reference to the evidence being sought for the post.

It is important that all members of the selection panel listen to the responses given by candidates to all questions, not just the ones that they are asking. At the same time judgements will need to be made about candidates on the basis of their non-verbal behaviour. It is to be expected that a candidate will show signs of nervousness during an interview but other non-verbal factors are also important. What impression does the candidate's appearance give? Is the candidate able to relax? Does the candidate make eye contact with the panel members? How significant these signals are is open to debate but they do influence opinion and, since this is the case, they should be discussed openly as part of the process of reaching a decision. They should not, however, take precedence over the main criteria derived from the job description and person specification.

If listening and observing provide evidence on which judgements can be made it is the skill of questioning that can trigger the responses that help to provide the most significant evidence. Interviews should be reflective and thoughtful rather than interrogative. A small number of carefully chosen questions is far better than a large number of ill conceived ones. Questions should be linked so that they follow a theme, topic or idea and should normally be open so that the candidate can give a detailed and considered response. Thus, for the post of teacher with an incentive allowance for mathematics across the primary school curriculum, the following sequence might be used to explore one aspect of the evidence required to make a judgement. The main question might be:

- What experience have you had of providing school-based inservice support in mathematics?

Depending on the answer one or more supplementary questions such as the ones below might be asked:

- How did you involve colleagues in identifying the needs to be addressed by your inservice programme?
- What benefits did your school gain from the programme?
- Did you encounter any problems in providing your programme? How did you overcome them?
- How did you evaluate the programme?
- What did you learn from that evaluation that would influence your planning for your next inservice programme?

Such a sequence of questions would enable a selection panel to glean a significant amount of evidence about each candidate's experience in providing one form of inservice support to colleagues. The focus might now be shifted to look at what experience the candidate has in providing support to colleagues within their classrooms. The extent to which this line of questioning is continued will be determined by how important that particular aspect of the person specification is for the post under consideration. Each major area of the person specification will need to be examined in this way. After each interview it is useful to summarise briefly what the candidate has said so that the panel bases its judgements on a common understanding of what takes place during the interview.

Towards the end of each interview candidates should be given the opportunity to volunteer information which they feel might support their case but which has not been covered adequately or at all by the selection panel's questioning. Candidates should also be able to ask questions about the post and the school. At the end of the interview each candidate should be reminded of how and when the decision will be reached and communicated. Finally the candidates should be thanked for their interest in the post.

Reaching the decision

At the end of the interviews the selection panel will be faced with the task of digesting, assessing and interpreting the information about each candidate and reaching a decision. Most selection panels reflect on the merits of each candidate in broad terms of strengths, weaknesses and special circumstances and then try to decide by either elimination of most candidates or the advocacy of a particular candidate as the best available. It is very tempting to seek an early consensus on who should be appointed. This can, however, lead to the wrong choice being made. Each candidate must be looked at carefully. For this to happen the information has to be processed in a systematic way. An interview analysis sheet helps in this process because it relates directly to the person specification (see Figures 7.7a–c). It also provides a combination of professional judgement and measurement of relevant attributes, experience and qualifications.

The interview analysis sheet is simply a list of the items identified in the person specification with some indication of how important each item is for the post. This importance is given a numerical expression through the importance weighting column. The weightings need to be agreed in advance by the selection panel who also have to focus their questioning of the candidates so as to elicit the required information. In the example in Figure 7.7(a) a higher weighting is given to a B.Ed. or similar qualification than to any other. In this example further differentiation is also made. Thus, Mrs Green has an upper-second class honours degree with mathematics as her main subject while Mrs Lilac has a pass degree. Mr White's PGCE was for mathematics and science in the primary age range.

Similarly, more weighting is given to junior school teaching experience than to any other type. This also helps to focus the discussion. While there may be some disagreement about the extent of Mr White's experience as a class teacher, this can be considered on the basis of evidence rather than guesswork and assumption if questions to him are carefully prepared. Some of the evidence that is included on the interview analysis sheet can be obtained from the applications and references, but the real assessment of much of it takes place during the interview. The score given to each candidate in the weighted score column is the actual score, arrived at by looking at the documentary and interview evidence multiplied by the importance weighting shown for each item in column one. This gives an overall result for each candidate. This outcome and the evidence on which it is based needs detailed consideration in the post-interview discussion.

The interview analysis sheet is helpful because it relates directly to the person specification and to relevant evidence. Further discussion might be developed by encouraging the selection panel to:

- assemble the facts of the candidate's career in chronological order;
- superimpose in as many areas of the interview analysis sheet as possible the candidate's own explanations and responses by using his or her own words;
- consider his or her likely performance in specific situations.

All judgements must be based on evidence that is shared with the whole of the selection panel. It is all too easy to forget the person specification and concentrate on the personalities of the candidates. It would be unfair to the candidates, the existing staff of the school and the children to appoint somebody who did not meet the criteria. It is better not to appoint. Beware also of appointing the cheapest candidate, although cost is a very real consideration for many schools with delegated budgets and high staffing costs. The cheapest candidate may be the least experienced and the least able to do the job. Such an appointment may have high hidden costs in the longer term. Once the selection panel has identified the candidate that it wishes to appoint then the reasons for recommending that person should be reviewed in the light of the evidence, the job description and the person specification.

Once the decision has been made a formal notification of the candidate to be appointed can be made to the LEA by the appointing panel acting on behalf of the governors. It should also be reported to the governors at their next meeting. The selected candidate can be informed and discussions held about salary. These can be legally binding and so should only take place once the relevant details are available and understood. Other details will also need to be considered such as the date of appointment, arrangements for medicals, and visits to the school.

Teacher with special responsibility for mathematics	Importance weighting	Mrs Green		Mrs Lilac		Mr White	
		Actual score	Weighted score	Actual score	Weighted score	Actual score	Weighted score
Qualifications							
Teaching certificate	2	0	0	0	0	0	0
B.Ed. or similar	5	2	10	3	15	0	0
PGCE	4	0	0	0	0	2	8
Higher degree	2	0	0	0	0	0	0
Other advanced courses	3	2	6	1	3	3	9
INSET courses	4	3	12	1	4	2	8
Sub-total		7	28	5	22	7	25
Experience							
Infant	3	1	3	1	3	0	0
Junior	4	3	12	2	8	2	8
Other	1	0	0	2	2	0	0
Curriculum change in maths	2	2	4	0	0	0	0
Coordinating work of colleagues	3	4	12	3	9	1	3
Providing school-based INSET	3	2	6	1	3	1	3
Sub-total		12	37	9	25	4	14

Figure 7.7(a) Interview analysis sheet

Teacher with special responsibility for mathematics	Importance weighting	Mrs Green		Mrs Lilac		Mr White	
		Actual score	Weighted score	Actual score	Weighted score	Actual score	Weighted score
Aptitudes							
Successful class teaching	5	4	20	5	25	3	15
Providing curriculum leadership	5	4	20	2	10	1	5
Organising resources	1	3	3	4	4	1	1
Diagnosing learning difficulties and identifying strategies	2	4	8	5	10	2	4
Communication with colleagues in other schools	1	0	0	1	1	0	0
Communication with parents	1	2	2	3	3	1	1
Recent developments in mathematics	3	3	9	3	9	2	6
Sub-total		20	62	23	62	10	32
Interests							
Commitment to multicultural education	4	3	12	4	16	5	20
PE/Games	3	0	0	2	6	1	3
Sub-total		4	12	6	22	6	23

Figure 7.7(b) Interview analysis sheet

Teacher with special responsibility for mathematics	Importance weighting	Mrs Green		Mrs Lilac		Mr White	
		Actual score	Weighted score	Actual score	Weighted score	Actual score	Weighted score
Other comments							
Suitability as colleague	5	4	20	5	25	4	20
Ambition	1	3	3	3	3	5	5
Interested in PTA	2	3	6	2	4	4	8
Sub-total		10	29	10	32	13	33
Total weighted scores		53	164	52	163	36	128
Discussion points							

Candidate appointed: Mrs Green

Notes: The weighting on this table is provided as a guide to interviewers. The scoring on this form should be on a 1–5 scale where, on the basis of the evidence, 5 is the highest unweighted score which can be awarded to any candidate in any category, 3 indicates an average rating and 1 is low. The weighted score for each item is arrived at by multiplying the actual score for each item by the figure in the *importance weighting* column. Thus, on the available evidence Mrs Green was given an actual score of 4 for her success as a class teacher. This has an importance weighting of 5. Therefore her weighted score is 20.

Figure 7.7(c) Interview analysis sheet

Unsuccessful candidates should also be notified as quickly as possible. Some of them may request feedback on their performance at the interview and this should be given to them. All papers relating to the appointment should be kept for six months in case there are any queries or disputes, after which time those pertaining to the unsuccessful candidates should be destroyed. Those relating to the successful candidate will go into his or her personal file.

Induction

The selection process does not end when the successful candidate has accepted the post. The appointment is, in fact, the start of another stage, that of induction. Induction should begin by informing existing staff of the appointment that has been made and giving them a few details about their new colleague and about his or her first visit to the school. For all newly appointed staff the first visit to the school can be rather difficult, especially if there have been internal candidates on the staff. It should, as far as possible, be social rather than inductive, enabling the new teacher to meet colleagues and children and to become familiar with the school and its environment.

The first visit also gives the new teacher a chance to ask questions and to deal with any immediate concerns that may have arisen since the interview. When taking on a new role such as teacher with responsibility for mathematics across the primary school curriculum, the new colleague may wish to arrange future visits and meetings with the people with whom she will be working and to find out more about the available books and equipment. This is also a good opportunity to check that the new teacher has copies of the school handbook, the staff handbook, curriculum guidelines, the school development plan and relevant timetables. She may also wish to have information about stock suppliers, available funds and the process for ordering materials. Some of this may have been given to all candidates for the post but it is advisable to ensure that the new colleague has a complete set of relevant information.

The initial visit may be followed by others, perhaps in the holidays, one of which might be a formal induction when all the relevant details of the appointment are discussed and confirmed. Figure 7.8 outlines some of the information that a newly appointed member of staff may find useful. Some schools may consider compiling a pack of information to give to new teachers and also to new governors whose needs, while not the same as a newly appointed teacher, are similar. Once colleagues have such information at their finger tips they can concentrate on their professional duties and responsibilities.

1 *Terms of employment and conditions of service*

- Normally provided by LEA but may need checking and explaining
- Salary and methods/date of payment

2 *School organisation*

- Details of start/break/meal/finish times and dates of terms
- List of duties and playground supervision
- Basic routines for entering, leaving building, playtime, lunchtime, visits, out of school activities
- Staff meetings and parent meetings
- Fire drill and first aid material
- Arrangements of staff facilities, provision and payment for refreshments

3 *The school*

- Names and responsibilities of staff including ancillaries, helpers, caretaker and secretary
- Policy on marking, discipline, pupil and staff records, registers, dinner money, absenteeism
- Arrangements for children with special needs
- Layout of the school
- Organisation and allocation of classroom and other facilities such as the hall, library and special equipment
- Arrangements for consulting and being consulted by other colleagues, headteacher and parents
- Governors' meetings and names of governors
- Arrangements for Assembly

4 *The post*

- Timetable and working arrangements
- Curriculum documents
- Stock and equipment availability and ordering
- Responsibilities and duties
- Agreed targets and priorities
- Staff development and further training
- Arrangements for staff review interviews
- Communication within the school

5 *The locality*

- Details of catchment area including transport and shopping facilities
- Other local amenities
- Teachers' centre
- Community involvement in school
- Accommodation and nearby schools

Figure 7.8 Checklist for induction programme

Chapter 8

Managing human resources

The most valuable resource available in any school is its staff. Teachers and support staff make the most significant contribution to the success of any school. As was seen in the previous chapter, much thought and effort goes into the effective selection and induction of staff. If the staff are to give their best to the school and its children then as much care has to be devoted to managing them, the human resources in the school, as was taken over appointing them in the first place.

The effective management of staff begins with the creation of a framework within which teachers can teach and children can learn. Headteachers and senior staff have the major responsibility for creating these conditions. The governing body also has an important role to play in supporting the staff as they seek to create the ideal conditions in which children may develop. Furthermore, the soundest of frameworks is based on a clear, agreed sense of purpose within which roles and responsibilities are defined and understood. This sense of purpose will find its expression in the school development plan. The roles and responsibilities will be defined in and communicated by the job description. It should be noted, however, that, whereas responsibilities are clearly defined, the same is not always true of roles, such as that of deputy headteacher or curriculum coordinator. People often need time to grow into such roles. The processes of appraisal, review, induction and development play an important part in enabling both teaching and non-teaching staff to do this.

The creation of a good learning environment in primary schools is a responsibility shared by the headteacher and staff who must all play a significant part through effectively managing the human resources in the school. We have seen in earlier chapters that the aims statement and the school development plan are used to establish a common purpose for the school. In turn careful organisation of the curriculum and the provision of opportunities for teacher professional development can provide a sound foundation on which the management of the school can be based. Headteachers and senior staff will also need to:

- set high professional standards in such areas as teaching, displaying children's work, and communicating with parents;
- show a high level of personal involvement so that they are seen to be playing a full part in the daily routines of school life;
- be available to their colleagues for discussions on professional matters and to give help, advice and support;
- be interested in individual teacher development and take an active part in the professional development of all staff;
- give a lead in establishing and using the aims of the school and in achieving the objectives embodied in the school development plan;
- encourage the participation of all staff in the setting and achieving of objectives, the formulation of plans and decision-making;
- help staff to evaluate their own work and that of the children and to use those evaluations to inform planning for the future.

(adapted from Nias 1980: 260)

If all of this is to be achieved all staff must be part of a communication system that works. They must have responsibilities and tasks delegated to them effectively. Above all, they must make the best use of the time that they have at their disposal. If the staff of any school are its most valuable resource, time is the scarcest resource. One of the most useful management skills that any teacher can have is to be able to manage time well. Effective time management is vital for all members of the staff in every school because people must be able to organise themselves before they can manage others or create the conditions in which others can work or learn to the best of their ability.

THE EFFECTIVE MANAGEMENT OF TIME

Different people work best in different ways and at different times. Some work best in the morning, others in the afternoon or evening. Some work best in a quiet, well-organised environment, while others may be happiest working in noise and chaos. Staff in primary schools have limited choice over when they work, but to manage time effectively they need to know something about their own work patterns. There is no single best work pattern, nor is there a best way to manage time. It is possible to establish some clear guidelines to help all colleagues make even more effective use of the time that they have at their disposal. This begins with knowing accurately how the available time is being used.

One way of finding this out is to keep an activity log. This involves recording all the things that are done during at least three working days. Note for each separate activity the time started and finished and a brief description of what was taking place (see Figure 8.1). Although it is difficult to do, the activity log should be kept up to date throughout the day because

Method

Start a new sheet for each day, and use as many sheets as you need for the day.

Record each separate activity in the order in which it occurs. Enter start time, finish time, a brief description of what happened and a note of the total time spent.

If an activity is unplanned, but requires immediate action, mark your entry with a star *.

Keep the log up to date during the day.

If you find it inconvenient to carry separable log sheets around, use a notebook.

At the end of each day's entries note anything which made that day different or caused special problems (e.g. teacher off sick).

Example

From–to	Activity	Time spent
8.15–8.35	Drive to School	20 mins
8.35–9.00	Daily administration	25 mins
9.00–9.20	Assembly	20 mins
9.20–10.00	Interview with parent	40 mins
10.00–10.45	Teaching	45 mins

Remember: An activity is anything you do, including meal breaks, driving, talking, waiting, etc.

Figure 8.1 Keeping an activity log

at the end of the day it is not easy to remember the times and precise nature of events with any degree of accuracy. A note should be made of anything during the day that caused problems or made the day atypical.

Once the log is completed it is possible to analyse how the time was spent and to consider ways of using time more effectively. To do this it is necessary to know what the main priorities, tasks or targets were for the period of time for which the log was being kept and also what were the important tasks and what were the urgent ones. Important tasks contribute towards achieving main objectives or completing main tasks, while urgent tasks may be relatively trivial. Important tasks should, therefore, be given significant amounts of time, while urgent tasks should have less time expended on them.

As a result of this analysis it might be asked, Was too much time spend on trivial but urgent work rather than on important tasks? Other questions can also be asked about the activity log to help identify actions that can be reduced or eliminated. Was too much time spend at the start and the end of the day in social chatting? This question should not be taken to imply that social contact is unimportant. Effective school management depends, in part, on giving attention to social as well as professional concerns. Structured times should exist for staff to talk with each other, but this has to be placed in the context of the whole working day. This can lead to a further question: Was the best use made of times when most people are together? Similarly, was too much time used waiting to see colleagues or making unnecessary journeys? Was sufficient time allocated to handle paperwork as soon as it comes in or at a pre-determined time so that the in-tray does not overflow and information can be passed on quickly to colleagues who might need it? It helps to try to handle paperwork a limited number of times. If time can be set aside to deal with post regularly then most items only need to be handled once or, at most twice. To achieve this a decision must be made immediately about every item's importance, urgency and the action to be taken, if any. A few items, such as requests for detailed information about children or budget matters, may have to be left until relevant information can be collected, but this should be initiated immediately and time planned to write the necessary report.

The activity log can also be used to identify ways of reducing unplanned events that take up time. What were the unplanned events on the activity log? How much time did they take up? It may not be possible to predict when such events will happen, but we can plan time in such a way as to create the opportunity to deal with them while not wasting that time. Try not to organise time so that every scheduled event follows on immediately from the next. Leave small gaps so that simple tasks can be dealt with and tasks not completed through unforeseen events finished. Is it possible to use the knowledge that we all have about the ways things happen in school to predict events such as parents requiring urgent attention and to allow time for them? This time might be allocated to relatively trivial tasks that can easily be re-scheduled in the event of an interruption. Is it possible to spot other problems before they happen? If an unplanned event seems to be urgent, what might happen if it is not dealt with? Could it be left, dealt with at a more convenient time or delegated to a colleague? The answer to many of these questions depends on having a clear view about what the current priorities are.

In many primary schools, however, the only person able to respond to the urgent or unusual situation, however, trivial it may be, is the headteacher. Many headteachers are tempted to troubleshoot or deal with trivia which could well be left to somebody else at another time (Laws and Dennison 1991). In some schools the deputy may also be free, and in a few schools coordinators have non-contact time. Care must be taken to use this time wisely and to avoid, as far as possible, erosion by allowing staff to deal with the trivial and unimportant.

Similarly, the headteacher might be the only person available to cover the teaching of a staff member who is sick or out of school for professional reasons. Headteachers may also want to teach to provide examples of good practice, to have the opportunity to work with colleagues or with specific groups of children. In some schools the headteacher may be the only person with a particular curriculum expertise. This all has to be taken into account when analysing the use made of staff time. Headteachers should be clear about why they are doing various tasks and should prioritise their use of time.

All members of staff should be clear about what their priorities are. In some cases those priorities will be derived from the school development plan. In others they will be related to whole school, curriculum, year group or classroom responsibilities. These priorities can then be used to plan time on a weekly or longer-term basis. It is unrealistic to expect that any teacher can control all of his or her time. There are too many competing demands in schools for this to be the case. Classroom teachers may only be in direct control of between 10 per cent and 20 per cent of their total time in school, while headteachers may be able to control 70 per cent or more of their working day. Nevertheless every teacher will have some time that can be allocated to specific tasks.

This is done by making a list of all the jobs that may have to be done over the planning time period of, say, a week. Each job should then be given a rating of A, B or C. A tasks are important because they make a vital contribution to achieving main priorities, and urgent because they must be done in the next week. B jobs are important but not necessarily urgent at the present time. C tasks are those that it would be nice to do if time allows. Now look again at the A jobs and rank them in order of importance, calling the most important A1, the next most important A2 and so on. Having graded the tasks, the jobs to do list can be used to plan how time will be spent during the next week.

For the jobs rated A, estimate how much time each one will take; identify those jobs like writing a report, that depend on receiving information from colleagues; make a distinction between those jobs that need a large block of uninterrupted time and those which, although they may need a long time, can be done in small sections or can easily be picked up and put down again. It is also important to establish if access to certain equipment, say a word processor or photocopier, may be necessary. Establish what time is available during the next week, that is what time is left unscheduled after meetings, teaching time and other pre-arranged events are taken into consideration. Decide what type of time it is. Is it likely to be protected time or time when interruptions are likely? It is now possible to begin to plan when A jobs will be done by fitting them in to the most appropriate time slots based on the amount and type of time required for each. Remember to allow time for unplanned events and for information to come from colleagues where this is necessary. If there is any time left over the B and C jobs can be treated in the same way.

Once the planning is completed, it should be implemented and reviewed. No plan is perfect and every plan will need to be revised. The estimates of the time required to complete particular tasks, especially key or routine ones, should be checked and the actual time taken recorded for future reference. Time for planning and thinking ahead can be incorporated. Headteachers and senior staff should be seen to be planning their own time effectively and should encourage their colleagues to do the same. Headteachers and deputies should also ensure that they spend some time together each week to discuss whole school issues. They, like every member of staff, must have a break in the middle of the day. All members of the primary school staff should also examine the effect of their time management on others, especially where they are responsible for the work of colleagues. Such responsibilities must be allocated fairly and carefully. This means that all delegation must be done effectively. This will also maximise the use of time throughout the school.

DELEGATION IN SCHOOLS

Delegation of tasks within primary schools is inevitable since no one person can do all the work or have all the necessary expertise. Common policies and systems, agreed priorities, objectives and targets and established practices provide a framework within which delegation can take place. All staff should be involved in making decisions about such matters. There are, however, some matters that cannot be delegated. Headteachers have the day-to-day responsibility for the organisation and management of the school. Where a task is delegated which is part of the work of the delegater, the responsibility for the task cannot be delegated. If, for example, a headteacher delegates the writing of a policy document to a teacher, the headteacher is responsible for the document when it is produced.

Delegation can be, in a very real sense, part of professional development if tasks are delegated effectively. Sometimes, however, tasks are dumped and the responsibility abdicated by senior staff who give tasks or parts of tasks that they do not want to do to junior colleagues without proper training, support resources or supervision. Delegation is, therefore, the transfer of a task, or set of tasks, and the resources and responsibility to carry out the work from one person to another with appropriate professional support. This may involve a headteacher delegating a curriculum task to a teacher with responsibility for that curriculum area. It may be a teacher giving a task to a classroom assistant or even to a parent helping in the classroom. It may be a school secretary assigning work to a part-time secretarial assistant. Whatever is being delegated, the process should always be carried out carefully.

Every act of delegation should be carefully planned. This plan will have five main elements. The first is the precise identification of what is to be delegated. The second is the identification of the person to whom the work will be delegated. The third is the training of that person prior to the work being delegated. The fourth is the identification of resources and the setting of appropriate deadlines. The fifth is monitoring and reviewing progress during and after the delegation process. A thorough delegation plan will be written out to ensure that all key questions have been answered and that none of the main stages have been omitted.

Delegation must begin by identifying appropriate whole tasks that might be delegated. This can be done by asking the following questions:

- Which of my tasks can be done by some or all members of the teaching, secretarial or support staff?
- Which of my tasks make only a small contribution to the total success of the school?
- Which of my tasks take up more time than I can afford or could be done more efficiently by someone else?
- Which of my tasks are not related to my key targets?
- Which of my tasks are really the day-to-day responsibilities of a colleague?
- Which of my tasks cause problems when I am away because nobody else can cover effectively for me?
- Which of my tasks would enhance the professional development of colleagues if they were given the responsibility?
- Which of my tasks do I do because I enjoy doing them, but which could be done by others?

Once tasks have been identified in response to these questions it should then be possible to identify named colleagues to whom some or all of the tasks might be delegated. It is necessary to bear in mind which members of staff should be performing the task in question; who can already perform the task or could do so after training; who might benefit from the experience; who is overloaded and who is not. The answer to these questions help to identify those to whom tasks can and should be delegated. These are the first stages in effective delegation (see Figure 8.2).

When identifying colleagues to whom tasks might be delegated it should be remembered that any individual's commitment to or membership of the staff team will vary over time and according to issues and tasks. Motivation is a significant factor in establishing and sustaining such commitment. All individuals have certain strengths and needs. Maslow (1954) suggested five factors that influence all teacher's commitment to their work. Each factor will influence everybody but in different degrees and combinations which help to determine the relationship between individual and their professional

Plan delegation	Decide what is to be delegated and to whom. Identify the objective. Decide standard of work required and success criteria. Consider suitability, experience and expertise.

Identify person	Decide how much training, guidance and support are
	    needed.
	Discuss plan with person. Make clear why task is
	    being delegated and the benefits to the person
	    and the school.

Organise training	Brief and train member of staff.
	Define the task and its limits clearly.
	Define authority limits clearly.
	Share expertise and arrange for skills to be practised
	    where necessary.
	Agree levels of resourcing.
	Discuss and agree success criteria.
	Establish time limits and deadlines.
	Agree how performance will be monitored and
	    reviewed.

Implement plan	Inform all relevant people of what has been delegated and to whom. Be available to give advice. Monitor outcomes not process. Encourage but do not interfere.
Evaluate plan	Appreciate and praise what colleague has achieved. Ask colleague to review performance. Ask if problems arose and how they were overcome. Check that objectives were achieved and success criteria met. Discuss process adopted. Agree any follow-up tasks and who does them. Identify ways to improve performance next time.

Figure 8.2 Stages in effective delegation

activities. Colleagues might, for example, have basic needs-related survival. They will obviously be motivated by the need to earn money and, to the extent that they believe that they are justly rewarded, they can be expected to function reasonably well. When, on the other hand, such people feel that their rewards are not adequate for what is being expected of them, then motivating them will involve paying attention to basic rewards. Closely related to the survival need is that of security. This is especially powerful in times of change and reorganisation if redundancy, redeployment or being required to face something new and unknown may be involved. The remaining three needs constitute what Maslow termed higher order needs. These are the need to have an acceptable self image, the need to be able to do things that are useful and meaningful and the need to have opportunities for personal growth and development. McClelland (1951) restated these higher order needs as the need for achievement, for affiliation or friendship and for power.

- The need for achievement expresses itself in a desire to improve one's own job performance through personal effort and the wish to receive feedback on the quality of that performance. Colleagues with a strong achievement need may have tasks delegated to them which give more responsibility, a more interesting activity, freedom to plan, control and implement a change or an opportunity to improve and use skills and expertise.
- The affiliation need leads colleagues to be concerned with developing and maintaining good relationships within the staff team. Appropriate delegated tasks here will include those which provide opportunities to work with, support or help other members of the primary school team.
- The power need finds expression in a desire to achieve results by working through other people. This can be met by delegating tasks which give responsibility for the work of colleagues, which involve planning and implementing a long- or medium-term project across the school or which link to the management of the school as a whole.

Delegation should always be based on an understanding of the person to whom the task responsibility is to be delegated. It should never be undertaken without some form of training or practical support, although this is unlikely to mean a long-term secondment or an in-service course. Training prior to delegation should be done in school, normally by the person whose job is being delegated. Government grants for in-service training are now delegated to schools and each school has training days available. These are intended to do far more than provide training for delegated tasks but they can provide resources, especially time, for such training to take place within the school's existing budget. Briefing, demonstration, coaching or working alongside a more experienced colleague will normally be used to prepare a colleague to receive a delegated task. Such preparation is vital to gain the commitment of the person to whom the task is being delegated.

Any necessary training should be done before delegation, not after the person to whom the task has been delegated has started to carry out his or her new responsibilities. Training should cover a number of areas.

- It should begin by explaining what is to be delegated and why.
- The areas of responsibility and the nature of the tasks must be clearly and precisely defined, the objectives agreed and the scope of the authority to be delegated established. People to whom the tasks are being delegated

need to know what they are able to do and when they must consult or ask for advice. Can they sign letters, order materials, involve colleagues or take decisions without referring back?

- If the delegated task requires the person to whom it has been delegated to exercise new skills or to use ones which have become rusty through lack of practice, then relevant practice, guidance and support must be given. This must be organised in such a way as to enable mistakes to be made without damaging the confidence of the person or inhibiting the performance of the task.

- The resource limitations of the task must be defined. How much money is available, if any? Can money be spent up to an agreed total without reference to a higher authority? How much staff time can be used and how much secretarial and support help will be forthcoming?

- It must be agreed how performance will be judged. Nobody can ever be expected to take on new responsibilities without making mistakes, but what are the success criteria that the person receiving the task has to achieve and by when? This should be specified as part of the initial briefing before delegation takes place. There may also be times when a written note confirming the details for the delegation will be useful and may prevent later confusion. The success criteria should be specified. If this is done the colleague to whom work is being delegated will be able to assess how well the job is being done, as will the person who was responsible for delegating it.

Once decisions have been taken then the person delegating the task must ensure that everyone knows what has been delegated to whom and what the implications are for the work of other colleagues in the school. In this way confusion about areas of responsibility can be avoided and effective communication maintained.

The delegator must agree with her colleague on how performance will be monitored and when reporting back will be necessary. The monitoring of somebody attempting a complex task for the first time should be regular and frequent. Evaluating a small task may be left until the work is finished. It is the outcomes or results that should be evaluated rather than the process. If the success criteria are being achieved then the process is appropriate even if it is different from that employed by the person who previously carried out the work. Possible improvements in the process used can be discussed when the whole task is reviewed after completion.

Delegation is most likely to be effective if all parties are well-prepared and the process is well-structured. The delegator must also take into account the likely future career development of the person to whom the task is being delegated. Will the task, for example, enable a classroom teacher to gain or extend expertise in a curriculum area and thus enhance his or her prospects of promotion? Is it possible to identify whole-school tasks to delegate to more senior and experienced staff to improve their prospects of successfully obtaining a promotion if they so wish? Do the tasks delegated to the deputy reflect her position and career development needs?

Some of the most onerous tasks in the management of primary schools involve the establishing, implementing, monitoring and reviewing of policy. Deputy headteachers who are regarded by their headteachers as having the potential for promotion may benefit by having such tasks delegated to them. Deputy headteachers who want promotion may need to show that they have managed aspects of the school, have curriculum expertise, can produce written reports and have experience of conducting appraisals. Delegation in this context can be both developmental to the deputy headteacher and supportive for the headteacher.

The essence of effective delegation is planning, empowerment, monitoring and communication. The appropriate information must be communicated both to the person being given the new responsibilities and to all other relevant members of the school community, including governors, parents and even children where necessary. Communication with the staff team is as vital to the success of the delegation process as it is to all other aspects of primary school management.

COMMUNICATION IN SCHOOLS

Attentive communication in primary schools is an extremely complex topic. A thorough coverage of it would deal with everything from formal policy-making at senior management level to informal discussions with parents. Such an analysis is beyond the scope of this book. Instead this section will examine the ways in which day-to-day communications within schools can be made more effective than they often are.

Before looking at this in detail, however, some of the more general problems with communication systems in schools will be identified and suggestions made about how these might be overcome. Problems with communication in schools tend to be associated with four aspects of the process:

1 The senders of the communication

- Do they have something to communicate?
- Do they really want to share it?
- Do they understand it sufficiently to communicate it?
- Is the meaning clear to the receiver?

2 The receivers of the communication

- Have they interpreted the message accurately?
- Is the message important enough to demand attention?
- Are they able to respond to the message?
- Do they want to respond to the message?

3 The method of communicating

- Has the most appropriate method been chosen?
- Has the best time to communicate been chosen?
- Can the message be distorted in delivery?

4 The purpose or intended outcome

- Is the purpose clear?
- Are the receivers able to achieve the purpose?
- Will they want to achieve the purpose?
- Are the deadlines and other constraints realistic?

From the above list of potential problems it can be deduced that effective communication is about initiating or preventing action, or providing or requesting information on which future action can be based.

If communication in primary schools is to be effective then this must be recognised. All communication, therefore, must focus the nature and quality of the action that is required as a result of communicating with colleagues.

Communication is often treated as an end in itself rather than what it should be, a means to an end. Thus, the well-produced and apt memo, the carefully chosen phrase are regarded as the epitome of good communication when, in fact, this is far from being the case. Effective communication in the context of primary school management is the link between thought and action or behaviour. It is the transmission of ideas, hopes, data, feelings, intentions or opinions in order to generate actions. Where such action does not take place or is not carried out in the way intended by the communicator, then the communication has not been effective, however elegant it may appear.

Within a group such as the staff of a primary school there is often so much that has to be communicated that the tendency is to try to communicate too much at any one time. This leads to confusion and to a failure by both sender and receiver to identify clearly who is meant to do what as a result of the communication. Communication overload can also mean that inappropriate types and styles of communication are used. Colleagues may be given complex information verbally when it ought to be put in writing; people are asked for a decision on an important matter without being given time to consider it; individuals or groups are told about certain matters when they should have been consulted or asked when they should have been instructed.

Both the sender and the receiver of the communication should be clear about what the objectives of it are: whether it is simply to inform or request information or whether it requires specific action by a certain time. This should be unambiguously stated. Effective communication demands that the message should be clear and transmitted in a style that is acceptable and

Why?
The basic reason for communication is to get someone else to do
something.

What?
Spell out exactly what the received is to do. Making the messages precise
and to the point saves time (and money, if using the telephone).

Who?
When something has to be done tell the person who has responsibility for
it and make sure that everyone affected by it is told.

When?
If there is a message for someone it is usually best to tell her now. Putting
off communications can result in forgetting, or in a build-up of work. If there
is a deadline a reminder can be given at the right time.

How?
Choose the simplest and most direct method to communicate.

Check
Check that the other person grasps what she has to do. Check that it has
been done.

Figure 8.3 Making communication work

understandable. Figure 8.3 outlines a number of points to be considered if simple communication is to work effectively.

Communication in primary schools will be more effective if all the staff recognise that they have responsibility to ensure that the system works. This means that they play their part by reading notices, opening letters and dealing with them, checking pigeon holes and providing information when requested to do so. Communication can always be improved. A good way to start this improvement is by asking staff to describe and comment on existing practices. This enables them to begin to evaluate the school's communication system, to say how it works from their point of view and to make recommendations for its improvement.

The communication system within the primary school should also be managed by identifying its main components and their purposes, and then giving to specific people the responsibility for ensuring that the different parts of the system work (see Figure 8.4).

Everyone can make communication more successful by bearing in mind the following questions:

- What is the purpose of my communication?
- What are my objectives and are they clear?

Staff room noticeboard
Relevant information is displayed on the noticeboard under the headings of: Administration, Inset Courses and General Information. A hall timetable, together with assembly and playground rotas are on permanent display. (Deputy headteacher responsible. All staff to read).

White noticeboard
Notices which require the immediate attention of all staff are recorded on a separate, white noticeboard. (All staff use and read daily.)

Weekly notices
Current information is filed in a blue ring binder and stored in the staff room. This information is updated each week. (School secretary responsible. All staff to read).

Staff diary
Special events, meetings, courses and visits are recorded in the staff diary which is kept on the staff room table at all times. The majority of these dates are entered by the headteacher at the beginning of each week. However, staff are asked to enter information which is specific to them or their area of responsiblity. This diary serves to inform all staff about current activities and must be ready each day. (Headteacher responsible. All staff to read daily.)

Busy book
A Busy book which contains day-to-day information requiring the attention of specific members of staff, is circulated by the deputy headteacher.

Minutes of meetings
The minutes of both staff and senior management meetings are confidential. They are recorded in appropriate books and circulated by the deputy headteacher to relevant staff.

Miscellaneous
Medicines
All medicines must be given by parents to secretary to record in the medicine book. Medicine is stored in the school office and administered by the secretary or the headteacher and the book signed. (Secretary and headteacher responsible).
Building maintenance
All staff are required to complete a building maintenance form for all building repairs. This should be given directly to the caretaker for action. (All relevant staff responsible.)
First Aid
Minor injuries are dealt with by the ancillary staff, dinner ladies or teacher first aider. First Aid equipment is stored in the cupbard in the school office together with a list of the children with specific medical conditions. LEA Guidelines concerning First Aid are adhered to.

Figure 8.4 Communication in school

- Is the method chosen the most appropriate for the audience and the content of the message?
- Who is the message for?
- Are they the most appropriate people to receive this message?
- How should I communicate? Which method or combination of methods should be used and which style is best suited to my target audience?
- When should I communicate? Is one particular time better than another?
- Where – to what address or location – am I sending this communication?
- If the communication is written how do I check that it has been received?
- Have I established controls to get feedback on whether the message has been correctly received and acted upon?

Sometimes communication in a school can break down almost completely. This can result in a disciplinary or grievance procedure. Some guidelines about how to conduct such procedures and how to avoid them are given in Appendix 1. Fortunately such procedures are rare. Primary school colleagues normally work well together and communicate well.

Successful communication in primary schools can take a variety of forms which may be divided into three main categories:

- verbal, including planned or unplanned discussions, face-to-face encounters, small or large meetings and use of telephones;
- written, including notices, notes, memos, reports, letters, position papers and policy documents.
- visual, including posters, diagrams, displays of work, photographs, pictures, year planners and flow charts.

Much of the daily communication in primary schools is spoken rather than written. This may be informal, as in a brief discussion of a professional matter or formal, as in a pre-arranged and planned meeting between a group of teachers. Where any such verbal communication is part of the total process of school management, rather than a social activity, there are a number of ways to improve its effectiveness. Preparing, checking understanding, listening and building agreements are all part of that process. In order to be successful in face-to-face communication where it is important to influence or to negotiate an agreement:

1 Prepare

- Define your own aim clearly.
- Predict the other person's aim and whether there might be a point of compromise.
- Prepare your case, collecting any information you need.
- Predict and plan how to overcome any major objections that may be raised.

2 Question

- Use closed questions to check facts.

  How many children did you take?
  Precisely when did it happen?

- Use open questions to encourage others to talk, explain or put a point of view.

  What are your opinions about—?
  Can you explain what happened—?
  How do you think we should tackle—?

- Use probing and reflecting questions to check or explore a point further.

  What makes you say that?
  Can you tell me more about—?
  How do you know?
  What changes have you noticed since—?

- Avoid using leading questions because they produce false impressions of agreement and consensus.
- Avoid a series of questions because only one may be answered at a time.
- Avoid jumping in too quickly because you will miss a good point or an agreement.
- Listen.
- Do not interrupt: it only irritates. Let the other person finish speaking unless she is straying too far from the point.
- Concentrate on what is being said. Do not think about the next point that you want to make.
- Hear what is actually being said not what you want to hear.
- Note key points. Summarise the most important points either mentally or in writing.
- Be objective. Do not let your judgement or interpretation be clouded by your opinion of the other person.
- Evaluate. Weigh up what is being said.
- Separate fact from opinion and base your view on fact.
- Decide the real meaning. Sometimes you have to look beyond the words and consider tone of voice, body language and what is not being said.
- Communicate: present your case, keeping it brief and using a few strong facts and as little opinion as you can to support your argument. Put your case with confidence, emphasising essential points to hold the other person's attention.
- Listen carefully to what the other person says. Look for opportunities to agree.
- List objections. Itemise each one and deal with each in turn, checking understanding first. Choose the most persuasive way to respond to objections.

Objections often arise from misunderstandings, so clarify key points to avoid this happening. If the objections are based on new information or ideas, you will need to modify your approach rather than reject the other person's case.

- Question frequently to clarify points, to check understanding, to make progress and to get the other person to build on your case.
- Make positive proposals starting with those areas in which agreement is most likely, leaving difficult issues until last.

3 Agree

- Check feelings about proposals. Ask: 'How do you feel about—?'
- Look for solutions together. Ask: 'How can we—?'
- Bargain to reach agreement. Build consensus.
- Watch for signals that the other person is ready to agree a deal.
- Close the deal speedily, spelling out what has been agreed so that there is no misunderstanding.
- Agree actions, who will carry them out and by when.
- Make this clear by stating what you will do; by asking the other person to do things; and by writing this down together with agreed ways to follow up what is to be done and a time scale.

If all members of staff in primary schools can prepare themselves and conduct face-to-face discussions in this way, then such encounters will become even more productive. The key to all this is listening. All effective influencing and negotiating depends on listening rather than on putting a forceful case. A good negotiator will listen for about 80 per cent of the time and speak for only 20 per cent. The more colleagues feel that they are being listened to then the more amenable they are likely to be to reaching agreements. This is as true in meetings as it is in face-to-face discussions.

Meetings play an extremely important part in communicating in every primary school. Indeed, meetings are often regarded as a significant and integral part of the total system of communication. Unfortunately, many of them fail in this intent. Meetings must be well-planned, carefully organised, well-structured and productive if the time spent on them is to be justified. Many meetings, such as year, curriculum, staff, parents' and governors' meetings, can and should be scheduled on a regular basis over the school year. Those who are required to attend will then know on what dates, at what time and where the meetings will be held. A schedule of meetings can be published at the start of the school year, even if reminders, perhaps in the form of an agenda for the meeting have to be sent at a later stage. This gives people an opportunity to plan their use of time. The uncertainty about how long a meeting will last should also be removed. It is as important to have an agreed finishing time as it is to have a known starting time.

Careful planning of meetings starts with a decision about the purpose of the meeting. Some meetings are identified in terms of their membership, a year group or senior staff meeting for example. Others are defined by their frequency. Such designations give little clue as to the purpose of the meeting. In most cases this is because the meeting has several different purposes, depending on the items on the agenda. It is important to ensure that for each item, as well as for each meeting, the purpose is clear. Some of those purposes might include:

- **Giving information**   This might be about events, policies, arrangements or changes in administration and organisation. Here the meeting depends heavily on the person giving the information. The other members present will normally restrict their involvement to receiving the information and asking questions to clarify points that have not been understood.
- **Requesting information**   This may require the group to respond immediately or, more likely, to respond in a particular way by a given time to a specified person. All of this should be made clear to group members at the meeting, as should the limits to discussion. Staff at meetings of this kind may want to change the purpose to decision-making about whether or not the information is necessary, about the appropriateness of the method and the convenience of the deadline.
- **Giving instruction**   This is often in a staff development context when, for example, a group of teachers is being shown how to use an item of equipment or a new curriculum package. This needs to be organised so that staff have opportunities to practice and apply what they have learned.
- **Influencing colleagues**   This tends to take place when a course of action has been decided upon by the headteacher, governors or senior staff or has been imposed from outside. The staff team has to be persuaded to implement the decision. Here the main focus for discussion should be how to implement, rather than whether to implement. This can best be done by outlining to the group what the situation is and why the decision had to be taken in the way that it was. Comments can be invited but every effort should be made to elicit positive rather than negative points.
- **Motivating staff**   This often follows or coincides with an influencing meeting. The intention is to gain commitment from the group to a course of action and to generate enthusiasm for it rather than mere acceptance of it.
- **Problem solving**   Attempts at problem-solving in large groups are often unproductive but techniques such as brainstorming can be used to generate ideas from which a number of alternative solutions can be derived. These should then be examined in turn since the first suggestion may or may not be the best one. At the start of such meetings the problem and any possible time and resource constraints must be presented clearly and the discussion structured so that everybody has a real opportunity to make a contribution. Those who shout loudest do not necessarily have the best ideas.

- **Reaching a decision on a particular matter** Often these meetings are confused with other types of meetings because those who attend are not sure about the extent to which they are being informed of a decision that has already been made or are being asked to reach a decision during the meeting. This must be made clear from the outset together with the means of reaching the decision. Will this be done, for example, by majority vote of all those present or by the chair of the meeting after the 'feeling of the meeting' has emerged? When a decision is reached it should be announced in such a way as to leave no doubt in the minds of those present about what has been decided.

Knowing the intended outcome of any meeting and how it is to proceed will help to make meetings more effective. Other matters also require attention. Every meeting should have an agenda, items for which must be handed in to a specified person at least two weeks before the meeting to enable the agenda to be circulated at least a week before the meeting. This should state the date, place, time, duration of the meeting and who is to attend. It should list each item of business, making clear what the purpose is of that item by using terms such as: 'To inform . . .', 'To receive . . .', 'To consider . . .', 'To decide . . .'. The person introducing each item should also be identified. It helps with the smooth running of the meeting if the chair of the meeting has discussed each item in advance with the person presenting it to check on desired outcomes, possible alternatives and potential difficulties.

Where possible, a time limit should be imposed on the length of the discussion. Important items may thus receive sufficient time and urgent but trivial items are dealt with speedily. The sequencing of times on the agenda also requires some thought. After listing apologies from those unable to attend, which helps to ensure that they receive the details of the meeting, the minutes of the previous meeting should be considered and progress reported on various matters which were on the agenda of the last meeting. Briefing and information-giving items should always come before discussion of decision items to avoid decisions being taken without the benefit of the latest information. Items of business not included on the agenda may be raised at the end of the meeting under 'any other business', although it is a good idea to restrict these to notifications and requests rather than discussion or decision items. Those chairing meetings should remember that they do not have to deal with or answer all questions raised under any other business. It should not be a minefield full of the unexpected. The surprise question can be noted politely, and a forum for its discussion, or a timescale for its answer, arranged.

If papers are to be discussed they should either be included with the agenda or circulated a minimum of five working days before the meeting with an indication of what the outcome of considering the paper will be. Are members of the meeting being asked to receive, consider, accept, agree, or decide on some

Plan
Know the objectives of the meeting and what is to be achieved.

Communicate
Inform other team members what is to be discussed at the meeting and why.

Prepare
Prepare the room and the resources.
Put agenda in a sequence and allot appropriate time to each item.
Arrange your papers in agenda order.
Plan results for each agenda item.
Decide location, time, duration and notify all those involved.
Prepare yourself and brief those who are to lead the discussion.

Raise points
Declare aims and agenda at outset.
Work to agenda sequence, introduce each item in turn.
Put across information clearly and confidently.

Manage
Encourage constructive discussion.

Discussion
Keep discussion directed toward aims.
Remain in charge throughout.
Control the pace of the meeting.

Conclude
At the end of each agenda item present sharp, clear conclusions.

Report
Prepare a report on all important meetings. Make report short and concise, listing conclusions against each agenda item. If there are agreed follow-up actions, state who does what and when, and who will check.

Follow-up
Send out the minutes with highlighted decisions and actions to be taken, by whom and by when.

Check
That any agreed actions are successfully carried out.

Figure 8.5 The organisation of a meeting

aspect of the paper's contents? Are any recommendations in the paper easily identifiable? Is it known who will present the paper at the meeting and for how long that person will be allowed to speak? The chair of the meeting should discuss the paper with the person presenting it in advance of the meeting.

Those attending meetings should prepare themselves in advance by reading relevant papers and having views on what is being considered. This is especially true for the person chairing the meeting who must allow and encourage the discussion to flow. This can be done by prompting colleagues, asking open questions, suggesting alternatives and restraining the more vocal. This can be supplemented by inviting comments from specific individuals who have been briefed before the meeting or who have relevant expertise. Often the chair may need to clarify a point or check that everyone understands what is being said. Throughout the meeting the chair should summarise decisions taken and actions agreed.

Where a matter appears unclear it should not be ignored or left in the hope that it will become clearer at a later stage. Invariably this will not happen. Above all the chair must ensure that each item is concluded clearly and firmly.

A secretary and/or the chairperson should be responsible for recording the decisions and actions of the meeting. If absolutely necessary this can include voting figures, but voting should only be used as a last resort or to confirm a decision that is largely agreed. Where an action has been agreed and recorded, the name of the person responsible for it can also be minuted together with the deadlines set and, if relevant, the resources agreed. The minutes then provide both a record of decisions and a checklist for follow-up. Minutes should be circulated quickly so that staff can implement any necessary actions. The names of individuals responsible for actions can be highlighted on their copy of the minutes to draw attention to the relevant item.

To facilitate good decision-making and to prevent an overloaded agenda it is a good idea to specify the length of time which must elapse before any item can be reconsidered. This is useful where there is strong but divided opinion on a matter which can be tackled in different ways. It is less helpful where an item is subject to continual policy changes outside the school. Normally, however, the combination of a well-structured agenda, control from the chair and colleagues committed to making meetings work will enable those agenda items which are really important to the work of the primary school to be thoroughly discussed and sensible decisions taken. Equally, those matters which are not of central importance can be dealt with speedily and effectively.

From time to time it is worth evaluating the success of the meetings that take place in the school. This can be done by posing the following questions and taking appropriate action if the answer is unsatisfactory:

- Was the purpose of the meeting and/or of each agenda item clear to all those who attended?
- Was the attendance appropriate for the subjects being discussed?
- Were the participants adequately prepared for the meeting?
- Did the meeting achieve its purpose?

- What was the quality of the outcomes?
- Was there a clear definition of the actions to be taken, the person responsible, deadlines and a procedure for reporting back and following up?
- Was the time well used?

(adapted from Everard and Morris 1985: 52)

Effective meetings are not difficult to organise if they are well planned from the start and evaluated periodically. Figure 8.5 outlines what needs to be done from the earliest planning stage to circulating the outcomes. Meetings organised in this way will be an important and useful part of the communication system and time spend at meetings will be time well spent.

Chapter 9

Managing the financial and physical resources

The governing body is responsible for the allocation of the school's delegated budget and for the oversight of its financial management. Its decisions and processes parallel those in other areas of the management within the school, in that the authority and responsibilities of governors are largely delegated to the headteacher, senior staff, coordinators, postholders, class teachers and support staff. Each level of responsibility has its purpose, level of accountability and mandate to act. The common aim is to ensure that the budget is allocated as effectively as possible. The governors are publicly accountable to the annual meeting of parents. They must demonstrate that the finances allocated to the school have been used to best effect for the purchase of the staffing, premises, materials and externally provided services, required to ensure the effective delivery of the National Curriculum and religious education to the children who attend the school.

If the governing body chooses to delegate financial authority to the headteacher or to a finance sub-committee, this does not lessen or remove its ultimate accountability. All spending decisions should be made within the context of the school development plan, and provide the power to achieve its agreed priorities and objectives. The key role of the governors is to ensure the correct allocation of money, so that the essential resources of time, accommodation, staffing and materials are purchased in sufficient quantities and at the highest quality. In order to understand governors' responsibilities for the overall effective management of the school's financial and physical resources, and how they are supported in the day-to-day running of the school by the headteacher and staff, we need to consider the nature of delegated financial authority itself and the role of the finance sub-committee. We also need to consider the budget cycle, financial controls and systems, the management responsibility for effective audit and the need for a regular financial health check. The financial issues surrounding the school buildings which need to be considered include energy and maximising the use made of the premises as a suitable environment for teaching and learning.

DELEGATED AUTHORITY

Governing bodies, although accountable, must delegate genuine financial authority to either the headteacher, senior staff or a mandated finance sub-committee so that the day-to-day business of the school can proceed in an orderly manner. The Audit Commission makes it clear that: 'Schools should define the responsibilities of each person involved in the administration of school finances to avoid duplication or omission of functions and provide a framework of accountability for governors and staff' (1993: 4). It is the headteacher's responsibility to see established, and formally recorded in the minutes of a full governors meeting, exactly in which circumstances the governors, as a body, wish to make financial decisions and when and how financial authority is delegated elsewhere. There should be no room for misinterpretation. The regulations actively encourage governors to delegate financial responsibilities to the headteacher. This does not reduce or remove the governors' overall accountability or their right to make final decisions.

The governors should expect the headteacher to manage the day-to-day financial business of the school, to prepare budgets, present costed options for them to consider, and produce reports as required. The governing body should also minute its requirements for the management of non-public funds such as the school fund or the profits from fundraising events. Senior staff should be given clear discretionary rights to authorise expenditure to an agreed cost ceiling, and, when appropriate, authority to delegate funding to other members of staff, including the school secretary and caretaker. The school is going to obtain far more value for money if the person who is going to order and manage the stationery stock is given the stationery budget and authorised to find the best deal. The curriculum coordinator for science will not act with authority within the school if every decision for expenditure on science materials has to be made by the headteacher or a committee. If powers to authorise expenditure up to an agreed limit are to be delegated to the chair of governors, this too must be formally minuted. When considering to whom powers to authorise expenditure are given, governing bodies must be aware when there might be a conflict of interest and should keep a register of pecuniary interests of the governors and staff. Any links with local firms who might supply the school with goods and services must be public knowledge. 'It is important for anyone involved in spending public money to demonstrate that they do not benefit personally from decisions they make' (DES 1988b: para. 144)

THE FINANCE SUB-COMMITTEE

The governing body may decide to delegate some of its financial authority to a finance sub-committee so that an appropriate small group can manage the detail of the school budget. What it should do, what it should not do and how it does it, will be the individual decision of each governing body. Once agreed, the committee's purpose, powers, responsibilities, membership and quorum should be clearly stated in the minutes of a governors' meeting, where the quorum is two-thirds (rounded up) of those entitled to vote. The purpose of the sub-committee is to be helpful to the decision-making process, and not as a bureaucratic bottleneck. The governors should make clear exactly what levels and types of expenditure should be referred to the finance sub-committee, and which directly to the headteacher or members of staff. The finance sub-committee should not have to concern itself with minor expenses, or the allocation of budget heads which have already been agreed and authorised by the full governing body. It should feel empowered to advise on both the current year's budget, and be the focal point for budget building for subsequent years. It should expect to monitor accounts and advise on any budget which appears to be heading for an overspend or underspend long before the imbalance becomes a problem. This will require that the committee has high quality and up-to-date financial information.

The headteacher is entitled to attend, and should do so in order to inform and guide the committee as the accountable manager of the school. It is perfectly proper for non-governors to be co-opted on to the committee, but they may not vote. The exception to this, by the agreement of the governors, would be on matters relating to the use of school premises after school hours. It is not permissible for a member of the school staff to chair the committee. Decisions should be taken by majority vote, the chair having a second or casting vote. The committee must report back actions and decisions to the next full governors' meeting. The usual rules relating to notice of meetings, the record of those attending, the public availability of agenda, minutes and papers for inspection, apply also to sub-committees. If any governing body is uncertain of the regulations, it should seek legal advice from the LEA to ensure that correct practice is followed.

The responsibilities laid on a finance sub-committee might include:

- drawing up and recommending a budget for the year to the full governing body;
- monitoring, or assisting senior staff in monitoring the budget during the course of the year;
- in consultation with the headteacher, viring an agreed sum or percentage of the budget during the course of the year;
- ensuring that the school complies with the legal requirements of the LMS scheme, financial regulations and the local authority's contract standing orders;
- approving contracts above the value of the ceiling delegated to the headteacher;
- recommending a lettings policy to the full governing body and overseeing its implementation;

- preparing the finance section of the governors' annual report to parents;
- preparing papers which set out costed options for the consideration of the full governing body. An analysis of the financial impact of not replacing a retiring teacher, for example.

(adapted from Beckett and Hallworth 1993)

The finance sub-committee will work in close liaison with the full governing body and the headteacher, and within the framework of the annual budget cycle, in order to ensure that the money is allocated to the priority areas and budgets agreed by the governing body and as laid out in the development plan.

THE ANNUAL BUDGET CYCLE

The school receives its budget on an annual basis, usually at the very end of the previous financial year. Its size is determined by formula and by political decisions made at government and local level. Once the budget is known, governors need to make their key spending decisions, not in isolation, but as part of a cyclical planning process which probably started the previous autumn and has its rationale in the school development plan. The Audit Commission is clear in where priorities should be set:

The process of allocating the budget should not be an incremental process from one year to the next but should reflect, in monetary terms, the school's aims and objectives within the available budget. As the School Development Plan may lead to changes in priorities for expenditure in successive years, the emphasis should be on the objectives the school wants to achieve rather than on monetary inputs.

(Audit Commission 1993: 5)

Schools have become used to managing a budget which is allocated in the April, requiring them to produce an annual financial plan which does not coincide with the academic year. An April budget actually requires that the planning cycle starts in the previous September so that there is adequate time to cost and plan for the likely financial demands to be made upon it. As we demonstrated in Chapter 3, an effective development plan, must be subject to regular review in order to reaffirm that the objectives and priorities are still correct. The allocation of the budget is the mechanism which provides and empowers the staff to activate the plan and work towards the achievement of the objectives. They are thus inextricably linked, and any suggestion that the budget plan exists in separation from the curriculum plan is bound to reduce seriously the efficiency of the school. September, the start of the new academic year, is not only the point at which the revised development plan comes into force, but the point at which senior staff start to evaluate its validity, confirm their medium- and longer-term plans for the future, and identify ways in which the plan may have to be amended for the following year.

September to November

- Start of the school year and the implementation of the revised school development plan.
- Governors and staff confirm the centrality of the agreed aims and objectives for the school. This should be done formally at a staff meeting and at a governors meeting.
- Headteacher asks coordinators to carry out an initial audit of the likely curriculum, resource, professional development, premises and staffing needs for following September. Some items will continue from year to year, and will already have been agreed and included in the three-year plan. Other priorities will be identified in the audit of the current situation. Post-OFSTED inspection action plans may require a major re-examination of priorities and have staffing and resourcing implications.
- The headteacher and finance sub-committee monitor budget reports on a monthly basis. As this is the mid-point of the current financial year, it should be possible to transfer money from any underspending budget heads to overspending budgets or to contingency fund or to activate projects previously 'on hold'.
- Finance report to governors meeting.
- Priorities in development plan confirmed, three-year plan revised if necessary.
- Initial costing of prioritised budget for the following April.

Figure 9.1 The budget cycle from September to November

By January, the likely out-turn for the current year's budget should be reasonably clear. The unexpected and expensive still has plenty of time to happen, but the finance sub-committee should be able to spend most of the time available to them considering the probable size of the new budget and what it will mean for the school and its development plan.

In the majority of local authorities the final budget for the new financial year will be set in March. Calculations will be made and individual schools informed of their allocation.

In the April, the governing body will have come to terms with the size of the allocated budget and authorised spending allowance including the staffing budget for the new academic year.

The budget cycle we suggest above raises two fundamental questions: Is such a structured plan necessary in a small primary school where there is little time for managerial tasks? and Is it necessary when so large a proportion of the budget is spent on staffing and fixed costs? The answer to both questions is yes. Whatever the size of the school or the limited budget available for allocation, any expenditure has to be part of the overall plan for the school. The school exists in order to provide the best possible learning opportunities for its pupils. The way in which the school will work to achieve

January to February

- Indicative or likely budget announced.
- Indicative budget is matched with school's own prioritised budget for the following year. If this is to have any meaning, it must be derived directly from the costed development plan. This is why the revisions, and costing of the plan, should have taken place by the end of the previous term. If, for example, the plan calls for an alteration in staffing levels in the school, the budget implications must be clear and included in the figures to be matched against the indicative budget.
- Any likely carry forward or overspend from the current financial is added into the indicative budget.
- The development plan is revised in the light of the size of the revised budget. If the size of the budget demands a reduction in expenditure in the following year, the elements trimmed back must not be selected at random. The development plan should have laid out the priorities for the school in order of importance and the debate which produced the ranking order should have already taken place during the later stages of writing the plan.

Figure 9.2 The budget cycle from January to February

that objective is through its development plan. The correct allocation of the budget is the only way in which the plan can be effectively implemented. Therefore there has to be a plan, it has to be revised and recosted on a regular basis and it has to provide the framework within which all financial decisions are made. The headteacher should encourage the governors to establish such a planning cycle and to understand their role within it, the role of the finance sub-committee, the role of the headteacher and senior staff and the annual timetable which they must follow.

March
- Actual budget announced. Matched with indicative budget. SDP adjusted if necessary. Any reduction in budget should be managed within the priorities set out in the previously agreed development plan.
- Finance report and budget to governing body for ratification.
- SDP for September agreed. Budget heads allocated. The senior staff and coordinators are given their actual budgets for the following year, a clear statement of their authority to spend, and how and to whom they are accountable for obtaining value for money.

Figure 9.3 The budget in March

April

- Staffing implications of SDP implemented for September

- Budget holders free to spend within their agreed limits

- End of year out-turns calculated and audited

Figure 9.4 The budget in April

It is normal for the headteacher to be asked to prepare estimates of income and expenditure at appropriate periods in the budget cycle. As we have already demonstrated, much of the budget will have to be committed before the financial year starts, as it consists of the known and unavoidable costs of staffing, basic supplies and the school premises. Staffing will probably account for at least 80 per cent of the total net costs of the school. Staffing costs must be calculated accurately and allowance made for possible pay awards or incremental changes. Teachers salaries are agreed nationally, but the impact has to be carried within the school's budget, especially where governors have discretion over the precise point on a pay spine at which a teacher can be paid. The school development plan may call for a change in the staffing profile: more secretarial hours, the appointment of a maths specialist or a further classroom helper. Such major changes are only possible if the budget permits, or the departure of a colleague 'releases' a salary. Just because a Year 2 teacher has left, does not mean that a new Year 2 teacher is automatically appointed. If the audit stage in the development planning process has been accurate, the plan will show where the staffing need is greatest, and where the budget should be deployed. The plan may, in fact, suggest higher priorities than replacing the departing member of staff!

The headteacher must maintain an accurate staffing budget and profile it through to the end of the financial year. This will consist of a simple list of each member of staff employed within the school showing their individual salaries and on-costs and the total staffing budget. Several financial software packages used by schools do the monthly calculations automatically and show expenditure to date and the financial implications of each member of staff remaining in post until the end of the financial year. Vacancies and staff changes may result in budget availability, but all spending must be in accordance with the development plan. The costs of short-term supply cover must be allocated an adequate budget. Draft budgets can be based on previous years, but a school must never get into the position where teachers come into work when ill, because they feel guilty about 'costing the school money' in terms of a supply teacher. Any supply cover money left at the end of the financial year must be spent within the priorities in the development plan or carried forward. Such gains may be unexpected windfalls, but must be spent wisely and within the agreed plan. Unspent balances from government grants for training and professional development cannot usually be carried forward and the appropriate coordinator should ensure that such resources are spent during the year and according to the agreed priorities.

Schools are generally under-resourced and anxious to effect savings wherever possible. It is important to remember that any savings in staffing can only be achieved within the constraints of employment law and the statutory requirement to deliver a broad and balanced curriculum. Although we suggest a few ways to save money on the premises later in this chapter, savings on water and other energy costs must be realistic and achievable and are likely to be marginal at best. Health and safety priorities cannot be deferred. In extreme cases the LEA can carry out the necessary Health and Safety work without authorisation from the school and can forward the bill to the governors for payment. External maintenance contracts, for fixed PE equipment for example, cannot be dropped.

FINANCIAL CONTROL AND SYSTEMS

In order to safeguard both individual members of staff and the school itself, governors should lay down clear financial rules and regulations for the way the delegated budgets are to be managed. It should be absolutely clear what can be spent, how it should be spent, who controls the budget, who audits expenditure and who monitors the complete process. The protection of individual members of staff is also important, although the ideal might prove difficult to mange in smaller schools. At least two people, for example, should be involved in the receipt of money and the issuing of receipts. The governors' policies for financial systems and procedures should be recorded and reviewed on a regular basis and appropriate training and support provided for those who have to implement them. The governors should insist on some form of regular internal audit. This is not because of any suspicion that anyone is misusing public money, but is based on a recognition that genuine errors and miscodings can take place and are far better identified and corrected at an early stage and not months later when the error has compounded. Proper training is especially important if the school uses an administration and financial IT package.

If the school uses any sort of computer system to maintain records and process financial data it must ensure that it is registered in accordance with the Data Protection Act 1984. Back up copies should be made at least weekly and, preferably, kept off site. Disks kept on-site should be in a secure and fireproof container. Only named members of staff, such as the headteacher, deputy and school secretary should be able to access the data files. Only authorised software should be used to avoid possible pollution by viruses. Above all, the school's financial systems must permit audit and provide up-to-the-minute and accurate information to all those who need it. Governors and budget holders rely on this information as they make decisions and plan for the future.

The governors must ensure that adequate insurance cover is provided for all their liabilities, either through the school's own insurance policies or through the LEA. Such risks may include third party liability, property, money, personal accident, motor vehicles and fidelity guarantees to cover the loss of assets due to fraud or dishonesty on the part of employees. The school must guarantee total and appropriate insurance cover whenever pupils leave the school site during the working day or are in the care of staff. The staff must be completely aware of their personal responsibilities and insurance obligations if private cars are used for conveying pupils. Insurance arrangements should also cover the use of school property when off the premises. This will support a school policy which permits, for example, staff taking computers home or the school camera being used off-site on educational visits. Stockbooks, for all items over a value identified by the governors or LEA, must be maintained and checked on a regular basis. This is important so that the school list of resources is up-to-date, the principles of accountability are observed and accurate records are immediately available if the school is burgled. All but minor discrepancies in stockbooks must be reported to the governing body. Portable items should be coded with security markings. It is good practice to keep the main stockbook and supportive receipts off-site, so that they are readily available to insurance assessors in cases of fire or theft. The school must have a clear and public policy on loose money and personal valuables. Petty cash should never be left in desk drawers or handbags and wallets in places where opportunist sneak thieves can help themselves. Many schools provide a secure locker or cupboard for each member of staff, but everyone must be clear if there is any liability on the school or LEA if these are broken into. This knowledge must be available in the staff handbook, so that anyone leaving valuables in a locker or cupboard understands the potential risk they are taking. Advice on all security issues will be readily available from the crime prevention officer in the local police station, and on insurance matters from the local authority or the school's own insurer.

The proper administration of bank accounts is a fundamental financial control (Audit Commission 1993). In particular, regular bank reconciliations are essential. They prove that balances are correct and provide assurance that the underlying accounts have been properly compiled and are accurate. In considering petty cash, the Commission recommends that the governing body ensures that the size of the cash holding is appropriate, that it is only used for approved purposes, that proper records are maintained and that there are regular reconciliations and occasional spot checks to verify that the sums in hand are correct. The Commission further recommends that personal cheques should never be cashed against school funds, nor should short-term loans be permitted. If it is agreed that private telephone calls can be made from the school telephone, a proforma form requiring staff to record when they have made the call and its destination and duration is far better than an honesty box system. These can be totalled every half-term, and those billed asked to pay by cheque. This cuts down the amount of loose money in school, allows staff to use the telephone, and is more likely to be accurate. In any case, cash or postage stamps must never be kept in a desk drawer or convenient tin as this will be the first target of any sneak thief. The school secretary, or whoever is responsible for the office, should total the cash received at the end of every working day and lock it in the school safe. The school safe should never be used to store sums in excess of its insured limit. Headteachers must encourage those banking money to vary the time of day they do this and the route followed and to take every sensible precaution to ensure their personal safety. Non-public funds raised for the school by parent groups or the school itself, should be subject to the same financial rigour as other accounts.

At least two signatures should be required on any authorisation to withdraw money from all school bank or building society accounts, including those for school journeys and school funds. Money raised from school fêtes, concerts or from the sale of school photographs, should never be left in the school overnight, as thieves will know there are potential pickings to be had. If at all possible, two people should be present when envelopes containing sums of money are opened. This may seem labour-intensive in a busy school with slim resources, but it is sound financial practice.

PURCHASING

Governors should draw up guidelines to assist staff to whom the authority to purchase has been delegated, so that the delegated budget is spent to maximum effect for the benefit of the children. The governing body, as the final accountable authority, will delegate responsibility to the headteacher and senior staff, who in turn should give subject and phase coordinators the power to authorise spending to an agreed budget and within the framework established by the development plan. The normal decisions resulting from the comparison of the price and quality of like products will obviously continue in the case of most purchases, but governors are likely to set a single unit figure above which they will require written quotations and reserve to themselves the authority to purchase. The Audit Commission (1993) recommends that any decision to put an order out to tender should be framed within a policy set out by the governors. Such a policy should include the advertisement of the tender, compliance with EEC regulations, the procedure for the submission, receipt, opening and recording of tenders, the circumstances when financial or technical evaluation is necessary, acceptance of tenders, the form of contact documentation and cancellation clauses.

Orders for goods and services should always be written, preferably on pre-numbered forms. Any oral order must be confirmed in writing. Governors should make it clear that official order forms are only to be used to purchase items for the school itself and not to assist individuals to buy goods for their private use. This is especially important in relation to the purchase of computer equipment when the educational 'mark down' can be very attractive. As soon as an order has been placed, the appropriate budget must show the estimated costs as a commitment, so that accurate budget balances can be seen at any time. Ideally the person ordering the goods should not be the person signing for their receipt, although this is often not practical in smaller schools. No account should be passed for payment until the goods have been received, checked, coded and certified for payment. Any school with doubts about its financial procedures should take advice from the LEA.

AUDIT

The 1988 Education Reform Act makes it clear that the accounts of schools with delegated budgets will be subject to regular audit. In the case of LEA schools, the auditors will be appointed by the Audit Commission with a brief to assess the legality and regularity of financial affairs and to ensure that the authorities have made proper arrangements to secure value for money (Audit Commission 1993). Grant maintained schools are required to appoint external auditors upon incorporation. Schools are expected to give auditors full access to any premises, documents and assets the auditors consider necessary, and to provide any necessary explanations. The headteacher is to consider and respond to recommendations, report the results of audit reports to the governing body and detail any action to be taken by the school. The headteacher must also notify the auditors immediately of any suspected financial irregularity.

The Education (Schools) Act 1992 requires that the efficiency with which the financial resources made available to schools are managed must be inspected as part of formal OFSTED inspections. The 'efficiency' of the school is to be judged in terms of:

- the quality of financial management;
- the soundness of financial decisions;
- the efficiency and effectiveness with which resources are deployed to achieve the school's aims and objectives and to match its priorities;
- the efficiency of financial control;
- the assessment of any steps taken by the school to evaluate its cost-effectiveness.

(Audit Commission 1993: 2)

A FINANCIAL HEALTH CHECK

Schools will want to carry out a regular and systematic review of their various financial processes. *Keeping your Balance* (Audit Commission 1993) contains a very useful 'standards' questionnaire. It is used as the basis for OFSTED Inspections when inspectors report on the efficiency of the school. All schools would be well-advised to refer to it on a regular basis in order to reassure themselves that their financial systems are correct and functioning well. One section, for example, examines the organisation of responsibility and accountability. The key areas of role definition, limits of delegated authority, a register of pecuniary interests, internal control systems and compliance with financial regulations are set out in a table. Governors tick whether the required systems are in place, or whether action is needed to achieve it. The section on petty cash checks whether there is an agreed level of petty cash, whether clear responsibility is assigned, and that there is an agreement that personal cheques are not encashed. Concise, well thought through, non-bureaucratic systems, approved by the governors, mean that the machinery of the school functions smoothly, and releases the senior staff for their professional duties.

It is possible to lay out the roles and responsibilities of all those involved in the management of the school in the form of a table (Figure 9.5). Accountability will always stay with the governing body, but responsibility should be delegated as near to the point of delivery as possible. The governing body will commission the drawing up of trial and suggested budgets. The finance sub-committee will have its own specified responsibilities, will offer advice, provide information and commission detailed work from the headteacher and members of staff.

THE BUDGET AND THE SCHOOL PREMISES

Next to the staff themselves, the accommodation the school uses is the major resource available to advance the learning opportunities offered to the children. It is wrong to imagine that the quality of teaching and learning is bound to be better in bright, modern airy classrooms set in leafy suburbia, rather than in cramped neo-Victorian buildings where the windows are set too high to offer any view other than the sky. Thousands of such buildings have contained schools where the quality of teaching and learning have been second to none, but all teachers would agree that they would rather not work in adverse conditions. The governors and senior staff should, therefore, aim to use all parts of the school buildings as efficiently as possible, whatever the constraints, and have become adept in turning surplus accommodation into resource centres, parent rooms, library corners and work bases. As with any resource, the effective school will carry out a regular audit of its total accommodation, challenge current usage, evaluate the total needs of the children

Activity	Governors	Finance sub	Headteacher	S.staff/coords	Teachers	Support staff
Budget (overall)	Accountable delegators	Responsible advisers	Responsible adviser	Delegated responsibility advisers	Delegated responsibility advisers	Delegated responsibility advisers
Budget design	Accountable commissioner	Provider commissioner monitor	Provider commissioner monitor	Provider monitor	Provider	Provider
Budget links to SDP	Accountable commissioner	Provider	Main provider	Provider	Provider	Provider
Budget control	Accountable	Monitor	Information giver	Information giver	Information giver	Information giver
Purchaser	Commissioner	Monitor	Delegated responsibility advisers	Delegated responsibility advisers	Advisers	Delegated responsibility advisers

Figure 9.5 Accountability and responsibilty for finance

and seek to maximise the ways the building can be used. Some care needs to be exercised. If corridors are to be used as extensions to classrooms, this should not be at the expense of fire regulations. The teacher responsible for health and safety should use the annual visit by the local fire officer to check whether wall displays and corridor bookcases infringe fire regulations. It may mean that some areas contain fewer displays, but the safety of the children must be paramount.

A useful start point for the audit is an evaluation of the curriculum needs of the school. This might change if there is a major rise or fall in the school roll, but should quickly identify the need for a defined number of teaching spaces, resource and storage areas, areas for specialist work and teaching and an area where large numbers of children can all gather if wide spaces are necessary. If the curriculum needs of the children do not match the reality of the existing accommodation then, finance and physical constraints permitting, a programme to convert the building to something nearer the actual requirement should be part of the development plan.

Governors should be involved in the audit as they carry a wide range of responsibilities for the school buildings and will find being part of the audit extremely useful in giving them the curriculum context in which their plans for improving the accommodation can be based. A number of criteria can be used within the audit to see how well the school deploys its resources to the benefit of the children. These include the availability and condition of classrooms, storage and shared areas, toilets and the school ground and how they contribute to the raising of the standards of pupils' work and quality of learning. This analysis will lead into an evaluation of the efficiency with which the accommodation is used and whether specialist facilities are adequately provided. Are the curriculum needs of the children best met, for example, by housing all the library resources in the same room as that used by the peripatetic music staff for children's individual instrumental lessons? If not, how can the collective advice of staff and governors be used to improve the situation, and if not now, how in the future? What are the budget implications and how will any recommendation for expenditure be included in the school development plan, and at what level of priority? Every child has an equal right to physical access to the curriculum, and the removal of any constraints to mobility within the building should be a high priority. Governors and staff should evaluate whether the building is accessible to all pupils, including those with physical difficulties. Its acoustic and visual qualities should ensure access to the curriculum for all pupils including those with visual and hearing impairments. Toilets and changing facilities for pupils with physical disabilities should be suitably adapted and private. Support work should be in rooms of reasonable size and quality.

If the staff involve the governors in a detailed examination of the effectiveness of the ways in which the school uses its classrooms and teaching areas, they can give the governors a very wide range of information about how learning is managed in the modern classroom. Many governors were taught in different learning environments from those found in schools today and do not understand all of the implications of what they see in their own schools. It is important that they do so, and the accommodation audit is very useful in achieving understanding. Staff and governors can, for example, ask how appropriate is the accommodation for the teaching of specialist areas of the curriculum. If PE lessons are taking place in a hall also used for stacking dining tables and chairs, does this contravene health and safety regulations, and if so, what can be done? Is running water available in rooms used for art work? If not, how does this constrain the quality of the teaching and learning which has to take place there, and what can be done? Is television watched in rooms with suitable seating where each child can see the screen without straining? Are health and safety regulations observed? Do any lessons have to take place in inappropriate accommodation, and what is the impact of this on the learning outcomes?

Governors and staff must question whether the accommodation is appropriate to the age of the pupils as well as to any specialist subject being taught. Nursery and reception classes have different accommodation requirements from Year 6, not least in consideration of the need for sufficient space for the furniture. In each classroom, irrespective of the age band it serves, the reviewers need to check whether there is sufficient space for the grouping and re-grouping of pupils, and adequate space to accommodate practical areas as well as table-top work space for each child. Finally, everyone needs to assess whether the building is a good place to come to work in, either as a child, a teacher or member of the support staff.

The premises audit should include use at lunch times, in the evenings, at weekends and in the school holidays. Schools are a community asset and should seek to play their wider role through a positive attitude to availability outside the school day. Teachers are understandably concerned that misuse does not take place and good relations have been soured in the past by the thoughtless behaviour of those using the school in the evenings. Cigarette ends in classroom sinks, rifled cupboards and stiletto heel marks over a precious hall floor do not encourage invitations for return visits. Partnerships which respect the fact that the prime purpose of the building is its daytime use, but welcome responsible alternative users, form invaluable bridges between the school and the community it serves.

THE PREMISES: ENERGY

The school will need power and water in order to deliver the curriculum in an environment which is warm, safe, sanitary and well lit. It will also need to use energy directly within the curriculum as an essential learning and teaching resource. Energy costs are high and schools strive to reduce heating and electricity costs by sensible housekeeping, but savings will be comparatively small and senior staff will wish to guard against things taken to extreme. A decision not to turn on any lights on a very dark winter's morning may save a few pence, but is hardly in the best interests of the children or teachers. Some premises savings can be made after initial investment. Changing the heating system so that only the hall is heated may turn evening lettings into cost-effective sources of income. Sensible economies can be made by:

- **Monitoring fuel consumption** The caretaker should read meters regularly, keep personal records and look for unusual fluctuations in usage. The breakdown cost for each type of fuel should be recorded separately and compared with like quarters. Differences can be matched against unusual weather or other circumstances. Fuel bills should be checked before they are passed for payment and current agreements examined to see if the correct tariff is being used
- **Improving energy awareness** This should involve staff and children. Competitions can be run to find new ways to save energy or to produce 'eye catching' energy saving posters. Class energy monitors can make sure that when the room is vacated, lights are always turned off and doors closed. Energy issues should be included in the curriculum, and children made aware of the need to use precious resources wisely. Pupils should be praised for closing external doors, turning off dripping taps and unwanted lights. Key staff, including the caretaker should be offered training on energy conservation, and rewarded for energy saving ideas.
- **Operating the heating system efficiently** Check what happens to the system 'off peak', at weekends and during school holidays. Ensure that the time and temperature controls are set correctly and that clocks are reset promptly at the end and beginning of Summer Time. External lights which are triggered by photo-electric cells should be regularly checked to make sure that they are operating correctly. The caretaker should be familiar with all the various controls and, as part of the planning team, understand the school's needs and why sometimes heating will be needed out of normal school hours.
- **Identifying investment opportunities whenever possible** If a classroom is to be rewired, improve switching arrangements so that lights next to classroom windows can be turned off on days of reasonable light. Fit draught excluders to all external doors and, if possible, insulate walls and ceilings. Replace tungsten light bulbs with compact fluorescent lamps. Consider the installation of timers on urinals to prevent the wastage of water during weekends and school holidays.

(adapted from DFE 1993)

PREMISES MANAGEMENT AND THE GOVERNORS

Governors have a wide range of premises responsibilities. These include the day-to-day and planned maintenance of the buildings, the use of the delegated budget for minor improvements, health and safety, the payment of energy costs, building security and the quality assurance of school cleaning and grounds maintenance contracts. The governors should manage their responsibilities within the context and priorities of the development plan. These responsibilities should be expressed in a policy document which sets out a coherent strategy which might include:

- **A programme of planned maintenance** This should be a regular feature of the school development plan and authority could well be delegated to a small sub-committee of the governing body. Such a group should also include members of the teaching staff and the caretaker. There should be a regular inspection of the complete site, and proper examination of a suggestion notebook kept in the staffroom where anyone could note suggestions for improvements. The cycle of maintenance should be planned over a number of years so that each area receives proper attention.
- **A policy for reducing costs** By careful housekeeping, use of quality materials and avoidance of unnecessary work.
- **A policy for monitoring the performance of contractors** This is a responsibility which should be shared jointly between named governors and senior staff who should understand the conditions and terms of the contract, and who monitor progress and quality as the work proceeds.
- **A contingency fund for repairs and maintenance** The right to authorise expenditure should be delegated to the headteacher and caretaker. Emergency repairs should be carried out as fast as possible. The school should maintain a list of reliable contractors who will respond quickly if the occasion requires.
- **Encouragement of energy savings** By expecting the caretaker to monitor fuel consumption and make regular reports; by improving energy awareness and operating heating and water systems efficiently; and by using major structural alterations as opportunities to improve insulation and lighting systems.

Schools whose cleaning and grounds maintenance is covered as part of a compulsory competitive tender, should consider taking over this responsibility themselves when the existing contract expires.

A governors' premises sub-committee can be very supportive to the senior staff by managing many premises' issues on behalf of the school. If a staff member and the caretaker are coopted on to the committee it will include representatives of all those most affected by premises issues. As with the finance sub-committee, it is very important that the authority and responsibilities delegated to the committee are recorded in the minutes of a full governors' meeting, and that regular reports are fed back to the governing body.

Specific responsibilities delegated to a premises sub-committee could include:

- ensuring that the school complies with the legal requirements of the LMS scheme, financial regulations and the council's contract standing orders;
- approving contracts above a specified value;
- carrying out the governing body's responsibilities in relation to health and safety, including drawing up a health and safety policy;
- making arrangements for governors to inspect the premises on a regular basis;
- recommending a hiring policy to the full governing body and overseeing its implementation;
- preparing for the full governing body the premises section of governors' annual report to parents.

(based on Beckett and Hallworth 1993)

Governors will want to delegate many of their premises management responsibilities to those who work in the school. The caretaker or site manager, for example, should be given genuine authority, and encouraged to work with staff in order to maximise the ways the building is used on a day-to-day basis. The schools who include non-teaching staff in their regular planning staff meetings have found that the inclusion of the caretaker and school secretary leads to a fruitful partnership and often saves time. In the past, caretakers often felt excluded from the mainstream life of the school and did not understand much of what happened there. It was not suprising that they were resistant to changes. Inclusion of the caretaker in discussions about the conversion of an underused area of the premises will often reveal a wealth of ideas and practical help. All internal building costs are likely to be high, and a rolling programme of internal decoration planned by the staff and caretaker will feature in most development plans. Many schools have used delegated funds to make their entrance halls and facilities for parents more attractive and comfortable, or have painted display boards in suitable colours to save on the costs of backing paper. Other schools have recognised that school secretaries have often been required to work in unsatisfactory environments with antiquated equipment and have sought to recognise the key function of these important colleagues by making internal structural alterations to create better office space. Teaching staff sometimes feel uncomfortable about spending money on improving the staffroom. The guilt is misplaced. The staff will function more effectively if they have a comfortable and clean room for their rare moments of relaxation.

The introduction of local management of schools was seen by many as a distraction from the headteacher's principal role as curriculum manager. The new associated financial and premises responsibilities which passed through the governors to the headteacher were thought to be so heavy that the headteacher could never again have enough time to give sufficient thought to the quality of what was happening in classrooms. In the early years, and still in a minority of schools, this is the case, and the overall quality of provision and leadership has dropped. In better schools, governors and staff work together to ensure that the search to improve the quality of the curriculum is what drives the school. The premises and financial responsibilities they now share can be managed through practical systems and structures which ensure that the prime responsibilities of the staff are safeguarded and that the precious resources available to be used by the staff are deployed to the best effect. The ingredients of success are a clear understanding of role and responsibility, genuine delegated authority which trusts the person to whom responsibility has been given and a common aim and plan which is understood by all as the best possible agreed route to achieve the objectives for the children that everyone acknowledges as paramount.

Grievance and discipline procedures

Even in the best managed schools staff problems do occur. For this reason schools are required to have both a grievance and a discipline procedure. The responsibility for establishing such policies rests with the school's governing body, although LEAs normally have model procedures on which these might be based. Another model can be found in *The Conditions of Service for Teachers in England and Wales* (The Burgundy Book) published by the DFE at regular intervals to reflect changes in legislation. Both sets of procedures are intended to remedy the different types of human resource problems with which they deal.

GRIEVANCE PROCEDURES

Grievance procedures are used when members of staff feel dissatisfied with any aspect of their employment except payment or grading, or consider that they have been victims of harassment, harsh or unfair treatment. Such procedures are difficult, time-consuming and stressful. Avoid moving straight from a disagreement about employment matters to a grievance procedure by exploring as many informal means as are available. For example, meetings between the parties concerned may be held to discuss, and to try to resolve, the matter. Third-party mediation might be tried using a senior colleague, mentor or representative of a professional association.

If all the informal avenues fail then it is wise to take advice from an LEA officer and/or a senior and experienced member of a professional association before embarking on a formal grievance procedure. Such procedures are a means by which members of staff can seek to redress grievances related to employment issues as quickly as possible by, if necessary, referring it to the governors. It is a request for corrective action in which the initiative is taken by the member of staff. Any such procedure adopted must aim at conciliation as well as corrective action if the grievance is proved to be justified. To achieve this, grievances should be dealt with in stages. Each stage should be thought through carefully and, where agreements or courses of action are agreed, these must be clarified so that it is clear what has been agreed. All parties should continue to seek relevant professional and other advice, such as that available from LEA officers before the matter escalates throughout the process. Hume (1990) represents these stages as steps on a ladder where the seriousness and the level of management involved increases as each upward step is taken. The stages in a typical grievance procedure might be:

Stage 1

The member of staff who is aggrieved presents the grievance either orally or in writing to his or her immediate superior. If the grievance is against the superior then the procedure starts at stage 2 unless the immediate superior is the headteacher in which case it begins at stage 3. In many smaller primary schools there may not be an immediate superior other than the headteacher. In this case the procedure begins at stage 3. At stage 1 the immediate superior should give an oral or written response within five working days.

Stage 2

If the member of staff receives no response within the allotted time or if the response is unsatisfactory then the matter should be raised with the head of department, section, unit or equivalent as soon as possible. A response should be given within seven working days.

Stage 3

Again if no response is received after seven working days, or if an unsatisfactory one is received at stage 2, then the aggrieved party should submit the grievance in writing to the headteacher. The headteacher will invite the member of staff accompanied by a 'friend', often a representative from a professional association, together with appropriate other parties, to a meeting. The person against whom the complaint has been made will also attend with a friend. The headteacher should attempt to counsel and reconcile and should respond to the aggrieved person in writing within ten working days of the meeting taking place.

Stage 4

If the member of staff is not satisfied with the response at stage 3, or does not receive one, then an appeal may be made to the governing body. Such an appeal should normally be addressed in writing to the headteacher who will inform the chair of the governors. The governors will convene a grievance panel consisting of, under normal circumstances, the chair of governors and two other members of the governing body. This should meet within fifteen working days of the appeal being lodged. The parties to the grievance must attend and can be accompanied as at stage 3. Governors may also set up an appeals panel to consider further representations if this is thought to be desirable. This should be made clear at the start of stage 4. If the issue is not resolved at this stage then it becomes a more serious matter and beyond the scope for action of those within the school.

Hume (1990) also points out that all grievance procedures must be based on natural justice. This means that time must be given to all parties to prepare a case. Adequate opportunity has to be allowed for the case to be stated and evidence produced so that a decision can be reached on the basis of evidence. Each person involved has the right to be accompanied and each side to the grievance has a right to reply and to call and question witnesses. There must also be a known and specific right of appeal included in the procedure. Such procedures are complex and detailed in order to be fair to all parties to a grievance and, wherever possible, to restore and maintain sound working relationships within the school.

DISCIPLINARY PROCEDURES

If a grievance is based on the right of the individual in a school to appeal against unacceptable working conditions and management processes then discipline is founded on the right of managers to set and enforce minimum standards of work. Such standards exist in every school and are normally implemented through informal processes and widely recognised and accepted management procedures. Disciplinary procedures must proceed with even more urgency than those for grievance. This is required on the grounds of fairness to all parties and because the usual assumption on which discipline procedures are based is that minimum standards of conduct or performance are not being maintained. This has serious consequences, especially where children are involved, and can lead to the suspension of the person who is the subject of the procedure.

Any discipline procedure must be fair and consistent, not least because the outcome may involve an industrial tribunal. The basic principle that underpins disciplinary processes is that an attempt must be made to redeem some failing by a member of staff. Time and opportunity must be given for this to happen, but failure to respond by the subject of the disciplinary procedure leads to a progression up the ladder of seriousness in that procedure. Again, Hume's concept of staging is useful in helping to understand the main elements of a typical disciplinary procedure. The same reservations about the concept of stages apply here as in those concerning grievance procedures in primary schools. Since primary schools tend not to have a large number of levels of management some of the stages will not be found in many such schools. The stages are:

Stage 1

The immediate supervisor must consider if the work behaviour of the colleague is such as to warrant formal disciplinary steps being taken. The situation must be discussed with the member of staff involved but no record of this need to be kept. After six months this will be considered to have lapsed. Stage 2 must be initiated within this time scale. If, within the six month period the immediate supervisor is not satisfied with the response from the member of staff, the head of department will decide whether or not to proceed to stage 2.

Stage 2

The member of staff in question, accompanied by a representative, will be requested to attend a disciplinary interview. At least five working days notice must be given of this meeting. After this meeting the head of department must write to the member of staff either stating that no further action will be taken or giving a written warning. This warning must give an outline of the areas of concern, of the action required from the member of the staff, and a date for reviewing the situation which should be six months after the stage 2 interview. If the matter is resolved, then the written warning lapses and is removed from the file and a letter sent to the member of staff stating that no further disciplinary action is considered necessary.

Stage 3

The headteacher must decide whether or not to proceed to stage 3. At this stage the member of staff, with a representative, will be asked in writing to attend a disciplinary interview. Five working days notice must be given of this meeting and the invitation must outline the details of the subject to be discussed. Once the interview has been held the headteacher must write to the member of staff giving a final warning or stating that no further action will be taken. This final warning will be kept on file and will lapse after two years and be removed if no further action is taken.

Stage 4

At stage 4 the headteacher will involve the governors who will convene a disciplinary panel consisting of the chair of governors and two other members of the governing body. It should meet within fifteen working days of receiving the notification and the member of staff will be advised in writing as soon as the date of the panel has been arranged. The decision of the panel will be conveyed in writing to the member of staff within 24 hours of the decision being reached. The disciplinary panel is empowered to take any decision that it considers appropriate including dismissal if the terms of the relevant statutory provisions are met.

As Hume (1990) points out, these procedures must be conducted within the requirements of natural justice outlined above. If one person has a disciplinary action raised against him or her by governors, then a different set of governors must be involved. There must also be a special provision for cases of gross misconduct where criminal or similar offences are alleged to have been committed. Furthermore, there must be a provision for appeal at every stage in the procedure, while at stage 4 provision for an appeal against dismissal is a legal requirement.

An approach to human resource management based on care, consideration, clearly defined expectations and a professional approach which rests on sound communication and good delegation will minimise the extent to which grievance and disciplinary procedures are used. They need to exist to protect the rights of all the staff in schools and to help to ensure that children receive the best treatment possible within the primary school.

Bibliography

Alexander, R. (1992) *Policy and Practice in Primary Education*, London, Routledge.
Alexander, R., Rose, J., Woodhead, C. (1992) *Curriculum Organisation and Classrooom Practice in Primary Schools: a discussion paper*, London, Department of Education and Science.
Audit Commission (1991) *Management within Primary Schools*, London, The Audit Commission for Local Authorities and the National Health Service in England and Wales.
Audit Commission (1993) *Keeping the Balance: Standards for Financial Administration in Schools*, London, The Audit Commission for Local Authorities and the National Health Service in England and Wales.
Beckett, C. and Hallworth, A. (1993) *Organising your Governing Body*, Warwickshire LEA.
Beckett, C., Bell, L. and Rhodes, C. (1991) *Working with Governors in Schools*, Milton Keynes, Open University Press.
Bell, L.A. (1986) *The Organisation of Primary Schools: a Survey of Headteacher Perceptions*, Education Department, Coventry: University of Warwick.
Bell, L. (1992) *Managing Teams in Secondary Schools*, London, Routledge.
Blanchard, T., Lovell, B. and Ville, N. (1989) *Managing Finance in Schools*, London, Cassell Educational.
Bush, T., Glatter, R., Goodey, J. and Riches, C. (eds) (1980) *Approaches to School Management*, London, Harper and Row.
Campbell, J. (1994) 'Managing the Primary Curriculum: The Issue of Time Allocation', *Education*, March, pp. 3–13.
Campbell, J., Evans, L., St. J. Neill, S. and Packwood, A. (1993) *The Use and Management of Infant Teachers' Time: Some Policy Issues*, Stoke-on-Trent, Trentham Books.
Coopers and Lybrand (1993) *Good Management in Small Schools*, London, DFE.
Cowan, B. and Wright, N. (1990) 'Two Million Days Lost', *Education*, 2 February.
Dearing, R. (1993) *The National Curriculum and its Assessment: An Interim Report*, York, National Curriculum Council.
Dearing, R. (1994) *The National Curriculum and its Assessment: The Final Report*, London, School Curriculum and Assessment Authority.
DES (1977) *Ten Good Schools*, London, HMSO.
DES (1985) *Education Observed 3: Good Teachers*, London, HMSO.
DES (1986) *The Education Act*, London, HMSO.
DES (1988a) *The Education Reform Act*, London, HMSO.
DES (1988b) *Circular 7/88, Education Reform Act/Local Management of Schools*, London, HMSO.

DES (1991a) *Education (School Teacher Appraisal) Regulations*, London, HMSO.

DES (1991b) *Circular 12/91, School Teacher Appraisal*, London, HMSO.

DFE (1992) *Choice and Diversity: A New Framework for Schools*, London, HMSO.

DFE (1993) *Good Management in Small Schools*, London, Coopers and Lybrand.

DFE (1994a) *School Teachers' Pay and Conditions of Employment Document*, London, HMSO.

DFE (1994b) Circular 7/94, *School Teachers' Pay and Conditions of Employment 1994*, London, HMSO.

Everard, B. and Morris, G. (1985) *Effective School Management*, London, Harper and Row.

Field, D. (1985) 'Headship in the Secondary School' in Hughes, M.G., Ribbins, P. and Thomas, H. (eds) (1985) *Managing Education: The System and the Institution*, Eastbourne, Holt, Rinehart and Winston.

Hargreaves, D., Hopkins, D., Leask, M., Connolly, J. and Robinson, P. (1989) *Planning for School Development: Advice to Governors, Headteachers and Teachers*, London, HMSO.

Hughes, M.G. (1985) 'Leadership in Professionally Staffed Organisations' in Hughes, M.G., Ribbins, P. and Thomas, H. (eds) (1985) *Managing Education: The System and the Institution*, Eastbourne, Holt, Rinehart and Winston.

Hume, C. (1990) *Grievance and Discipline in Schools*, London, Longman.

Laws, J. and Dennison, W.F. (1991) 'The Use of Headteachers' Time: Leading Professional or Chief Executive' in *Education*, 3–13 March, pp. 54–66.

McClelland, D.C. (1951) *Personality*, New York, Sloane.

Maclure, S. (1989) 'Headship in Perspective', *Education*, October, pp. 11–12.

Maslow, A.H. (1954) *Motivation and Personality*, New York, Harper and Row.

Morgan, C., Hall, V. and Mackay, H. (1983) *The Selection of Secondary School Headteachers*, Milton Keynes, Open University Press.

Mortimer, P., Sammons, P., Stoll, L., Lewis, D. and Ecob, R. (1988) *School Matters: The Junior Years*, London, Open Books.

NAHT (1992) *Response to the Secretary of State's White Paper, 'Choice and Diversity'*, Haywards Heath, National Association of Headteachers.

National Curriculum Council (1989) *Information Pack Number 1*, York, NCC.

Nias, J. (1980) 'Leadership styles and job satisfaction in primary schools' in Bush, T., Glatter, R., Goodey, J. and Riches, C. (eds) (1980) *Approaches to School Management*, London, Harper and Row.

Nias, J. Southworth, J. and Yeomans, R. (1989) *Staff Relationships in Primary School*, London, Cassell.

OFSTED (1993) *Handbook for the Inspection of Schools*, London, HMSO.

OFSTED (1994a) *Handbook for the Inspection of Schools: Amendments*, London, HMSO.

OFSTED (1994b) *Guidance on the School Inspection Schedule*, London, HMSO.

Ormston, M., and Shaw, M. (1993) *Inspection: A Preparation Guide for Schools*, London: Longman.

Pascal, D. (1992) *Guardian*, 6 October, pp. 22–3.

Poster, C. and Poster, D. (1991) *Teacher Appraisal: A Guide to Training*, London, Routledge.

Reid, K., Hopkins, D. and Holly, P. (1987) *Towards the Effective School*, Oxford, Basil Blackwell.

Rust, W.B. (1985) *Management Guidelines for Teachers*, London, Pitman.

Sallis, E. (1993) *Total Quality Management in Education*, London, Kogan Page.

School Curriculum Development Committee (1988) *Guidelines for Review and*

Internal Development in Schools (GRIDS); Primary School Handbook, York, Longman for the SCDC.

Scottish Education Departmant (1989) *Effective Primary Schools*, London, HMSO.

Styan, D. (1989) *Times Educational Supplement*, 27 January.

Torrington, D. and Weightman, J. (1989) *The Reality of School Management*, Oxford, Blackwell.

West, N. (1992) *Primary Headship*, London, Longman.

West-Burnham, J. (1992) *Managing Quality in Schools*, London, Longman.

Index